Praise for *Growing Object-Oriented Software, Guided by Tests*

"The authors of this book have led a revolution in the craft of programming by controlling the environment in which software grows. Their Petri dish is the mock object, and their microscope is the unit test. This book can show you how these tools introduce a repeatability to your work that would be the envy of any scientist."

— *Ward Cunningham*

"At last a book, suffused with code, that exposes the deep symbiosis between TDD and OOD. The authors, pioneers in test-driven development, have packed it with principles, practices, heuristics, and (best of all) anecdotes drawn from their decades of professional experience. Every software craftsman will want to pore over the chapters of worked examples and study the advanced testing and design principles. This one's a keeper."

—*Robert C. Martin*

"Design is often discussed in depth, but without empiricism. Testing is often promoted, but within the narrow definition of quality that relates only to the presence or absence of defects. Both of these perspectives are valuable, but each on its own offers little more than the sound of one hand clapping. Steve and Nat bring the two hands together in what deserves—and can best be described as—applause. With clarity, reason, and humour, their tour de force reveals a view of design, testing, code, objects, practice, and process that is compelling, practical, and overflowing with insight."

—*Kevlin Henney*, co-author of *Pattern-Oriented Software Architecture* and 97 *Things Every Programmer Should Know*

"Steve and Nat have written a wonderful book that shares their software craftsmanship with the rest of the world. This is a book that should be studied rather than read, and those who invest sufficient time and energy into this effort will be rewarded with superior development skills."

—*David Vydra*, publisher, testdriven.com

"This book presents a unique vision of test-driven development. It describes the mature form of an alternative strain of TDD that sprang up in London in the early 2000s, characterized by a totally end-to-end approach and a deep emphasis on the messaging aspect of objects. If you want to be an expert in the state of the art in TDD, you need to understand the ideas in this book."

—*Michael Feathers*

"With this book you'll learn the rhythms, nuances in thinking, and effective programming practices for growing tested, well-designed object-oriented applications from the masters."

—*Rebecca Wirfs-Brock*

Growing Object-Oriented Software, Guided by Tests

Growing Object-Oriented Software, Guided by Tests

Steve Freeman and Nat Pryce

✦✦Addison-Wesley

Upper Saddle River, NJ • Boston • Indianapolis • San Francisco
New York • Toronto • Montreal • London • Munich • Paris • Madrid
Cape Town • Sydney • Tokyo • Singapore • Mexico City

Many of the designations used by manufacturers and sellers to distinguish their products are claimed as trademarks. Where those designations appear in this book, and the publisher was aware of a trademark claim, the designations have been printed with initial capital letters or in all capitals.

The authors and publisher have taken care in the preparation of this book, but make no expressed or implied warranty of any kind and assume no responsibility for errors or omissions. No liability is assumed for incidental or consequential damages in connection with or arising out of the use of the information or programs contained herein.

The publisher offers excellent discounts on this book when ordered in quantity for bulk purchases or special sales, which may include electronic versions and/or custom covers and content particular to your business, training goals, marketing focus, and branding interests. For more information, please contact:

U.S. Corporate and Government Sales
(800) 382–3419
corpsales@pearsontechgroup.com

For sales outside the United States please contact:

International Sales
international@pearson.com

Visit us on the Web: informit.com/aw

Library of Congress Cataloging-in-Publication Data:

Freeman, Steve, 1958-
  Growing object-oriented software, guided by tests / Steve Freeman and Nat Pryce.
    p. cm.
  ISBN 978-0-321-50362-6 (pbk. : alk. paper) 1. Object-oriented programming
(Computer science) 2. Computer software--Testing. I. Pryce, Nat. II. Title.
  QA76.64.F747 2010
  005.1'17--dc22
                              2009035239

ISBN-13: 978–0–321–50362–6
ISBN-10: 0–321–50362–7
Text printed in the United States on recycled paper at RR Donnelley in Crawfordsville, Indiana.
Ninth printing September 2015

To Paola, for all her support; to Philip, who sometimes missed out
—Steve

To Lamaan who put up with me spending time writing this book,
and Oliver Tarek who did not
—Nat

Contents

Foreword

Kent Beck

One of the dilemmas posed by the move to shorter and shorter release cycles is how to release more software in less time—and continue releasing indefinitely. A new perspective is necessary to resolve this dilemma. More than a shift in techniques is needed.

Growing Object-Oriented Software, Guided by Tests presents such a new perspective. What if software wasn't "made," like we make a paper airplane—finish folding it and fly it away? What if, instead, we treated software more like a valuable, productive plant, to be nurtured, pruned, harvested, fertilized, and watered? Traditional farmers know how to keep plants productive for decades or even centuries. How would software development be different if we treated our programs the same way?

I am most impressed by how this book presents both the philosophy and mechanics of such a shift in perspective. It is written by practitioners who code—and teach others to code—well. From it you can learn both how to program to sustain productivity and how to look at your programs anew.

The style of test-driven development presented here is different from what I practice. I can't yet articulate the difference, but I have learned from the clear, confident presentation of the authors' techniques. The diversity of dialects has given me a new source of ideas to further refine my own development. *Growing Object-Oriented Software, Guided by Tests*, presents a coherent, consistent system of development, where different techniques support each other.

I invite you to read *Growing Object-Oriented Software, Guided by Tests*, to follow along with the examples, to learn how the authors think about programming and how they program. The experience will enrich your software development style, help you program—and, just as important, see your programs differently.

Preface

What Is This Book About?

This book is a practical guide to the best way we've found to write object-oriented software: *test-driven development (TDD)*. It describes the processes we follow, the design principles we strive for, and the tools we use. It's founded on our decades of experience, working with and learning from some of the best programmers in the world.

Within the book, we address some of the questions and confusions we see coming up on project after project. How do I fit test-driven development into a software project? Where do I start? Why should I write both unit and end-to-end tests? What does it mean for tests to "drive" development? How do I test *difficult feature X*?

This book is also very much about design and the way our approach to design informs our approach to TDD. If there's one thing we've learned, it's that test-driven development works best when taken as a whole. We've seen teams that can do the raw practices (writing and running tests) but struggle with the result because they haven't also adopted the deeper processes that lie behind it.

Why "Growing" Object-Oriented Software?

We used the term "growing" because it gives a sense of how we develop incrementally. We have something working at all times, making sure that the code is always as well-structured as possible and thoroughly tested. Nothing else seems to be as effective at delivering systems that work. As John Gall wrote in [Gall03], "A complex system that works is invariably found to have evolved from a simple system that works."

"Growing" also hints at the biological quality we see in good software, the sense of coherence at every level of structure. It ties into our approach to object orientation which follows Alan Kay's[1] concept of objects being similar to biological cells that send each other messages.

Why "Guided" by Tests?

We write tests *first* because we find that it helps us write better code. Writing a test first forces us to clarify our intentions, and we don't start the next piece of work until we have an unambiguous description of what it should do. The *process* of writing a test first helps us see when a design is too rigid or unfocused. Then, when we want to follow through and fix a design flaw, the tests give us a safety net of regression coverage.

We use the term "guided" because the technique still requires skill and experience. We found test-driven development to be an effective design support tool—once we'd learned how to develop incrementally and to "listen to the tests." Like any serious design activity, TDD requires understanding and sustained effort to work.

We've seen teams that write tests and code at about the same time (and even teams that write the tests first) where the code is a mess and the tests just raise the cost of maintenance. They'd made a start but hadn't yet learned that the trick, as the title of the book suggests, is to let the tests *guide* development. Use the contents of the tests to stay focused on making progress and feedback from the tests to raise the quality of the system.

What about Mock Objects?

Our original motivation for writing the book was to finally explain the technique of using *mock objects*,[2] which we often see misunderstood. As we got deeper into writing, we realized that our community's discovery and use of mock objects was actually an expression of our approach to writing software; it's part of a larger picture.

In the course of the book, we will show how the mock objects technique works, using the jMock library. More specifically, we'll show where it fits into the TDD process and how it makes sense in the context of object-oriented development.

Who Is This Book For?

We wrote this book for the "informed reader." It's intended for developers with professional experience who probably have at least looked at test-driven

---

1. Alan Kay was one of the authors of Smalltalk and coined the term "object-oriented."
2. Mock objects are substitute implementations for testing how an object interacts with its neighbors.

development. When writing, we imagined we were explaining techniques to a colleague who hadn't come across them before.

To make room for the deeper material we wanted to cover, we've assumed some knowledge of the basic concepts and tools; there are other books that provide a good introduction to TDD.

Is This a Java Book?

We use the Java programming language throughout because it's common enough that we expect our readers to be able at least to understand the examples. That said, the book is really about a set of *techniques* that are applicable to any object-oriented environment.

If you're not using Java, there are equivalents of testing and mocking libraries we use (JUnit and jMock) in many other languages, including C#, Ruby, Python, Smalltalk, Objective-C, and (impressively) C++. There are even versions for more distant languages such as Scala. There are also other testing and mocking frameworks in Java.

Why Should You Listen to Us?

This book distills our experiences over a couple of decades, including nearly ten years of test-driven development. During that time, we have used TDD in a wide range of projects: large message-oriented enterprise-integration systems with an interactive web front-end backed by multiprocessor compute grids; tiny embedded systems that must run in tens of kilobytes of memory; free games used as advertising for business-critical systems; and back-end middleware and network services to highly interactive graphical desktop applications. In addition, we've written about and taught this material at events and companies across the world.

We've also benefited from the experience of our colleagues in the TDD community based in London. We've spent many hours during and after work having our ideas challenged and honed. We're grateful for the opportunity to work with such lively (and argumentative) colleagues.

What Is in This Book?

The book has six parts:

Part I, "Introduction," is a high-level introduction to test-driven development, mock objects, and object-oriented design within the context of a software development project. We also introduce some of the testing frameworks we use in the rest of the book. Even if you're already familiar with TDD, we stilll recommend reading through Chapters 1 and 2 since they describe our approach to software development. If you're familiar with JUnit and jMock, you might want to skip the rest of the introduction.

Part II, "The Process of Test-Driven Development," describes the process of TDD, showing how to get started and how to keep development moving. We dig into the relationship between our test-driven approach and object-oriented programming, showing how the principles of the two techniques support each other. Finally, we discuss how to work with external code. This part describes the concepts, the next part puts them to work.

Part III, "A Worked Example," is an extended example that gives a flavor of how we develop an object-oriented application in a test-driven manner. Along the way, we discuss the trade-offs and motivations for the decisions we take. We've made this quite a long example, because we want to show how some features of TDD become more significant as the code starts to scale up.

Part IV, "Sustainable Test-Driven Development," describes some practices that keep a system maintainable. We're very careful these days about keeping a codebase clean and expressive, because we've learned over the years the costs of letting things slip. This part describes some of the practices we've adopted and explains why we do them.

Part V, "Advanced Topics," looks at areas where TDD is more difficult: complex test data, persistence, and concurrency. We show how we deal with these issues and how this affects the design of the code and tests.

Finally, the appendices include some supporting material on jMock and Hamcrest.

What Is Not in This Book?

This is a technical book. We've left out all the other topics that make a project succeed, such as team organization, requirements management, and product design. Adopting an incremental test-driven approach to development obviously has a close relationship with how a project is run. TDD enables some new activities, such as frequent delivery, and it can be crippled by organizational circumstances, such as an early design freeze or team stakeholders that don't communicate. Again, there are plenty of other books to cover these topics.

Acknowledgments

The authors would like to thank everyone who provided their support and feedback during the writing of this book. Kent Beck and Greg Doench commissioned it in the first place, and Dmitry Kirsanov and Alina Kirsanova (with great patience) polished up the rough edges and turned it into print.

A great many people helped us by taking the trouble to read and review drafts, or just providing support and encouragement: Romilly Cocking, Jamie Dobson, Michael Feathers, Martin Fowler, Naresh Jain, Pete Keller, Tim Mackinnon, Duncan McGregor, Ivan Moore, Farshad Nayeri, Isaiah Perumalla, David Peterson, Nick Pomfret, J. B. Rainsberger, James Richardson, Lauren Schmitt, Douglas Squirrel, The Silicon Valley Patterns Group, Vladimir Trofimov, Daniel Wellman, and Matt Wynne.

Thanks to Dave Denton, Jonathan "Buck" Rogers, and Jim Kuo for modeling duties.

This book and the techniques we describe within it would not have existed without the Extreme Tuesday Club (XTC), a regular informal meet-up in London for people interested in agile, extreme programming and test-driven development. We are deeply grateful to all the people with whom we shared experiences, techniques, lessons learned, and rounds.

About the Authors

Steve Freeman

Steve Freeman is an independent consultant specializing in Agile software development (http://www.m3p.co.uk). He was joint winner, with Nat Pryce, of the 2006 Agile Alliance Gordon Pask award. A founding member of the London Extreme Tuesday Club, he was chair of the first London XP Day and is a frequent organizer and presenter at international conferences. Steve has worked in a wide variety of organizations, from developing shrink-wrap software for IBM to prototyping for major research labs. Steve has a PhD from Cambridge University, and degrees in statistics and music. Steve is based in London, UK.

Nat Pryce

After completing his PhD at Imperial College, Nat Pryce joined the dot-com boom just in time to watch it bust. Since then he has worked as a programmer, architect, trainer, and consultant in a variety of industries, including sports reportage, marketing communications, retail, telecoms, and finance. He has also worked on academic research projects and does occasional university teaching. An early adopter of XP, he has written or contributed to several open source libraries that support TDD and was one of the founding organizers of the London XP Day conference. He also regularly presents at international conferences. Nat is based in London, UK.

Part I

Introduction

Test-Driven Development (TDD) is a deceptively simple idea:
Write the tests for your code *before* writing the code itself. We
say "deceptively simple" because this transforms the role testing
plays in the development process and challenges our industry's
assumptions about what testing is for. Testing is no longer just
about keeping defects from the users; instead, it's about helping
the team to understand the features that the users need and to
deliver those features reliably and predictably. When followed
to its conclusions, TDD radically changes the way we develop
software and, in our experience, dramatically improves the
quality of the systems we build, in particular their reliability and
their flexibility in response to new requirements.

Test-driven development is widely used in "agile" software
development approaches. It is a core practice of Extreme Programming (XP) [Beck99], is recommended by Crystal Clear
[Cockburn04], and is often used in Scrum projects [Schwaber01].
We've used TDD on every agile project we've been involved in,
and have found uses for it in non-agile projects. We've even
found that it helps us make progress in pure research projects,
where the motivation is to explore ideas rather than deliver
features.

Chapter 1

What Is the Point of Test-Driven Development?

One must learn by doing the thing; for though you think you know it, you have no certainty, until you try.

—Sophocles

Software Development as a Learning Process

Almost all software projects are attempting something that nobody has done before (or at least that nobody in the organization has done before). That *something* may refer to the people involved, the application domain, the technology being used, or (most likely) a combination of these. In spite of the best efforts of our discipline, all but the most routine projects have elements of surprise. Interesting projects—those likely to provide the most benefit—usually have a lot of surprises.

Developers often don't completely understand the technologies they're using. They have to learn how the components work *whilst* completing the project. Even if they have a good understanding of the technologies, new applications can force them into unfamiliar corners. A system that combines many significant components (which means most of what a professional programmer works on) will be too complex for any individual to understand all of its possibilities.

For customers and end users, the experience is worse. The process of building a system forces them to look at their organization more closely than they have before. They're often left to negotiate and codify processes that, until now, have been based on convention and experience.

Everyone involved in a software project has to learn as it progresses. For the project to succeed, the people involved have to work together just to understand what they're supposed to achieve, and to identify and resolve misunderstandings along the way. They all know there will be changes, they just don't know *what* changes. They need a process that will help them cope with uncertainty as their experience grows—to *anticipate unanticipated changes*.

Feedback Is the Fundamental Tool

We think that the best approach a team can take is to use *empirical feedback* to learn about the system and its use, and then apply that learning back to the system. A team needs repeated cycles of activity. In each cycle it adds new features and gets feedback about the quantity and quality of the work already done. The team members split the work into *time boxes*, within which they analyze, design, implement, and deploy as many features as they can.

Deploying completed work to some kind of environment at each cycle is critical. Every time a team deploys, its members have an opportunity to check their assumptions against reality. They can measure how much progress they're really making, detect and correct any errors, and adapt the current plan in response to what they've learned. Without deployment, the feedback is not complete.

In our work, we apply feedback cycles at every level of development, organizing projects as a system of nested loops ranging from seconds to months, such as: pair programming, unit tests, acceptance tests, daily meetings, iterations, releases, and so on. Each loop exposes the team's output to empirical feedback so that the team can discover and correct any errors or misconceptions. The nested feedback loops reinforce each other; if a discrepancy slips through an inner loop, there is a good chance an outer loop will catch it.

Each feedback loop addresses different aspects of the system and development process. The inner loops are more focused on the technical detail: what a unit of code does, whether it integrates with the rest of the system. The outer loops are more focused on the organization and the team: whether the application serves its users' needs, whether the team is as effective as it could be.

The sooner we can get feedback about any aspect of the project, the better. Many teams in large organizations can release every few weeks. Some teams release every few days, or even hours, which gives them an order of magnitude increase in opportunities to receive and respond to feedback from real users.

Incremental and Iterative Development

In a project organized as a set of nested feedback loops, development is *incremental* and *iterative*.

Incremental development builds a system feature by feature, instead of building all the layers and components and integrating them at the end. Each feature is implemented as an end-to-end "slice" through all the relevant parts of the system. The system is always integrated and ready for deployment.

Iterative development progressively refines the implementation of features in response to feedback until they are good enough.

Practices That Support Change

We've found that we need two technical foundations if we want to grow a system reliably and to cope with the *unanticipated* changes that always happen. First, we need constant testing to catch regression errors, so we can add new features without breaking existing ones. For systems of any interesting size, frequent manual testing is just impractical, so we must automate testing as much as we can to reduce the costs of building, deploying, and modifying versions of the system.

Second, we need to keep the code as simple as possible, so it's easier to understand and modify. Developers spend far more time reading code than writing it, so that's what we should optimize for.[1] Simplicity takes effort, so we constantly *refactor* [Fowler99] our code as we work with it—to improve and simplify its design, to remove duplication, and to ensure that it clearly expresses what it does. The test suites in the feedback loops protect us against our own mistakes as we improve (and therefore change) the code.

The catch is that few developers enjoy testing their code. In many development groups, writing automated tests is seen as not "real" work compared to adding features, and boring as well. Most people do not do as well as they should at work they find uninspiring.

Test-Driven Development (TDD) turns this situation on its head. We write our tests *before* we write the code. Instead of just using testing to verify our work after it's done, TDD turns testing into a *design* activity. We use the tests to clarify our ideas about *what* we want the code to do. As Kent Beck described it to us, "I was finally able to separate logical from physical design. I'd always been told to do that but no one ever explained how." We find that the effort of writing a test first also gives us rapid feedback about the quality of our design ideas—that making code accessible for testing often drives it towards being cleaner and more modular.

If we write tests all the way through the development process, we can build up a safety net of automated regression tests that give us the confidence to make changes.

 "... you have nothing to lose but your bugs"

We cannot emphasize strongly enough how liberating it is to work on test-driven code that has thorough test coverage. We find that we can concentrate on the task in hand, confident that we're doing the right work and that it's actually quite hard to break the system—as long as we follow the practices.

---

1. Begel and Simon [Begel08] showed that new graduates at Microsoft spend most of their first year just reading code.

Test-Driven Development in a Nutshell

The cycle at the heart of TDD is: write a test; write some code to get it working; *refactor* the code to be as simple an implementation of the tested features as possible. Repeat.

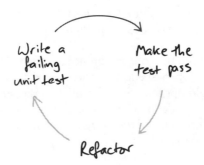

Figure 1.1   *The fundamental TDD cycle*

As we develop the system, we use TDD to give us feedback on the quality of both its *implementation* ("Does it work?") and *design* ("Is it well structured?"). Developing test-first, we find we benefit twice from the effort. *Writing* tests:

- makes us clarify the acceptance criteria for the next piece of work—we have to ask ourselves how we can tell when we're done (design);

- encourages us to write loosely coupled components, so they can easily be tested in isolation and, at higher levels, combined together (design);

- adds an executable description of what the code does (design); and,

- adds to a complete regression suite (implementation);

whereas *running* tests:

- detects errors while the context is fresh in our mind (implementation); and,

- lets us know when we've done enough, discouraging "gold plating" and unnecessary features (design).

This feedback cycle can be summed up by the Golden Rule of TDD:

The Golden Rule of Test-Driven Development

Never write new functionality without a failing test.

> **Refactoring. Think Local, Act Local**
>
> *Refactoring* means changing the internal structure of an existing body of code without changing its behavior. The point is to improve the code so that it's a better representation of the features it implements, making it more maintainable.
>
> Refactoring is a disciplined technique where the programmer applies a series of transformations (or "refactorings") that do not change the code's behavior. Each refactoring is small enough to be easy to understand and "safe"; for example, a programmer might pull a block of code into a helper method to make the original method shorter and easier to understand. The programmer makes sure that the system is still working after each refactoring step, minimizing the risk of getting stranded by a change; in test-driven code, we can do that by running the tests.
>
> Refactoring is a "microtechnique" that is driven by finding small-scale improvements. Our experience is that, applied rigorously and consistently, its many small steps can lead to significant structural improvements. Refactoring is not the same activity as *redesign*, where the programmers take a conscious decision to change a large-scale structure. That said, having taken a redesign decision, a team can use refactoring techniques to get to the new design incrementally and safely.
>
> You'll see quite a lot of refactoring in our example in Part III. The standard text on the concept is Fowler's [Fowler99].

The Bigger Picture

It is tempting to start the TDD process by writing unit tests for classes in the application. This is better than having no tests at all and can catch those basic programming errors that we all know but find so hard to avoid: fencepost errors, incorrect boolean expressions, and the like. But a project with only unit tests is missing out on critical benefits of the TDD process. We've seen projects with high-quality, well unit-tested code that turned out not to be called from anywhere, or that could not be integrated with the rest of the system and had to be rewritten.

How do we know where to start writing code? More importantly, how do we know when to *stop* writing code? The golden rule tells us what we need to do: *Write a failing test*.

When we're implementing a feature, we start by writing an *acceptance test*, which exercises the functionality we want to build. While it's failing, an acceptance test demonstrates that the system does not yet implement that feature; when it passes, we're done. When working on a feature, we use its acceptance test to guide us as to whether we actually need the code we're about to write—we only write code that's directly relevant. Underneath the acceptance test, we follow the *unit level* test/implement/refactor cycle to develop the feature; the whole cycle looks like Figure 1.2.

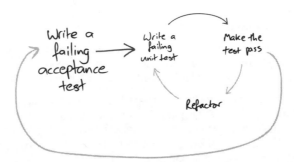

Figure 1.2   *Inner and outer feedback loops in TDD*

The outer test loop is a measure of demonstrable progress, and the growing suite of tests protects us against regression failures when we change the system. Acceptance tests often take a while to make pass, certainly more than one check-in episode, so we usually distinguish between acceptance tests we're working on (which are not yet included in the build) and acceptance tests for the features that have been finished (which are included in the build and must always pass).

The inner loop supports the developers. The unit tests help us maintain the quality of the code and should pass soon after they've been written. Failing unit tests should never be committed to the source repository.

Testing End-to-End

Wherever possible, an acceptance test should exercise the system end-to-end without directly calling its internal code. An *end-to-end test* interacts with the system only from the outside: through its user interface, by sending messages as if from third-party systems, by invoking its web services, by parsing reports, and so on. As we discuss in Chapter 10, the whole behavior of the system includes its interaction with its external environment. This is often the riskiest and most difficult aspect; we ignore it at our peril. We try to avoid acceptance tests that just exercise the internal objects of the system, unless we really need the speed-up and already have a stable set of end-to-end tests to provide cover.

The Importance of End-to-End Testing: A Horror Story

Nat was once brought onto a project that had been using TDD since its inception. The team had been writing acceptance tests to capture requirements and show progress to their customer representatives. They had been writing unit tests for the classes of the system, and the internals were clean and easy to change. They had been making great progress, and the customer representatives had signed off all the implemented features on the basis of the passing acceptance tests.

> But the acceptance tests did not run end-to-end—they instantiated the system's internal objects and directly invoked their methods. The application actually did nothing at all. Its entry point contained only a single comment:
>
> ```
> // TODO implement this
> ```
>
> Additional feedback loops, such as regular show-and-tell sessions, should have been in place and would have caught this problem.

For us, "end-to-end" means more than just interacting with the system from the outside—that might be better called "edge-to-edge" testing. We prefer to have the end-to-end tests exercise both the system *and* the process by which it's built and deployed. An automated build, usually triggered by someone checking code into the source repository, will: check out the latest version; compile and unit-test the code; integrate and package the system; perform a production-like deployment into a realistic environment; and, finally, exercise the system through its external access points. This sounds like a lot of effort (it is), but has to be done anyway repeatedly during the software's lifetime. Many of the steps might be fiddly and error-prone, so the end-to-end build cycle is an ideal candidate for automation. You'll see in Chapter 10 how early in a project we get this working.

A system is *deployable* when the acceptance tests all pass, because they should give us enough confidence that everything works. There's still, however, a final step of deploying to production. In many organizations, especially large or heavily regulated ones, building a deployable system is only the start of a release process. The rest, before the new features are finally available to the end users, might involve different kinds of testing, handing over to operations and data groups, and coordinating with other teams' releases. There may also be additional, nontechnical costs involved with a release, such as training, marketing, or an impact on service agreements for downtime. The result is a more difficult release cycle than we would like, so we have to understand our whole technical and organizational environment.

Levels of Testing

We build a hierarchy of tests that correspond to some of the nested feedback loops we described above:

Acceptance: Does the whole system work?

Integration: Does our code work against code we can't change?

Unit: Do our objects do the right thing, are they convenient to work with?

There's been a lot of discussion in the TDD world over the terminology for what we're calling *acceptance tests*: "functional tests," "customer tests," "system tests." Worse, our definitions are often not the same as those used by professional software testers. The important thing is to be clear about our intentions. We use "acceptance tests" to help us, with the domain experts, understand and agree on what we are going to build next. We also use them to make sure that we haven't broken any existing features as we continue developing.

Our preferred implementation of the "role" of acceptance testing is to write *end-to-end tests* which, as we just noted, should be as end-to-end as possible; our bias often leads us to use these terms interchangeably although, in some cases, acceptance tests might not be end-to-end.

We use the term *integration tests* to refer to the tests that check how some of our code works with code from outside the team that we can't change. It might be a public framework, such as a persistence mapper, or a library from another team within our organization. The distinction is that integration tests make sure that any abstractions we build over third-party code work as we expect. In a small system, such as the one we develop in Part III, acceptance tests might be enough. In most professional development, however, we'll want integration tests to help tease out configuration issues with the external packages, and to give quicker feedback than the (inevitably) slower acceptance tests.

We won't write much more about techniques for acceptance and integration testing, since both depend on the technologies involved and even the culture of the organization. You'll see some examples in Part III which we hope give a sense of the motivation for acceptance tests and show how they fit in the development cycle. Unit testing techniques, however, are specific to a style of programming, and so are common across all systems that take that approach—in our case, are object-oriented.

External and Internal Quality

There's another way of looking at what the tests can tell us about a system. We can make a distinction between external and internal quality: *External* quality is how well the system meets the needs of its customers and users (is it functional, reliable, available, responsive, etc.), and *internal* quality is how well it meets the needs of its developers and administrators (is it easy to understand, easy to change, etc.). Everyone can understand the point of external quality; it's usually part of the contract to build. The case for internal quality is equally important but is often harder to make. Internal quality is what lets us cope with continual and unanticipated change which, as we saw at the beginning of this chapter, is a fact of working with software. The point of maintaining internal quality is to allow us to modify the system's behavior safely and predictably, because it minimizes the risk that a change will force major rework.

Running end-to-end tests tells us about the external quality of our system, and *writing* them tells us something about how well we (the whole team) understand the domain, but end-to-end tests don't tell us how well we've written the code. *Writing* unit tests gives us a lot of feedback about the quality of our code, and *running* them tells us that we haven't broken any classes—but, again, unit tests don't give us enough confidence that the system as a whole works. Integration tests fall somewhere in the middle, as in Figure 1.3.

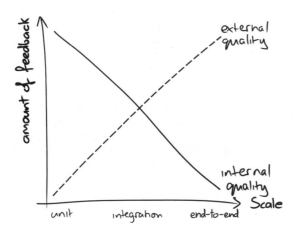

Figure 1.3 *Feedback from tests*

Thorough unit testing helps us improve the internal quality because, to be tested, a unit has to be structured to run outside the system in a test fixture. A unit test for an object needs to create the object, provide its dependencies, interact with it, and check that it behaved as expected. So, for a class to be easy to unit-test, the class must have explicit dependencies that can easily be substituted and clear responsibilities that can easily be invoked and verified. In software engineering terms, that means that the code must be *loosely coupled* and *highly cohesive*—in other words, well-designed.

When we've got this wrong—when a class, for example, is tightly coupled to distant parts of the system, has implicit dependencies, or has too many or unclear responsibilities—we find unit tests difficult to write or understand, so writing a test first gives us valuable, immediate feedback about our design. Like everyone, we're tempted not to write tests when our code makes it difficult, but we try to resist. We use such difficulties as an opportunity to investigate why the test is hard to write and refactor the code to improve its structure. We call this "listening to the tests," and we'll work through some common patterns in Chapter 20.

Coupling and Cohesion

Coupling and *cohesion* are metrics that (roughly) describe how easy it will be to change the behavior of some code. They were described by Larry Constantine in [Yourdon79].

Elements are *coupled* if a change in one forces a change in the other. For example, if two classes inherit from a common parent, then a change in one class might require a change in the other. Think of a combo audio system: It's tightly coupled because if we want to change from analog to digital radio, we must rebuild the whole system. If we assemble a system from separates, it would have low coupling and we could just swap out the receiver. "Loosely" coupled features (i.e., those with low coupling) are easier to maintain.

An element's *cohesion* is a measure of whether its responsibilities form a meaningful unit. For example, a class that parses both dates and URLs is not coherent, because they're unrelated concepts. Think of a machine that washes both clothes and dishes—it's unlikely to do both well.[2] At the other extreme, a class that parses only the punctuation in a URL is unlikely to be coherent, because it doesn't represent a whole concept. To get anything done, the programmer will have to find other parsers for protocol, host, resource, and so on. Features with "high" coherence are easier to maintain.

---

2. Actually, there was a combined clothes and dishwasher. The "Thor Automagic" was manufactured in the 1940s, but the idea hasn't survived.

Chapter 2

Test-Driven Development with Objects

Music is the space between the notes.

—Claude Debussy

A Web of Objects

Object-oriented design focuses more on the communication between objects than on the objects themselves. As Alan Kay [Kay98] wrote:

> The big idea is "messaging" [...] The key in making great and growable systems is much more to design how its modules communicate rather than what their internal properties and behaviors should be.

An object communicates by messages: It receives messages from other objects and reacts by sending messages to other objects as well as, perhaps, returning a value or exception to the original sender. An object has a *method* of handling every type of message that it understands and, in most cases, encapsulates some internal state that it uses to coordinate its communication with other objects.

An object-oriented system is a web of collaborating objects. A system is built by creating objects and plugging them together so that they can send messages to one another. The behavior of the system is an emergent property of the composition of the objects—the choice of objects and how they are connected (Figure 2.1).

This lets us change the behavior of the system by changing the composition of its objects—adding and removing instances, plugging different combinations together—rather than writing procedural code. The code we write to manage this composition is a *declarative* definition of the how the web of objects will behave. It's easier to change the system's behavior because we can focus on *what* we want it to do, not *how*.

Values and Objects

When designing a system, it's important to distinguish between *values* that model unchanging quantities or measurements, and *objects* that have an identity, might change state over time, and model *computational processes*. In the

13

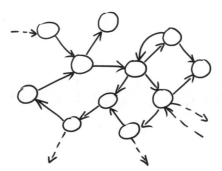

Figure 2.1   *A web of objects*

object-oriented languages that most of us use, the confusion is that both concepts are implemented by the same language construct: classes.

Values are immutable instances that model fixed quantities. They have no individual identity, so two value instances are effectively the same if they have the same state. This means that it makes no sense to compare the identity of two values; doing so can cause some subtle bugs—think of the different ways of comparing two copies of new Integer(999). That's why we're taught to use string1.equals(string2) in Java rather than string1 == string2.

Objects, on the other hand, use mutable state to model their behavior over time. Two objects of the same type have separate identities even if they have exactly the same state now, because their states can diverge if they receive different messages in the future.

In practice, this means that we split our system into two "worlds": values, which are treated functionally, and objects, which implement the stateful behavior of the system. In Part III, you'll see how our coding style varies depending on which world we're working in.

In this book, we will use the term *object* to refer only to instances with identity, state, and processing—not values. There doesn't appear to be another accepted term that isn't overloaded with other meanings (such as *entity* and *process*).

Follow the Messages

We can benefit from this high-level, declarative approach only if our objects are designed to be easily pluggable. In practice, this means that they follow common *communication patterns* and that the dependencies between them are made explicit. A communication pattern is a set of rules that govern how a group of objects talk each other: the roles they play, what messages they can send and when, and so on. In languages like Java, we identify object roles with (abstract) interfaces, rather than (concrete) classes—although interfaces don't define everything we need to say.

In our view, *the domain model is in these communication patterns*, because they are what gives meaning to the universe of possible relationships between the objects. Thinking of a system in terms of its dynamic, communication structure is a significant mental shift from the static classification that most of us learn when being introduced to objects. The domain model isn't even obviously visible because the communication patterns are not explicitly represented in the programming languages we get to work with. We hope to show, in this book, how tests and mock objects help us see the communication between our objects more clearly.

Here's a small example of how focusing on the communication between objects guides design.

In a video game, the objects in play might include: *actors*, such as the player and the enemies; *scenery*, which the player flies over; *obstacles*, which the player can crash into; and *effects*, such as explosions and smoke. There are also *scripts* spawning objects behind the scenes as the game progresses.

This is a good classification of the game objects from the players' point of view because it supports the decisions they need to make when playing the game—when interacting with the game from *outside*. This is not, however, a useful classification for the implementers of the game. The game engine has to display objects that are *visible*, tell objects that are *animated* about the passing of time, detect collisions between objects that are *physical*, and delegate decisions about what to do when physical objects collide to *collision resolvers*.

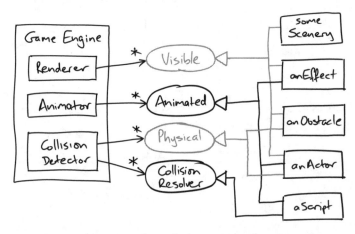

Figure 2.2   *Roles and objects in a video game*

As you can see in Figure 2.2, the two views, one from the game engine and one from the implementation of the in-play objects, are not the same. An Obstacle, for example, is *Visible* and *Physical*, while a Script is a *Collision Resolver* and *Animated* but not *Visible*. The objects in the game play different roles depending on what the engine needs from them at the time. This mismatch between static classification and dynamic communication means that we're unlikely to come up with a tidy class hierarchy for the game objects that will also suit the needs of the engine.

At best, a class hierarchy represents one dimension of an application, providing a mechanism for sharing implementation details between objects; for example, we might have a base class to implement the common features of frame-based animation. At worst, we've seen too many codebases (including our own) that suffer complexity and duplication from using one mechanism to represent multiple concepts.

Roles, Responsibilities, Collaborators

We try to think about objects in terms of roles, responsibilities, and collaborators, as best described by Wirfs-Brock and McKean in [Wirfs-Brock03]. An object is an implementation of one or more *roles*; a role is a set of related *responsibilities*; and a responsibility is an obligation to perform a task or know information. A *collaboration* is an interaction of objects or roles (or both).

Sometimes we step away from the keyboard and use an informal design technique that Wirfs-Brock and McKean describe, called *CRC cards* (Candidates, Responsibilities, Collaborators). The idea is to use low-tech index cards to explore the potential object structure of an application, or a part of it. These index cards allow us to experiment with structure without getting stuck in detail or becoming too attached to an early solution.

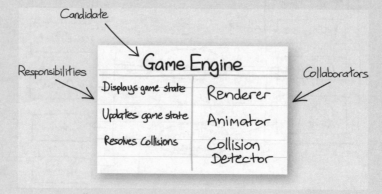

Figure 2.3   *CRC card for a video game*

Tell, Don't Ask

We have objects sending each other messages, so what do they say? Our experience is that the calling object should describe what it wants *in terms of the role* that its neighbor plays, and let the called object decide how to make that happen. This is commonly known as the *"Tell, Don't Ask"* style or, more formally, the *Law of Demeter*. Objects make their decisions based only on the information they hold internally or that which came with the triggering message; they avoid navigating to other objects to make things happen. Followed consistently, this style produces more flexible code because it's easy to swap objects that play the same role. The caller sees nothing of their internal structure or the structure of the rest of the system behind the role interface.

When we don't follow the style, we can end up with what's known as *"train wreck"* code, where a series of getters is chained together like the carriages in a train. Here's one case we found on the Internet:

```
((EditSaveCustomizer) master.getModelisable()
  .getDockablePanel()
    .getCustomizer())
      .getSaveItem().setEnabled(Boolean.FALSE.booleanValue());
```

After some head scratching, we realized what this fragment was *meant* to say:

```
master.allowSavingOfCustomisations();
```

This wraps all that implementation detail up behind a single call. The client of `master` no longer needs to know anything about the types in the chain. We've reduced the risk that a design change might cause ripples in remote parts of the codebase.

As well as hiding information, there's a more subtle benefit from "Tell, Don't Ask." It forces us to make explicit and so name the interactions between objects, rather than leaving them implicit in the chain of getters. The shorter version above is much clearer about *what* it's for, not just *how* it happens to be implemented.

But Sometimes Ask

Of course we don't "tell" everything;[1] we "ask" when getting information from values and collections, or when using a factory to create new objects. Occasionally, we also ask objects about their state when searching or filtering, but we still want to maintain expressiveness and avoid "train wrecks."

For example (to continue with the metaphor), if we naively wanted to spread reserved seats out across the whole of a train, we might start with something like:

---

1. Although that's an interesting exercise to try, to stretch your technique.

```java
public class Train {
  private final List<Carriage> carriages [...]
  private int percentReservedBarrier = 70;

  public void reserveSeats(ReservationRequest request) {
    for (Carriage carriage : carriages) {
      if (carriage.getSeats().getPercentReserved() < percentReservedBarrier) {
        request.reserveSeatsIn(carriage);
        return;
      }
    }
    request.cannotFindSeats();
  }
}
```

We shouldn't expose the internal structure of Carriage to implement this, not least because there may be different types of carriages within a train. Instead, we should ask the question we really want answered, instead of asking for the information to help us figure out the answer ourselves:

```java
public void reserveSeats(ReservationRequest request) {
  for (Carriage carriage : carriages) {
    if (carriage.hasSeatsAvailableWithin(percentReservedBarrier)) {
      request.reserveSeatsIn(carriage);
      return;
    }
  }
  request.cannotFindSeats();
}
```

Adding a query method moves the behavior to the most appropriate object, gives it an explanatory name, and makes it easier to test.

We try to be sparing with queries on objects (as opposed to values) because they can allow information to "leak" out of the object, making the system a little bit more rigid. At a minimum, we make a point of writing queries that describe the intention of the calling object, not just the implementation.

Unit-Testing the Collaborating Objects

We appear to have painted ourselves into a corner. We're insisting on focused objects that send commands to each other and don't expose any way to query their state, so it looks like we have nothing available to assert in a unit test. For example, in Figure 2.4, the circled object will send messages to one or more of its three neighbors when invoked. How can we test that it does so correctly without exposing any of its internal state?

One option is to replace the target object's neighbors in a test with substitutes, or *mock objects*, as in Figure 2.5. We can specify how we expect the target object to communicate with its mock neighbors for a triggering event; we call these specifications *expectations*. During the test, the mock objects assert that they

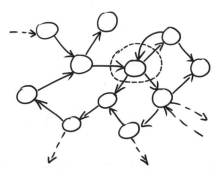

Figure 2.4   *Unit-testing an object in isolation*

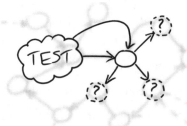

Figure 2.5   *Testing an object with mock objects*

have been called as expected; they also implement any stubbed behavior needed to make the rest of the test work.

With this infrastructure in place, we can change the way we approach TDD. Figure 2.5 implies that we're just trying to test the target object and that we already know what its neighbors look like. In practice, however, those collaborators don't need to exist when we're writing a unit test. We can use the test to help us tease out the supporting roles our object needs, defined as Java interfaces, and fill in real implementations as we develop the rest of the system. We call this *interface discovery*; you'll see an example when we extract an `AuctionEventListener` in Chapter 12.

Support for TDD with Mock Objects

To support this style of test-driven programming, we need to create mock instances of the neighboring objects, define expectations on how they're called and then check them, and implement any stub behavior we need to get through the test. In practice, the runtime structure of a test with mock objects usually looks like Figure 2.6.

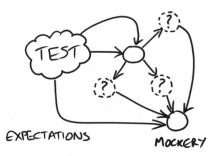

Figure 2.6   *Testing an object with mock objects*

We use the term *mockery*[2] for the object that holds the context of a test, creates mock objects, and manages expectations and stubbing for the test. We'll show the practice throughout Part III, so we'll just touch on the basics here. The essential structure of a test is:

- Create any required mock objects.

- Create any real objects, including the target object.

- Specify how you *expect* the mock objects to be called by the target object.

- Call the triggering method(s) on the target object.

- Assert that any resulting values are valid and that all the expected calls have been made.

The unit test makes explicit the relationship between the target object and its environment. It creates all the objects in the cluster and makes assertions about the interactions between the target object and its collaborators. We can code this infrastructure by hand or, these days, use one of the multiple mock object frameworks that are available in many languages. The important point, as we stress repeatedly throughout this book, is to make clear the intention of every test, distinguishing between the tested functionality, the supporting infrastructure, and the object structure.

---

2. This is a pun by Ivan Moore that we adopted in a fit of whimsy.

Chapter 3

An Introduction to the Tools

Man is a tool-using animal. Without tools he is nothing, with tools he is all.

—Thomas Carlyle

Stop Me If You've Heard This One Before

This book is about the techniques of using tests to guide the development of object-oriented software, not about specific technologies. To demonstrate the techniques in action, however, we've had to pick *some* technologies for our example code. For the rest of the book we're going to use Java, with the JUnit 4, Hamcrest, and jMock2 frameworks. If you're using something else, we hope we've been clear enough so that you can apply these ideas in your environment.

In this chapter we briefly describe the programming interfaces for these three frameworks, just enough to help you make sense of the code examples in the rest of the book. If you already know how to use them, you can skip this chapter.

A Minimal Introduction to JUnit 4

We use JUnit 4 (version 4.6 at the time of writing) as our Java test framework.[1] In essence, JUnit uses reflection to walk the structure of a class and run whatever it can find in that class that represents a test. For example, here's a test that exercises a `Catalog` class which manages a collection of `Entry` objects:

```java
public class CatalogTest {
  private final Catalog catalog = new Catalog();
  @Test public void containsAnAddedEntry() {
    Entry entry = new Entry("fish", "chips");
    catalog.add(entry);
    assertTrue(catalog.contains(entry));
  }
  @Test public void indexesEntriesByName() {
    Entry entry = new Entry("fish", "chips");
    catalog.add(entry);
    assertEquals(entry, catalog.entryFor("fish"));
    assertNull(catalog.entryFor("missing name"));
  }
}
```

---

1. JUnit is bundled with many Java IDEs and is available at www.junit.org.

Test Cases

JUnit treats any method annotated with @Test as a test case; test methods must have neither a return value nor parameters. In this case, CatalogTest defines two tests, called containsAnAddedEntry() and indexesEntriesByName().

To run a test, JUnit creates a new instance of the test class and calls the relevant test method. Creating a new test object each time ensures that the tests are isolated from each other, because the test object's fields are replaced before each test. This means that a test is free to change the contents of any of the test object fields.

 NUnit Behaves Differently from JUnit

Those working in .Net should note that NUnit reuses the same instance of the test object for all the test methods, so any values that might change must either be reset in [Setup] and [TearDown] methods (if they're fields) or made local to the test method.

Assertions

A JUnit test invokes the object under test and then makes *assertions* about the results, usually using assertion methods defined by JUnit which generate useful error messages when they fail.

CatalogTest, for example, uses three of JUnit's assertions: assertTrue() asserts that an expression is true; assertNull() asserts that an object reference is null; and assertEquals() asserts that two values are equal. When it fails, assertEquals() reports the expected and actual values that were compared.

Expecting Exceptions

The @Test annotation supports an optional parameter expected that declares that the test case should throw an exception. The test fails if it does *not* throw an exception or if it throws an exception of a different type.

For example, the following test checks that a Catalog throws an IllegalArgumentException when two entries are added with the same name:

```
@Test(expected=IllegalArgumentException.class)
public void cannotAddTwoEntriesWithTheSameName() {
  catalog.add(new Entry("fish", "chips"));
  catalog.add(new Entry("fish", "peas"));
}
```

Test Fixtures

A *test fixture* is the fixed state that exists at the start of a test. A test fixture ensures that a test is repeatable—every time a test is run it starts in the same state so it should produce the same results. A fixture may be *set up* before the test runs and *torn down* after it has finished.

The fixture for a JUnit test is managed by the class that defines the test and is stored in the object's fields. All tests defined in the same class start with an identical fixture and may modify that fixture as they run. For `CatalogTest`, the fixture is the empty `Catalog` object held in its `catalog` field.

The fixture is usually set up by field initializers. It can also be set up by the constructor of the test class or instance initializer blocks. JUnit also lets you identify methods that set up and tear down the fixture with annotations. JUnit will run all methods annotated with `@Before` before running the tests, to set up the fixture, and those annotated by `@After` after it has run the test, to tear down the fixture. Many JUnit tests do not need to explicitly tear down the fixture because it is enough to let the JVM garbage collect any objects created when it was set up.

For example, all the tests in `CatalogTest` initialize the `catalog` with the same entry. This common initialization can be moved into a field initializer and `@Before` method:

```
public class CatalogTest {
  final Catalog catalog = new Catalog();
  final Entry entry = new Entry("fish", "chips");

  @Before public void fillTheCatalog() {
    catalog.add(entry);
  }

  @Test public void containsAnAddedEntry() {
    assertTrue(catalog.contains(entry));
  }

  @Test public void indexesEntriesByName() {
    assertEquals(equalTo(entry), catalog.entryFor("fish"));
    assertNull(catalog.entryFor("missing name"));
  }

  @Test(expected=IllegalArgumentException.class)
  public void cannotAddTwoEntriesWithTheSameName() {
    catalog.add(new Entry("fish", "peas"));
  }
}
```

Test Runners

The way JUnit reflects on a class to find tests and then runs those tests is controlled by a *test runner*. The runner used for a class can be configured with the `@RunWith` annotation.[2] JUnit provides a small library of test runners. For example, the `Parameterized` test runner lets you write data-driven tests in which the same test methods are run for many different data values returned from a static method.

As we'll see below, the jMock library uses a custom test runner to automatically verify mock objects at the end of the test, before the test fixture is torn down.

Hamcrest Matchers and assertThat()

Hamcrest is a framework for writing declarative match criteria. While not a testing framework itself, Hamcrest is used by several testing frameworks, including JUnit, jMock, and WindowLicker, which we use in the example in Part III.

A Hamcrest *matcher* reports whether a given object matches some criteria, can describe its criteria, and can describe why an object does not meet its criteria. For example, this code creates matchers for strings that contain a given substring and uses them to make some assertions:

```
String s = "yes we have no bananas today";

Matcher<String> containsBananas = new StringContains("bananas");
Matcher<String> containsMangoes = new StringContains("mangoes");

assertTrue(containsBananas.matches(s));
assertFalse(containsMangoes.matches(s));
```

Matchers are not usually instantiated directly. Instead, Hamcrest provides static factory methods for all of its matchers to make the code that creates matchers more readable. For example:

```
assertTrue(containsString("bananas").matches(s));
assertFalse(containsString("mangoes").matches(s));
```

In practice, however, we use matchers in combination with JUnit's `assertThat()`, which uses matcher's self-describing features to make clear exactly what went wrong when an assertion fails.[3] We can rewrite the assertions as:

```
assertThat(s, containsString("bananas"));
assertThat(s, not(containsString("mangoes")));
```

The second assertion demonstrates one of Hamcrest's most useful features: defining new criteria by combining existing matchers. The `not()` method is a factory function that creates a matcher that reverses the sense of any matcher passed to it. Matchers are designed so that when they're combined, both the code and the failure messages are self-explanatory. For example, if we change the second assertion to fail:

---

2. By the time of publication, JUnit will also have a `Rule` annotation for fields to support objects that can "intercept" the lifecycle of a test run.

3. The `assertThat()` method was introduced in JUnit 4.5.

```
assertThat(s, not(containsString("bananas")));
```

the failure report is:

```
java.lang.AssertionError:
Expected: not a string containing "bananas"
     got: "Yes, we have no bananas"
```

Instead of writing code to explicitly check a condition and to generate an informative error message, we can pass a matcher expression to `assertThat()` and let it do the work.

Hamcrest is also user-extensible. If we need to check a specific condition, we can write a new matcher by implementing the `Matcher` interface and an appropriately-named factory method, and the result will combine seamlessly with the existing matcher expressions. We describe how to write custom Hamcrest matchers in Appendix B.

jMock2: Mock Objects

jMock2 plugs into JUnit (and other test frameworks) providing support for the mock objects testing style introduced in Chapter 2. jMock creates mock objects dynamically, so you don't have to write your own implementations of the types you want to mock. It also provides a high-level API for specifying how the object under test should invoke the mock objects it interacts with, and how the mock objects will behave in response.

 ### Understanding jMock

jMock is designed to make the expectation descriptions as clear as possible. We used some unusual Java coding practices to do so, which can appear surprising at first. jMock's design was motivated by the ideas presented in this book, backed by many years of experience in real projects. If the examples don't make sense to you, there's more description in Appendix A and at www.jmock.org. We (of course) believe that it's worth suspending your judgment until you've had a chance to work through some of the examples.

The core concepts of the jMock API are the *mockery*, *mock objects*, and *expectations*. A mockery represents the context of the object under test, its neighboring objects; mock objects stand in for the real neighbors of the object under test while the test runs; and expectations describe how the object under test should invoke its neighbors during the test.

An example will show how these fit together. This test asserts that an `AuctionMessageTranslator` will parse a given message text to generate an `auctionClosed()` event. For now, just concentrate on the structure; the test will turn up again in context in Chapter 12.

```
@RunWith(JMock.class) ❶
public class AuctionMessageTranslatorTest {
  private final Mockery context = new JUnit4Mockery(); ❷
  private final AuctionEventListener listener =
                          context.mock(AuctionEventListener.class); ❸
  private final AuctionMessageTranslator translator =
                          new AuctionMessageTranslator(listener); ❹

  @Test public void
  notifiesAuctionClosedWhenCloseMessageReceived() {
    Message message = new Message();
    message.setBody("SOLVersion: 1.1; Event: CLOSE;"); ❺

    context.checking(new Expectations() {{ ❻
      oneOf(listener).auctionClosed(); ❼
    }});

    translator.processMessage(UNUSED_CHAT, message); ❽
  } ❾
}
```

❶ The @RunWith(JMock.class) annotation tells JUnit to use the jMock test runner, which automatically calls the mockery at the end of the test to check that all mock objects have been invoked as expected.

❷ The test creates the Mockery. Since this is a JUnit 4 test, it creates a JUnit4Mockery which throws the right type of exception to report test failures to JUnit 4. By convention, jMock tests hold the mockery in a field named context, because it represents the context of the object under test.

❸ The test uses the mockery to create a mock AuctionEventListener that will stand in for a real listener implementation during this test.

❹ The test instantiates the object under test, an AuctionMessageTranslator, passing the mock listener to its constructor. The AuctionMessageTranslator does not distinguish between a real and a mock listener: It communicates through the AuctionEventListener interface and does not care how that interface is implemented.

❺ The test sets up further objects that will be used in the test.

❻ The test then tells the mockery how the translator should invoke its neighbors during the test by defining a block of expectations. The Java syntax we use to do this is obscure, so if you can bear with us for now we explain it in more detail in Appendix A.

❼ This is the significant line in the test, its one expectation. It says that, during the action, we expect the listener's auctionClosed() method to be called exactly once. Our definition of success is that the translator will notify its listener that an `auctionClosed()` event has happened whenever it receives a raw `Close` message.

❽ This is the call to the object under test, the outside event that triggers the behavior we want to test. It passes a raw `Close` message to the translator which, the test says, should make the translator call `auctionClosed()` once on the listener. The mockery will check that the mock objects are invoked as expected while the test runs and fail the test immediately if they are invoked unexpectedly.

❾ Note that the test does not require any assertions. This is quite common in mock object tests.

Expectations

The example above specifies one very simple expectation. jMock's expectation API is very expressive. It lets you precisely specify:

- The minimum and maximum number of times an invocation is expected;

- Whether an invocation is expected (the test should fail if it is not received) or merely allowed to happen (the test should pass if it is not received);

- The parameter values, either given literally or constrained by Hamcrest matchers;

- The ordering constraints with respect to other expectations; and,

- What should happen when the method is invoked—a value to return, an exception to throw, or any other behavior.

An expectation block is designed to stand out from the test code that surrounds it, making an obvious separation between the code that *describes* how neighboring objects should be invoked and the code that actually *invokes* objects and tests the results. The code within an expectation block acts as a little declarative language that describes the expectations; we'll return to this idea in "Building Up to Higher-Level Programming" (page 65).

There's more to the jMock API which we don't have space for in this chapter; we'll describe more of its features in examples in the rest of the book, and there's a summary in Appendix A. What really matters, however, is not the implementation we happened to come up with, but its underlying concepts and motivations. We will do our best to make them clear.

Part II

The Process of Test-Driven Development

So far we've presented a high-level introduction to the concept of, and motivation for, incremental test-driven development. In the rest of the book, we'll fill in the practical details that actually make it work.

In this part we introduce the concepts that define our approach. These boil down to two core principles: continuous incremental development and expressive code.

Chapter 4

Kick-Starting the Test-Driven Cycle

We should be taught not to wait for inspiration to start a thing. Action
always generates inspiration. Inspiration seldom generates action.

—Frank Tibolt

Introduction

The TDD process we described in Chapter 1 assumes that we can grow the system by just slotting the tests for new features into an existing infrastructure. But what about the very first feature, before we have this infrastructure? As an acceptance test, it must run end-to-end to give us the feedback we need about the system's external interfaces, which means we must have implemented a whole automated build, deploy, and test cycle. This is a lot of work to do before we can even see our first test fail.

Deploying and testing right from the start of a project forces the team to understand how their system fits into the world. It flushes out the "unknown unknown" technical and organizational risks so they can be addressed while there's still time. Attempting to deploy also helps the team understand who they need to liaise with, such as system administrators or external vendors, and start to build those relationships.

Starting with "build, deploy, and test" on a nonexistent system sounds odd, but we think it's essential. The risks of leaving it to later are just too high. We have seen projects canceled after months of development because they could not reliably deploy their system. We have seen systems discarded because new features required months of manual regression testing and even then the error rates were too high. As always, we view feedback as a fundamental tool, and we want to know as early as possible whether we're moving in the right direction. Then, once we have our first test in place, subsequent tests will be much quicker to write.

31

First, Test a Walking Skeleton

The quandary in writing and passing the first acceptance test is that it's hard to build both the tooling and the feature it's testing at the same time. Changes in one disrupt any progress made with the other, and tracking down failures is tricky when the architecture, the tests, and the production code are all moving. One of the symptoms of an unstable development environment is that there's no obvious first place to look when something fails.

We can cut through this "first-feature paradox" by splitting it into two smaller problems. First, work out how to build, deploy, and test a "walking skeleton," then use that infrastructure to write the acceptance tests for the first meaningful feature. After that, everything will be in place for test-driven development of the rest of the system.

A "walking skeleton" is an implementation of the thinnest possible slice of real functionality that we can automatically build, deploy, and test end-to-end [Cockburn04]. It should include just enough of the automation, the major components, and communication mechanisms to allow us to start working on the first feature. We keep the skeleton's application functionality so simple that it's obvious and uninteresting, leaving us free to concentrate on the infrastructure. For example, for a database-backed web application, a skeleton would show a flat web page with fields from the database. In Chapter 10, we'll show an example that displays a single value in the user interface and sends just a handshake message to the server.

It's also important to realize that the "end" in "end-to-end" refers to the process, as well as the system. We want our test to start from scratch, build a deployable system, *deploy it into a production-like environment*, and then run the tests through the deployed system. Including the deployment step in the testing process is critical for two reasons. First, this is the sort of error-prone activity that should not be done by hand, so we want our scripts to have been thoroughly exercised by the time we have to deploy for real. One lesson that we've learned repeatedly is that nothing forces us to understand a process better than trying to automate it. Second, this is often the moment where the development team bumps into the rest of the organization and has to learn how it operates. If it's going to take six weeks and four signatures to set up a database, we want to know *now*, not two weeks before delivery.

In practice, of course, real end-to-end testing may be so hard to achieve that we have to start with infrastructure that implements our *current understanding* of what the real system will do and what its environment is. We keep in mind, however, that this is a stop-gap, a temporary patch until we can finish the job, and that unknown risks remain until our tests really run end-to-end. One of the weaknesses of our Auction Sniper example (Part III) is that the tests run against a dummy server, not the real site. At some point before going live, we would have had to test against Southabee's On-Line; the earlier we can do that, the easier it will be for us to respond to any surprises that turn up.

Whilst building the "walking skeleton," we concentrate on the structure and don't worry too much about cleaning up the test to be beautifully expressive. The walking skeleton and its supporting infrastructure are there to help us work out how to start test-driven development. It's only the first step toward a complete end-to-end acceptance-testing solution. When we write the test for the first feature, *then* we need to "write the test you want to read" (page 42) to make sure that it's a clear expression of the behavior of the system.

The Importance of Early End-to-End Testing

We joined a project that had been running for a couple of years but had never tested their entire system end-to-end. There were frequent production outages and deployments often failed. The system was large and complex, reflecting the complicated business transactions it managed. The effort of building an automated, end-to-end test suite was so large that an entire new team had to be formed to perform the work. It took them months to build an end-to-end test environment, and they never managed to get the entire system covered by an end-to-end test suite.

Because the need for end-to-end testing had not influenced its design, the system was difficult to test. For example, the system's components used internal timers to schedule activities, some of them days or weeks into the future. This made it very difficult to write end-to-end tests: It was impractical to run the tests in real-time but the scheduling could not be influenced from outside the system. The developers had to redesign the system itself so that periodic activities were triggered by messages sent from a remote scheduler which could be replaced in the test environment; see "Externalize Event Sources" (page 326). This was a significant architectural change—and it was very risky because it had to be performed without end-to-end test coverage.

Deciding the Shape of the Walking Skeleton

The development of a "walking skeleton" is the moment when we start to make choices about the high-level structure of our application. We can't automate the build, deploy, and test cycle without *some* idea of the overall structure. We don't need much detail yet, just a broad-brush picture of what major system components will be needed to support the first planned release and how they will communicate. Our rule of thumb is that we should be able to draw the design for the "walking skeleton" in a few minutes on a whiteboard.

Mappa Mundi

We find that maintaining a public drawing of the structure of the system, for example on the wall in the team's work area as in Figure 4.1, helps the team stay oriented when working on the code.

Figure 4.1   *A broad-brush architecture diagram drawn on the wall of a team's work area*

To design this initial structure, we have to have *some* understanding of the purpose of the system, otherwise the whole exercise risks being meaningless. We need a high-level view of the client's requirements, both functional and non-functional, to guide our choices. This preparatory work is part of the chartering of the project, which we must leave as outside the scope of this book.

The point of the "walking skeleton" is to use the writing of the first test to draw out the context of the project, to help the team map out the landscape of their solution—the essential decisions that they must take before they can write any code; Figure 4.2 shows how the TDD process we drew in Figure 1.2 fits into this context.

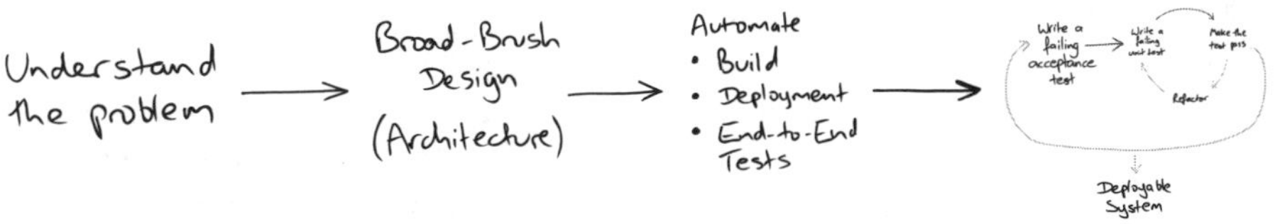

Figure 4.2   *The context of the first test*

Please don't confuse this with doing "Big Design Up Front" (BDUF) which has such a bad reputation in the Agile Development community. We're not trying to elaborate the whole design down to classes and algorithms before we start coding. Any ideas we have now are likely to be wrong, so we prefer to discover those details as we grow the system. We're making the smallest number of decisions we can to kick-start the TDD cycle, to allow us to start learning and improving from real feedback.

Build Sources of Feedback

We have no guarantees that the decisions we've taken about the design of our application, or the assumptions on which they're based, are right. We do the best we can, but the only thing we can rely on is validating them as soon as possible by building feedback into our process. The tools we build to implement the "walking skeleton" are there to support this learning process. Of course, these tools too will not be perfect, and we expect we will improve them incrementally as we learn how well they support the team.

Our ideal situation is where the team releases regularly to a real production system, as in Figure 4.3. This allows the system's stakeholders to respond to how well the system meets their needs, at the same time allowing us to judge its implementation.

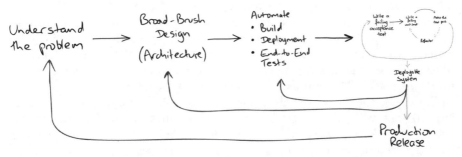

Figure 4.3   *Requirements feedback*

We use the automation of building and testing to give us feedback on qualities of the system, such as how easily we can cut a version and deploy, how well the design works, and how good the code is. The automated deployment helps us release frequently to real users, which gives us feedback on how well we have understood the domain and whether seeing the system in practice has changed our customer's priorities.

The great benefit is that we will be able to make changes in response to whatever we learn, because writing everything test-first means that we will have a thorough set of regression tests. No tests are perfect, of course, but in practice we've found that a substantial test suite allows us to make major changes safely.

Expose Uncertainty Early

All this effort means that teams are frequently surprised by the time it takes to get a "walking skeleton" working, considering that it does hardly anything. That's because this first step involves establishing a lot of infrastructure and asking (and answering) many awkward questions. The time to implement the first few features will be unpredictable as the team discovers more about its requirements and target environment. For a new team, this will be compounded by the social stresses of learning how to work together.

Fred Tingey, a colleague, once observed that incremental development can be disconcerting for teams and management who aren't used to it because it frontloads the stress in a project. Projects with late integration start calmly but generally turn difficult towards the end as the team tries to pull the system together for the first time. Late integration is unpredictable because the team has to assemble a great many moving parts with limited time and budget to fix any failures. The result is that experienced stakeholders react badly to the instability at the start of an incremental project because they expect that the end of the project will be much worse.

Our experience is that a well-run incremental development runs in the opposite direction. It starts unsettled but then, after a few features have been implemented and the project automation has been built up, settles in to a routine. As a project approaches delivery, the end-game should be a steady production of functionality, perhaps with a burst of activity before the first release. All the mundane but brittle tasks, such as deployment and upgrades, will have been automated so that they "just work." The contrast looks rather like Figure 4.4.

This aspect of test-driven development, like others, may appear counterintuitive, but we've always found it worth taking enough time to structure and automate the basics of the system—or at least a first cut. Of course, we don't want to spend the whole project setting up a perfect "walking skeleton," so we limit ourselves to whiteboard-level decisions and reserve the right to change our mind when we have to. But the most important thing is to have a sense of direction and a concrete implementation to test our assumptions.

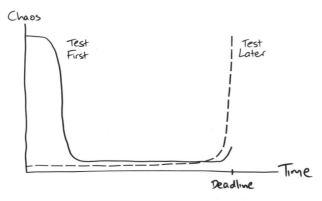

Figure 4.4 *Visible uncertainty in test-first and test-later projects*

A "walking skeleton" will flush out issues early in the project when there's still time, budget, and goodwill to address them.

Brownfield Development

We don't always have the luxury of building a new system from the ground up. Many of our projects have started with an existing system that must be extended, adapted, or replaced. In such cases, we can't start by building a "walking skeleton"; we have to work with what already exists, no matter how hostile its structure.

That said, the process of kick-starting TDD of an existing system is not fundamentally different from applying it to a new system—although it may be orders of magnitude more difficult because of the technical baggage the system already carries. Michael Feathers has written a whole book on the topic, [Feathers04].

It is risky to start reworking a system when there are no tests to detect regressions. The safest way to start the TDD process is to automate the build and deploy process, and then add end-to-end tests that cover the areas of the code we need to change. With that protection, we can start to address internal quality issues with more confidence, refactoring the code and introducing unit tests as we add functionality.

The easiest way to start building an end-to-end test infrastructure is with the simplest path through the system that we can find. Like a "walking skeleton," this lets us build up some supporting infrastructure before we tackle the harder problems of testing more complicated functionality.

Chapter 5

Maintaining the Test-Driven Cycle

> *Every day you may make progress. Every step may be fruitful. Yet there will stretch out before you an ever-lengthening, ever-ascending, ever-improving path. You know you will never get to the end of the journey. But this, so far from discouraging, only adds to the joy and glory of the climb.*
>
> —Winston Churchill

Introduction

Once we've kick-started the TDD process, we need to keep it running smoothly. In this chapter we'll show how a TDD process runs once started. The rest of the book explores in some detail how we ensure it runs smoothly—how we write tests as we build the system, how we use tests to get early feedback on internal and external quality issues, and how we ensure that the tests continue to support change and do not become an obstacle to further development.

Start Each Feature with an Acceptance Test

As we described in Chapter 1, we start work on a new feature by writing failing acceptance tests that demonstrate that the system does not yet have the feature we're about to write and track our progress towards completion of the feature (Figure 5.1).

We write the acceptance test using only terminology from the application's domain, not from the underlying technologies (such as databases or web servers). This helps us understand what the system should do, without tying us to any of our initial assumptions about the implementation or complicating the test with technological details. This also shields our acceptance test suite from changes to the system's technical infrastructure. For example, if a third-party organization changes the protocol used by their services from FTP and binary files to web services and XML, we should not have to rework the tests for the system's application logic.

We find that writing such a test before coding makes us clarify what we want to achieve. The precision of expressing requirements in a form that can be automatically checked helps us uncover implicit assumptions. The failing tests keep

39

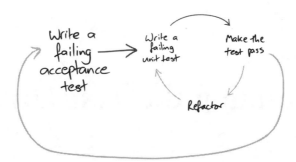

Figure 5.1   *Each TDD cycle starts with a failing acceptance test*

us focused on implementing the limited set of features they describe, improving our chances of delivering them. More subtly, starting with tests makes us look at the system from the users' point of view, understanding what *they* need it to do rather than speculating about features from the implementers' point of view.

Unit tests, on the other hand, exercise objects, or small clusters of objects, in isolation. They're important to help us design classes and give us confidence that they work, but they don't say anything about whether they work together with the rest of the system. Acceptance tests both test the integration of unit-tested objects and push the project forwards.

Separate Tests That Measure Progress from Those That Catch Regressions

When we write acceptance tests to describe a new feature, we expect them to fail until that feature has been implemented; new acceptance tests describe work yet to be done. The activity of turning acceptance tests from red to green gives the team a measure of the progress it's making. A regular cycle of passing acceptance tests is the engine that drives the nested project feedback loops we described in "Feedback Is the Fundamental Tool" (page 4). Once passing, the acceptance tests now represent completed features and should not fail again. A failure means that there's been a regression, that we've broken our existing code.

We organize our test suites to reflect the different roles that the tests fulfill. Unit and integration tests support the development team, should run quickly, and should always pass. Acceptance tests for completed features catch regressions and should always pass, although they might take longer to run. New acceptance tests represent work in progress and will not pass until a feature is ready.

If requirements change, we must move any affected acceptance tests out of the regression suite back into the in-progress suite, edit them to reflect the new requirements, and change the system to make them pass again.

Start Testing with the Simplest Success Case

Where do we start when we have to write a new class or feature? It's tempting to start with degenerate or failure cases because they're often easier. That's a common interpretation of the XP maxim to do "the simplest thing that could possibly work" [Beck02], but *simple* should not be interpreted as *simplistic*. Degenerate cases don't add much to the value of the system and, more importantly, don't give us enough feedback about the validity of our ideas. Incidentally, we also find that focusing on the failure cases at the beginning of a feature is bad for morale—if we only work on error handling it feels like we're not achieving anything.

We prefer to start by testing the simplest *success* case. Once that's working, we'll have a better idea of the real structure of the solution and can prioritize between handling any possible failures we noticed along the way and further success cases. Of course, a feature isn't complete until it's robust. This isn't an excuse not to bother with failure handling—but we can choose when we want to implement first.

We find it useful to keep a notepad or index cards by the keyboard to jot down failure cases, refactorings, and other technical tasks that need to be addressed. This allows us to stay focused on the task at hand without dropping detail. The feature is finished only when we've crossed off everything on the list—either we've done each task or decided that we don't need to.

Iterations in Space

We're writing this material around the fortieth anniversary of the first Moon landing. The Moon program was an excellent example of an incremental approach (although with much larger stakes than we're used to). In 1967, they proposed a series of seven missions, each of which would be a step on the way to a landing:

1. Unmanned Command/Service Module (CSM) test

2. Unmanned Lunar Module (LM) test

3. Manned CSM in low Earth orbit

4. Manned CSM and LM in low Earth orbit

5. Manned CSM and LM in an elliptical Earth orbit with an apogee of 4600 mi (7400 km)

6. Manned CSM and LM in lunar orbit

7. Manned lunar landing

At least in software, we can develop incrementally without building a new rocket each time.

Write the Test That You'd Want to Read

We want each test to be as clear as possible an expression of the behavior to be performed by the system or object. While writing the test, we ignore the fact that the test won't run, or even compile, and just concentrate on its text; we act as if the supporting code to let us run the test already exists.

When the test reads well, we then build up the infrastructure to support the test. We know we've implemented enough of the supporting code when the test fails in the way we'd expect, with a clear error message describing what needs to be done. Only then do we start writing the code to make the test pass. We look further at making tests readable in Chapter 21.

Watch the Test Fail

We *always* watch the test fail before writing the code to make it pass, and check the diagnostic message. If the test fails in a way we didn't expect, we know we've misunderstood something or the code is incomplete, so we fix that. When we get the "right" failure, we check that the diagnostics are helpful. If the failure description isn't clear, someone (probably us) will have to struggle when the code breaks in a few weeks' time. We adjust the test code and rerun the tests until the error messages guide us to the problem with the code (Figure 5.2).

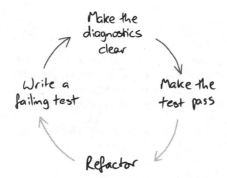

Figure 5.2   *Improving the diagnostics as part of the TDD cycle*

As we write the production code, we keep running the test to see our progress and to check the error diagnostics as the system is built up behind the test. Where necessary, we extend or modify the support code to ensure the error messages are always clear and relevant.

There's more than one reason for insisting on checking the error messages. First, it checks our assumptions about the code we're working on—sometimes we're wrong. Second, more subtly, we find that our emphasis on (or, perhaps, mania for) expressing our intentions is fundamental for developing reliable, maintainable systems—and for us that includes tests and failure messages. Taking the trouble to generate a useful diagnostic helps us clarify what the test, and therefore the code, is supposed to do. We look at error diagnostics and how to improve them in Chapter 23.

Develop from the Inputs to the Outputs

We start developing a feature by considering the events coming into the system that will trigger the new behavior. The end-to-end tests for the feature will simulate these events arriving. At the boundaries of our system, we will need to write one or more objects to handle these events. As we do so, we discover that these objects need supporting services from the rest of the system to perform their responsibilities. We write more objects to implement these services, and discover what services these new objects need in turn.

In this way, we work our way through the system: from the objects that receive external events, through the intermediate layers, to the central domain model, and then on to other boundary objects that generate an externally visible response. That might mean accepting some text and a mouse click and looking for a record in a database, or receiving a message in a queue and looking for a file on a server.

It's tempting to start by unit-testing new domain model objects and then trying to hook them into the rest of the application. It seems easier at the start—we feel we're making rapid progress working on the domain model when we don't have to make it fit into anything—but we're more likely to get bitten by integration problems later. We'll have wasted time building unnecessary or incorrect functionality, because we weren't receiving the right kind of feedback when we were working on it.

Unit-Test Behavior, Not Methods

We've learned the hard way that just writing lots of tests, even when it produces high test coverage, does not guarantee a codebase that's easy to work with. Many developers who adopt TDD find their early tests hard to understand when they revisit them later, and one common mistake is thinking about testing *methods*. A test called testBidAccepted() tells us what it does, but not what it's *for*.

We do better when we focus on the *features* that the object under test should provide, each of which may require collaboration with its neighbors and calling more than one of its methods. We need to know how to use the class to achieve a goal, not how to exercise all the paths through its code.

The Importance of Describing Behavior, Not API Features

Nat used to run a company that produced online advertising and branded content for clients sponsoring sports teams. One of his clients sponsored a Formula One racing team. Nat wrote a fun little game that simulated Formula One race strategies for the client to put on the team's website. It took him two weeks to write, from initial idea to final deliverable, and once he handed it over to the client he forgot all about it.

It turned out, however, that the throw-away game was by far the most popular content on the team's website. For the next F1 season, the client wanted to capitalize on its success. They wanted the game to model the track of each Grand Prix, to accommodate the latest F1 rules, to have a better model of car physics, to simulate dynamic weather, overtaking, spin-outs, and more.

Nat had written the original version test-first, so he expected it to be easy to change. However, going back to the code, he found the tests very hard to understand. He had written a test for each method of each object but couldn't understand from those tests how each object was meant to behave—what the responsibilities of the object were and how the different methods of the object worked together.

It helps to choose test names that describe how the object behaves in the scenario being tested. We look at this in more detail in "Test Names Describe Features" (page 248).

Listen to the Tests

When writing unit and integration tests, we stay alert for areas of the code that are difficult to test. When we find a feature that's difficult to test, we don't just ask ourselves *how* to test it, but also *why* is it difficult to test.

Our experience is that, when code is difficult to test, the most likely cause is that our design needs improving. The same structure that makes the code difficult to test now will make it difficult to change in the future. By the time that future comes around, a change will be more difficult still because we'll have forgotten what we were thinking when we wrote the code. For a successful system, it might even be a completely different team that will have to live with the consequences of our decisions.

Our response is to regard the process of writing tests as a valuable early warning of potential maintenance problems and to use those hints to fix a problem while it's still fresh. As Figure 5.3 shows, if we're finding it hard to write the next failing test, we look again at the design of the production code and often refactor it before moving on.

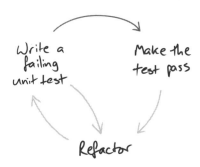

Figure 5.3   *Difficulties writing tests may suggest a need to fix production code*

This is an example of how our maxim—"Expect Unexpected Changes"—guides development. If we keep up the quality of the system by refactoring when we see a weakness in the design, we will be able to make it respond to whatever changes turn up. The alternative is the usual "software rot" where the code decays until the team just cannot respond to the needs of its customers. We'll return to this topic in Chapter 20.

Tuning the Cycle

There's a balance between exhaustively testing execution paths and testing integration. If we test at too large a grain, the combinatorial explosion of trying all the possible paths through the code will bring development to a halt. Worse, some of those paths, such as throwing obscure exceptions, will be impractical to test from that level. On the other hand, if we test at too fine a grain—just at the class level, for example—the testing will be easier but we'll miss problems that arise from objects not working together.

How much unit testing should we do, using mock objects to break external dependencies, and how much integration testing? We don't think there's a single answer to this question. It depends too much on the context of the team and its environment. The best we can get from the testing part of TDD (which is a lot) is the confidence that we can change the code without breaking it: Fear kills progress. The trick is to make sure that the confidence is justified.

So, we regularly reflect on how well TDD is working for us, identify any weaknesses, and adapt our testing strategy. Fiddly bits of logic might need more unit testing (or, alternatively, simplification); unhandled exceptions might need more integration-level testing; and, unexpected system failures will need more investigation and, possibly, more testing throughout.

Chapter 6

Object-Oriented Style

Always design a thing by considering it in its next larger context—a chair in a room, a room in a house, a house in an environment, an environment in a city plan.

—Eliel Saarinen

Introduction

So far in Part II, we've talked about how to get started with the development process and how to keep going. Now we want to take a more detailed look at our design goals and our use of TDD, and in particular *mock objects*, to guide the structure of our code.

We value code that is easy to maintain over code that is easy to write.[1] Implementing a feature in the most direct way can damage the maintainability of the system, for example by making the code difficult to understand or by introducing hidden dependencies between components. Balancing immediate and longer-term concerns is often tricky, but we've seen too many teams that can no longer deliver because their system is too brittle.

In this chapter, we want to show something of what we're trying to achieve when we design software, and how that looks in an object-oriented language; this is the "opinionated" part of our approach to software. In the next chapter, we'll look at the mechanics of how to guide code in this direction with TDD.

Designing for Maintainability

Following the process we described in Chapter 5, we grow our systems a slice of functionality at a time. As the code scales up, the only way we can continue to understand and maintain it is by structuring the functionality into objects, objects into packages,[2] packages into programs, and programs into systems. We use two principal heuristics to guide this structuring:

---

1. As the Agile Manifesto might have put it.
2. We're being vague about the meaning of "package" here since we want it to include concepts such as modules, libraries, and namespaces, which tend to be confounded in the Java world—but you know what we mean.

Separation of concerns

When we have to change the behavior of a system, we want to change as little code as possible. If all the relevant changes are in one area of code, we don't have to hunt around the system to get the job done. Because we cannot predict when we will have to change any particular part of the system, we gather together code that will change for the same reason. For example, code to unpack messages from an Internet standard protocol will not change for the same reasons as business code that interprets those messages, so we partition the two concepts into different packages.

Higher levels of abstraction

The only way for humans to deal with complexity is to avoid it, by working at higher levels of abstraction. We can get more done if we program by combining components of useful functionality rather than manipulating variables and control flow; that's why most people order food from a menu in terms of dishes, rather than detail the recipes used to create them.

Applied consistently, these two forces will push the structure of an application towards something like Cockburn's "ports and adapters" architecture [Cockburn08], in which the code for the business domain is isolated from its dependencies on technical infrastructure, such as databases and user interfaces. We don't want technical concepts to leak into the application model, so we write interfaces to describe its relationships with the outside world *in its terminology* (Cockburn's *ports*). Then we write bridges between the application core and each technical domain (Cockburn's *adapters*). This is related to what Eric Evans calls an "anticorruption layer" [Evans03].

The bridges implement the interfaces defined by the application model and map between application-level and technical-level objects (Figure 6.1). For example, a bridge might map an order book object to SQL statements so that orders are persisted in a database. To do so, it might query values from the application object or use an object-relational tool like Hibernate[3] to pull values out of objects using Java reflection. We'll show an example of refactoring to this architecture in Chapter 17.

The next question is how to find the facets in the behavior where the interfaces should be, so that we can divide up the code cleanly. We have some second-level heuristics to help us think about that.

---

3. http://www.hibernate.org

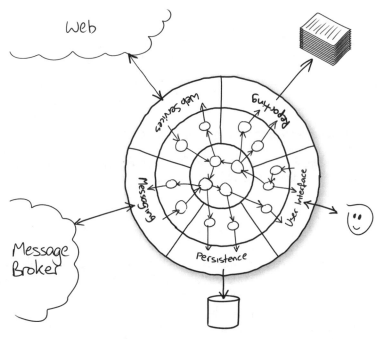

Figure 6.1 *An application's core domain model is mapped onto technical infrastructure*

Encapsulation and Information Hiding

We want to be careful with the distinction between "encapsulation" and "information hiding." The terms are often used interchangeably but actually refer to two separate, and largely orthogonal, qualities:

Encapsulation

> Ensures that the behavior of an object can only be affected through its API. It lets us control how much a change to one object will impact other parts of the system by ensuring that there are no unexpected dependencies between unrelated components.

Information hiding

> Conceals how an object implements its functionality behind the abstraction of its API. It lets us work with higher abstractions by ignoring lower-level details that are unrelated to the task at hand.

We're most aware of encapsulation when we haven't got it. When working with badly encapsulated code, we spend too much time tracing what the potential effects of a change might be, looking at where objects are created, what common data they hold, and where their contents are referenced. The topic has inspired two books that we know of, [Feathers04] and [Demeyer03].

Many object-oriented languages support encapsulation by providing control over the visibility of an object's features to other objects, but that's not enough. Objects can break encapsulation by sharing references to mutable objects, an effect known as *aliasing*. Aliasing is essential for conventional object- oriented systems (otherwise no two objects would be able to communicate), but *accidental* aliasing can couple unrelated parts of a system so it behaves mysteriously and is inflexible to change.

We follow standard practices to maintain encapsulation when coding: define immutable value types, avoid global variables and singletons, copy collections and mutable values when passing them between objects, and so on. We have more about information hiding later in this chapter.

Internals vs. Peers

As we organize our system, we must decide what is inside and outside each object, so that the object provides a coherent abstraction with a clear API. Much of the point of an object, as we discussed above, is to encapsulate access to its internals through its API and to hide these details from the rest of the system. An object communicates with other objects in the system by sending and receiving messages, as in Figure 6.2; the objects it communicates with directly are its *peers*.

Figure 6.2   *Objects communicate by sending and receiving messages*

This decision matters because it affects how easy an object is to use, and so contributes to the internal quality of the system. If we expose too much of an object's internals through its API, its clients will end up doing some of its work. We'll have distributed behavior across too many objects (they'll be *coupled* together), increasing the cost of maintenance because any changes will now ripple across the code. This is the effect of the "train wreck" example on page 17:

```
((EditSaveCustomizer) master.getModelisable()
  .getDockablePanel()
    .getCustomizer())
      .getSaveItem().setEnabled(Boolean.FALSE.booleanValue());
```

Every getter in this example exposes a structural detail. If we wanted to change, say, the way customizations on the master are enabled, we'd have to change all the intermediate relationships.

Different Levels of Language

As you'll see in Part III, we often write helper methods to make code more readable. We're not afraid of adding very small methods if they clarify the meaning of the feature they represent. We name these methods to make the calling code read as naturally as possible; we don't have to conform to external conventions since these methods are only there to support other code. For example, in Chapter 15 we have a line in a test that reads:

```
allowing(sniperListener).sniperStateChanged(with(aSniperThatIs(BIDDING)));
```

We'll explain what this means at the time. What's relevant here is that aSniperThatIs() is a local method that constructs a value to be passed to the with() method, and that its name is intended to describe its intent *in this context*. In effect, we're constructing a very small embedded language that defines, in this case, a part of a test.

As well as distinguishing between value and object types (page 13), we find that we tend towards different programming styles at different levels in the code. Loosely speaking, we use the *message-passing* style we've just described *between* objects, but we tend to use a more *functional* style *within* an object, building up behavior from methods and values that have no side effects.

Features without side effects mean that we can assemble our code from smaller components, minimizing the amount of risky shared state. Writing large-scale functional programs is a topic for a different book, but we find that a little immutability within the implementation of a class leads to much safer code and that, if we do a good job, the code reads well too.

So how do we choose the right features for an object?

No And's, Or's, or But's

Every object should have a single, clearly defined responsibility; this is the "single responsibility" principle [Martin02]. When we're adding behavior to a system, this principle helps us decide whether to extend an existing object or create a new service for an object to call.

Our heuristic is that we should be able to describe what an object does without using any conjunctions ("and," "or"). If we find ourselves adding clauses to the description, then the object probably should be broken up into collaborating objects, usually one for each clause.

This principle also applies when we're combining objects into new abstractions. If we're packaging up behavior implemented across several objects into a single construct, we should be able to describe its responsibility clearly; there are some related ideas below in the "Composite Simpler Than the Sum of Its Parts" and "Context Independence" sections.

Object Peer Stereotypes

We have objects with single responsibilities, communicating with their peers through messages in clean APIs, but what do they say to each other?

We categorize an object's peers (loosely) into three types of relationship. An object might have:

Dependencies
Services that the object requires from its peers so it can perform its responsibilities. The object cannot function without these services. It should not be possible to create the object without them. For example, a graphics package will need something like a screen or canvas to draw on—it doesn't make sense without one.

Notifications
Peers that need to be kept up to date with the object's activity. The object will notify interested peers whenever it changes state or performs a significant action. Notifications are "fire and forget"; the object neither knows nor cares which peers are listening. Notifications are so useful because they decouple objects from each other. For example, in a user interface system, a button component promises to notify any registered listeners when it's clicked, but does not know what those listeners will do. Similarly, the listeners expect to be called but know nothing of the way the user interface dispatches its events.

Adjustments
Peers that adjust the object's behavior to the wider needs of the system. This includes policy objects that make decisions on the object's behalf (the Strategy pattern in [Gamma94]) and component parts of the object if it's a composite. For example, a Swing `JTable` will ask a `TableCellRenderer` to draw a cell's value, perhaps as RGB (Red, Green, Blue) values for a color. If we change the renderer, the table will change its presentation, now displaying the HSB (Hue, Saturation, Brightness) values.

These stereotypes are only heuristics to help us think about the design, not hard rules, so we don't obsess about finding just the right classification of an object's peers. What matters most is the context in which the collaborating objects are used. For example, in one application an auditing log could be a dependency, because auditing is a legal requirement for the business and no object should be created without an audit trail. Elsewhere, it could be a notification, because auditing is a user choice and objects will function perfectly well without it.

Another way to look at it is that notifications are one-way: A notification listener may not return a value, call back the caller, or throw an exception, since there may be other listeners further down the chain. A dependency or adjustment, on the other hand, may do any of these, since there's a direct relationship.

"New or new not. There is no try."[4]

We try to make sure that we always create a valid object. For dependencies, this means that we pass them in through the constructor. They're required, so there's no point in creating an instance of an object until its dependencies are available, and using the constructor enforces this constraint in the object's definition.

Partially creating an object and then finishing it off by setting properties is brittle because the programmer has to remember to set all the dependencies. When the object changes to add new dependencies, the existing client code will still compile even though it no longer constructs a valid instance. At best this will cause a `NullPointerException`, at worst it will fail misleadingly.

Notifications and adjustments can be passed to the constructor as a convenience. Alternatively, they can be initialized to safe defaults and overwritten later (note that there is no safe default for a dependency). Adjustments can be initialized to common values, and notifications to a null object [Woolf98] or an empty collection. We then add methods to allow callers to change these default values, and add or remove listeners.

Composite Simpler Than the Sum of Its Parts

All objects in a system, except for primitive types built into the language, are composed of other objects. When composing objects into a new type, we want the new type to exhibit simpler behavior than all of its component parts considered together. The composite object's API must hide the existence of its component parts and the interactions between them, and expose a simpler abstraction to its peers. Think of a mechanical clock: It has two or three hands for output and one pull-out wheel for input but packages up dozens of moving parts.

---

4. Attributed to Yoda.

In software, a user interface component for editing money values might have two subcomponents: one for the amount and one for the currency. For the component to be useful, its API should manage both values together, otherwise the client code could just control it subcomponents directly.

```
moneyEditor.getAmountField().setText(String.valueOf(money.amount()));
moneyEditor.getCurrencyField().setText(money.currencyCode());
```

The "Tell, Don't Ask" convention can start to hide an object's structure from its clients but is not a strong enough rule by itself. For example, we could replace the getters in the first version with setters:

```
moneyEditor.setAmountField(money.amount());
moneyEditor.setCurrencyField(money.currencyCode());
```

This still exposes the internal structure of the component, which its client still has to manage explicitly.

We can make the API much simpler by hiding within the component everything about the way money values are displayed and edited, which in turn simplifies the client code:

```
moneyEditor.setValue(money);
```

This suggests a rule of thumb:

 Composite Simpler Than the Sum of Its Parts

The API of a composite object should not be more complicated than that of any of its components.

Composite objects can, of course, be used as components in larger-scale, more sophisticated composite objects. As we grow the code, the "composite simpler than the sum of its parts" rule contributes to raising the level of abstraction.

Context Independence

While the "composite simpler than the sum of its parts" rule helps us decide whether an object hides enough information, the "context independence" rule helps us decide whether an object hides too much or hides the wrong information.

A system is easier to change if its objects are *context-independent*; that is, if each object has no built-in knowledge about the system in which it executes. This allows us to take units of behavior (objects) and apply them in new situations. To be context-independent, whatever an object needs to know about the larger environment it's running in must be passed in. Those relationships might be "permanent" (passed in on construction) or "transient" (passed in to the method that needs them).

In this "paternalistic" approach, each object is told just enough to do its job and wrapped up in an abstraction that matches its vocabulary. Eventually, the chain of objects reaches a process boundary, which is where the system will find external details such as host names, ports, and user interface events.

 One Domain Vocabulary

A class that uses terms from multiple domains might be violating *context independence*, unless it's part of a bridging layer.

The effect of the "context independence" rule on a system of objects is to make their relationships explicit, defined separately from the objects themselves. First, this simplifies the objects, since they don't need to manage their own relationships. Second, this simplifies managing the relationships, since objects at the same scale are often created and composed together in the same places, usually in mapping-layer factory objects.

Context independence guides us towards coherent objects that can be applied in different contexts, and towards systems that we can change by reconfiguring how their objects are composed.

Hiding the Right Information

Encapsulation is almost always a good thing to do, but sometimes information can be hidden in the wrong place. This makes the code difficult to understand, to integrate, or to build behavior from by composing objects. The best defense is to be clear about the difference between the two concepts when discussing a design. For example, we might say:

- "Encapsulate the data structure for the cache in the `CachingAuctionLoader` class."

- "Encapsulate the name of the application's log file in the `PricingPolicy` class."

These sound reasonable until we recast them in terms of information hiding:

- "Hide the data structure used for the cache in the `CachingAuctionLoader` class."

- "Hide the name of the application's log file in the `PricingPolicy` class."

Context independence tells us that we have no business hiding details of the log file in the `PricingPolicy` class—they're concepts from different levels in the "Russian doll" structure of nested domains. If the log file name is necessary, it should be packaged up and passed in from a level that understands external configuration.

An Opinionated View

We've taken the time to describe what we think of as "good" object-oriented design because it underlies our approach to development and we find that it helps us write code that we can easily grow and adapt to meet the changing needs of its users. Now we want to show how our approach to *test-driven* development supports these principles.

Chapter 7

Achieving Object-Oriented Design

In matters of style, swim with the current; in matters of principle, stand like a rock.

—Thomas Jefferson

How Writing a Test First Helps the Design

The design principles we outlined in the previous chapter apply to finding the right boundaries for an object so that it plays well with its neighbors—a caller wants to know what an object does and what it depends on, but not how it works. We also want an object to represent a coherent unit that makes sense in its larger environment. A system built from such components will have the flexibility to reconfigure and adapt as requirements change.

There are three aspects of TDD that help us achieve this scoping. First, starting with a test means that we have to describe *what* we want to achieve before we consider *how*. This focus helps us maintain the right level of abstraction for the target object. If the intention of the unit test is unclear then we're probably mixing up concepts and not ready to start coding. It also helps us with information hiding as we have to decide what needs to be visible from outside the object.

Second, to keep unit tests understandable (and, so, maintainable), we have to limit their scope. We've seen unit tests that are dozens of lines long, burying the point of the test somewhere in its setup. Such tests tell us that the component they're testing is too large and needs breaking up into smaller components. The resulting composite object should have a clearer separation of concerns as we tease out its implicit structure, and we can write simpler tests for the extracted objects.

Third, to construct an object for a unit test, we have to pass its dependencies to it, which means that we have to know what they are. This encourages context independence, since we have to be able to set up the target object's environment before we can unit-test it—a unit test is just another context. We'll notice that an object with implicit (or just too many) dependencies is painful to prepare for testing—and make a point of cleaning it up.

In this chapter, we describe how we use an incremental, test-driven approach to nudge our code towards the design principles we described in the previous chapter.

Communication over Classification

As we wrote in Chapter 2, we view a running system as a web of communicating objects, so we focus our design effort on how the objects collaborate to deliver the functionality we need. Obviously, we want to achieve a well-designed class structure, but we think the communication patterns between objects are more important.

In languages such as Java, we can use interfaces to define the available messages between objects, but we also need to define their patterns of communication—their *communication protocols*. We do what we can with naming and convention, but there's nothing *in the language* to describe relationships between interfaces or methods within an interface, which leaves a significant part of the design implicit.

 Interface and Protocol

Steve heard this useful distinction in a conference talk: an interface describes whether two components will *fit* together, while a protocol describes whether they will *work* together.

We use TDD with mock objects as a technique to make these communication protocols visible, both as a tool for discovering them during development and as a description when revisiting the code. For example, the unit test towards the end of Chapter 3 tells us that, given a certain input message, the `translator` should call `listener.auctionClosed()` exactly once—and nothing else. Although the `listener` interface has other methods, this test says that its protocol requires that `auctionClosed()` should be called on its own.

```
@Test public void
notifiesAuctionClosedWhenCloseMessageReceived() {
  Message message = new Message();
  message.setBody("SOLVersion: 1.1; Event: CLOSE;");

  context.checking(new Expectations() {{
    oneOf(listener).auctionClosed();
  }});

  translator.processMessage(UNUSED_CHAT, message);
}
```

TDD with mock objects also encourages information hiding. We should mock an object's peers—its dependencies, notifications, and adjustments we categorized on page 52—but not its internals. Tests that highlight an object's neighbors help us to see whether they *are* peers, or should instead be internal to the target object. A test that is clumsy or unclear might be a hint that we've exposed too much implementation, and that we should rebalance the responsibilities between the object and its neighbors.

Value Types

Before we go further, we want to revisit the distinction we described in "Values and Objects" (page 13): *values* are immutable, so they're simpler and have no meaningful identity; *objects* have state, so they have identity and relationships with each other.

The more code we write, the more we're convinced that we should define types to represent value concepts in the domain, even if they don't do much. It helps to create a consistent domain model that is more self-explanatory. If we create, for example, an `Item` type in a system, instead of just using `String`, we can find all the code that's relevant for a change without having to chase through the method calls. Specific types also reduce the risk of confusion—as the Mars Climate Orbiter disaster showed, feet and metres may both be represented as numbers but they're different things.[1] Finally, once we have a type to represent a concept, it usually turns out to be a good place to hang behavior, guiding us towards using a more object-oriented approach instead of scattering related behavior across the code.

We use three basic techniques for introducing value types, which we've called (in a fit of alliteration): *breaking out*, *budding off*, and *bundling up*.

Breaking out

> When we find that the code in an object is becoming complex, that's often a sign that it's implementing multiple concerns and that we can break out coherent units of behavior into helper types. There's an example in "Tidying Up the Translator" (page 135) where we break a class that handles incoming messages into two parts: one to parse the message string, and one to interpret the result of the parsing.

Budding off

> When we want to mark a new domain concept in the code, we often introduce a placeholder type that wraps a single field, or maybe has no fields at all. As the code grows, we fill in more detail in the new type by adding fields and methods. With each type that we add, we're raising the level of abstraction of the code.

Bundling up

> When we notice that a group of values are always used together, we take that as a suggestion that there's a missing construct. A first step might be to create a new type with fixed public fields—just giving the group a name highlights the missing concept. Later we can migrate behavior to the new

---

1. In 1999, NASA's Mars Climate Orbiter burned up in the planet's atmosphere because, amongst other problems, the navigation software confused metric with imperial units. There's a brief description at http://news.bbc.co.uk/1/hi/sci/tech/514763.stm.

type, which might eventually allow us to hide its fields behind a clean interface, satisfying the "composite simpler than the sum of its parts" rule.

We find that the discovery of value types is usually motivated by trying to follow our design principles, rather than by responding to code stresses when writing tests.

Where Do Objects Come From?

The categories for discovering object types are similar (which is why we shoe-horned them into these names), except that the design guidance we get from writing unit tests tends to be more important. As we wrote in "External and Internal Quality" (page 10), we use the effort of unit testing to maintain the code's *internal* quality. There are more examples of the influence of testing on design in Chapter 20.

Breaking Out: Splitting a Large Object into a Group of Collaborating Objects

When starting a new area of code, we might temporarily suspend our design judgment and just write code without attempting to impose much structure. This allows us to gain some experience in the area and test our understanding of any external APIs we're developing against. After a short while, we'll find our code becoming too complex to understand and will want to clean it up. We can start pulling out cohesive units of functionality into smaller collaborating objects, which we can then unit-test independently. Splitting out a new object also forces us to look at the dependencies of the code we're pulling out.

We have two concerns about deferring cleanup. The first is how long we should wait before doing something. Under time pressure, it's tempting to leave the un-structured code as is and move on to the next thing ("after all, it works and it's just one class..."). We've seen too much code where the intention wasn't clear and the cost of cleanup kicked in when the team could least afford it. The second concern is that occasionally it's better to treat this code as a *spike*—once we know what to do, just roll it back and reimplement cleanly. Code isn't sacred just because it exists, and the second time won't take as long.

 The Tests Say...

Break up an object if it becomes too large to test easily, or if its test failures become difficult to interpret. Then unit-test the new parts separately.

Looking Ahead...

In Chapter 12, when extracting an `AuctionMessageTranslator`, we avoid including its interaction with `MainWindow` because that would give it too many responsibilities. Looking at the behavior of the new class, we identify a missing dependency, `AuctionEventListener`, which we define while writing the unit tests. We repackage the existing code in `Main` to provide an implementation for the new interface. `AuctionMessageTranslator` satisfies both our design heuristics: it introduces a separation of concerns by splitting message translation from auction display, and it abstracts message-handling code into a new domain-specific concept.

Budding Off: Defining a New Service That an Object Needs and Adding a New Object to Provide It

When the code is more stable and has some degree of structure, we often discover new types by "pulling" them into existence. We might be adding behavior to an object and find that, following our design principles, some new feature doesn't belong inside it.

Our response is to create an interface to define the service that the object needs *from the object's point of view*. We write tests for the new behavior as if the service already exists, using mock objects to help describe the relationship between the target object and its new collaborator; this is how we introduced the `AuctionEventListener` we mentioned in the previous section.

The development cycle goes like this. When implementing an object, we discover that it needs a service to be provided by another object. We give the new service a name and mock it out in the client object's unit tests, to clarify the relationship between the two. Then we write an object to provide that service and, in doing so, discover what services *that* object needs. We follow this chain (or perhaps a directed graph) of collaborator relationships until we connect up to existing objects, either our own or from a third-party API. This is how we implement "Develop from the Inputs to the Outputs" (page 43).

We think of this as "on-demand" design: we "pull" interfaces and their implementations into existence from the needs of the client, rather than "pushing" out the features that we think a class should provide.

The Tests Say...

When writing a test, we ask ourselves, "If this worked, who would know?" If the right answer to that question is not in the target object, it's probably time to introduce a new collaborator.

Looking Ahead...

In Chapter 13, we introduce an Auction interface. The concept of making a bid would have been an additional responsibility for AuctionSniper, so we introduce a new service for bidding—just an interface without any implementation. We write a new test to show the relationship between AuctionSniper and Auction. *Then* we write a concrete implementation of Auction—initially as an anonymous class in Main, later as XMPPAuction.

Bundling Up: Hiding Related Objects into a Containing Object

This is the application of the "composite simpler than the sum of its parts" rule (page 53). When we have a cluster of related objects that work together, we can package them up in a containing object. The new object hides the complexity in an abstraction that allows us to program at a higher level.

The process of making an implicit concept concrete has some other nice effects. First, we have to give it a name which helps us understand the domain a little better. Second, we can scope dependencies more clearly, since we can see the boundaries of the concept. Third, we can be more precise with our unit testing. We can test the new composite object directly, and use a mock implementation to simplify the tests for code from which it was extracted (since, of course, we added an interface for the role the new object plays).

The Tests Say...

When the test for an object becomes too complicated to set up—when there are too many moving parts to get the code into the relevant state—consider bundling up some of the collaborating objects. There's an example in "Bloated Constructor" (page 238).

Looking Ahead...

In Chapter 17, we introduce XMPPAuctionHouse to package up everything to do with the messaging infrastructure, and SniperLauncher for constructing and attaching a Sniper. Once extracted, the references to Swing behavior in SniperLauncher stand out as inappropriate, so we introduce SniperCollector to decouple the domains.

Identify Relationships with Interfaces

We use Java interfaces more liberally than some other developers. This reflects our emphasis on the relationships between objects, as defined by their communication protocols. We use interfaces to name the roles that objects can play and to describe the messages they'll accept.

We also prefer interfaces to be as narrow as possible, even though that means we need more of them. The fewer methods there are on an interface, the more obvious is its role in the calling object. We don't have to worry which other methods are relevant to a particular call and which were included for convenience. Narrow interfaces are also easier to write adapters and decorators for; there's less to implement, so it's easier to write objects that compose together well.

"Pulling" interfaces into existence, as we described in "Budding Off," helps us keep them as narrow as possible. Driving an interface from its client avoids leaking excess information about its implementers, which minimizes any implicit coupling between objects and so keeps the code malleable.

Impl Classes Are Meaningless

Sometimes we see code with classes named by adding "Impl" to the single interface they implement. This is better than leaving the class name unchanged and prefixing an "I" to the interface, but not by much. A name like `BookingImpl` is duplication; it says exactly the same as `implements Booking`, which is a "code smell." We would not be happy with such obvious duplication elsewhere in our code, so we ought to refactor it away.

It might just be a naming problem. There's always something specific about an implementation that can be included in the class name: it might use a bounded collection, communicate over HTTP, use a database for persistence, and so on. A bridging class is even easier to name, since it will belong in one domain but implement interfaces in another.

If there really isn't a good implementation name, it might mean that the interface is poorly named or designed. Perhaps it's unfocused because it has too many responsibilities; or it's named after its implementation rather than its role in the client; or it's a value, not an object—this discrepancy sometimes turns up when writing unit tests, see "Don't Mock Values" (page 237).

Refactor Interfaces Too

Once we have interfaces for protocols, we can start to pay attention to similarities and differences. In a reasonably large codebase, we often start to find interfaces that look similar. This means we should look at whether they represent a single concept and should be merged. Extracting common roles makes the design more malleable because more components will be "plug-compatible," so we can work at a higher level of abstraction. For the developer, there's a secondary advantage that there will be fewer concepts that cost time to understand.

Alternatively, if similar interfaces turn out to represent different concepts, we can make a point of making them distinct, so that the compiler can ensure that we only combine objects correctly. A decision to separate similar-looking interfaces is a good time to reconsider their naming. It's likely that there's a more appropriate name for at least one of them.

Finally, another time to consider refactoring interfaces is when we start implementing them. For example, if we find that the structure of an implementing class is unclear, perhaps it has too many responsibilities which might be a hint that the interface is unfocused too and should be split up.

Compose Objects to Describe System Behavior

TDD at the unit level guides us to decompose our system into value types and loosely coupled computational objects. The tests give us a good understanding of how each object behaves and how it can be combined with others. We then use lower-level objects as the building blocks of more capable objects; this is the *web of objects* we described in Chapter 2.

In jMock, for example, we assemble a description of the expected calls for a test in a context object called a `Mockery`. During a test run, the `Mockery` will pass calls made to any of its mocked objects to its `Expectations`, each of which will attempt to match the call. If an `Expectation` matches, that part of the test succeeds. If none matches, then each `Expectation` reports its disagreement and the test fails. At runtime, the assembled objects look like Figure 7.1:

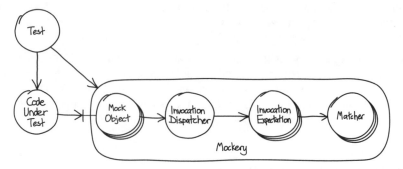

Figure 7.1   *jMock* Expectations *are assembled from many objects*

The advantage of this approach is that we end up with a flexible application structure built from relatively little code. It's particularly suitable where the code has to support many related scenarios. For each scenario, we provide a different assembly of components to build, in effect, a subsystem to plug into the rest of the application. Such designs are also easy to extend—just write a new plug-compatible component and add it in; you'll see us write several new Hamcrest matchers in Part III.

For example, to have jMock check that a method `example.doSomething()` is called exactly once with an argument of type `String`, we set up our test context like this:

```
InvocationExpectation expectation = new InvocationExpectation();
expectation.setParametersMatcher(
  new AllParametersMatcher(Arrays.asList(new IsInstanceOf(String.class))));
expectation.setCardinality(new Cardinality(1, 1));
expectation.setMethodMatcher(new MethodNameMatcher("doSomething"));
expectation.setObjectMatcher(new IsSame<Example>(example));

context.addExpectation(expectation);
```

Building Up to Higher-Level Programming

You have probably spotted a difficulty with the code fragment above: it doesn't explain very well what the expectation is testing. Conceptually, assembling a web of objects is straightforward. Unfortunately, the mainstream languages we usually work with bury the information we care about (objects and their relationships) in a morass of keywords, setters, punctuation, and the like. Just assigning and linking objects, as in this example, doesn't help us understand the behavior of the system we're assembling—it doesn't express our *intent*.[2]

Our response is to organize the code into two layers: an *implementation layer* which is the graph of objects, its behavior is the combined result of how its objects respond to events; and, a *declarative layer* which builds up the objects in the implementation layer, using small "sugar" methods and syntax to describe the purpose of each fragment. The declarative layer describes *what* the code will do, while the implementation layer describes *how* the code does it. The declarative layer is, in effect, a small *domain-specific language* embedded (in this case) in Java.[3]

The different purposes of the two layers mean that we use a different coding style for each. For the implementation layer we stick to the conventional object-oriented style guidelines we described in the previous chapter. We're more flexible for the declarative layer—we might even use "train wreck" chaining of method calls or static methods to help get the point across.

A good example is jMock itself. We can rewrite the example from the previous section as:

---

2. Nor does the common alternative of moving the object construction into a separate XML file.

3. This became clear to us when working on jMock. We wrote up our experiences in [Freeman06].

```
context.checking(new Expectations() {{
    oneOf(example).doSomething(with(any(String.class)));
}});
```

The Expectations object is a *Builder* [Gamma94] that constructs expectations. It defines "sugar" methods that construct the assembly of expectations and matchers and load it into the Mockery, as shown in Figure 7.2.

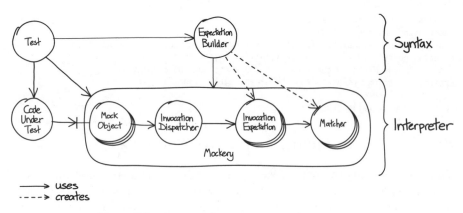

Figure 7.2   *A syntax-layer constructs the interpreter*

Most of the time, such a declarative layer emerges from continual "merciless" refactoring. We start by writing code that directly composes objects and keep factoring out duplication. We also add helper methods to push the syntax noise out of the main body of the code and to add explanation. Taking care to notice when an area of code is not clear, we add or move structure until it is; this is very easy to do in a modern refactoring IDE. Eventually, we find we have our two-layer structure. Occasionally, we start from the declarative code we'd like to have and work down to fill in its implementation, as we do with the first end-to-end test in Chapter 10.

Our purpose, in the end, is to achieve more with less code. We aspire to raise ourselves from programming in terms of control flow and data manipulation, to composing programs from smaller programs—where objects form the smallest unit of behavior. None of this is new—it's the same concept as programming Unix by composing utilities with pipes [Kernighan76],[4] or building up layers of language in Lisp [Graham93]—but we still don't see it in the field as often as we would like.

---

4. Kernighan and Plauger attribute the idea of pipes to Douglas McIlroy, who wrote a memo in 1964 suggesting the metaphor of data passing through a segmented garden hose. It's currently available at http://plan9.bell-labs.com/who/dmr/mdmpipe.pdf.

And What about Classes?

One last point. Unusually for a book on object-oriented software, we haven't said much about classes and inheritance. It should be obvious by now that we've been pushing the application domain into the gaps between the objects, the communication protocols. We emphasize interfaces more than classes because that's what other objects see: an object's type is defined by the roles it plays.

We view classes for objects as an "implementation detail"—a way of *implementing* types, not the types themselves. We discover object class hierarchies by factoring out common behavior, but prefer to refactor to delegation if possible since we find that it makes our code more flexible and easier to understand.[5] Value types, on the other hand, are less likely to use delegation since they don't have peers.

There's plenty of good advice on how to work with classes in, for example, [Fowler99], [Kerievsky04], and [Evans03].

---

5. The design forces, of course, are different in languages that support multiple inheritance well, such as Eiffel [Meyer91].

Chapter 8

Building on Third-Party Code

Programming today is all about doing science on the parts you have to work with.

—Gerald Jay Sussman

Introduction

We've shown how we pull a system's design into existence: discovering what our objects need and writing interfaces and further objects to meet those needs. This process works well for new functionality. At some point, however, our design will come up against a need that is best met by third-party code: standard APIs, open source libraries, or vendor products. The critical point about third-party code is that we don't control it, so we cannot use our process to guide its design. Instead, we must focus on the *integration* between our design and the external code.

In integration, we have an abstraction to implement, discovered while we developed the rest of the feature. With the third-party API pushing back at our design, we must find the best balance between elegance and practical use of someone else's ideas. We must check that we are using the third-party API correctly, and adjust our abstraction to fit if we find that our assumptions are incorrect.

Only Mock Types That You Own

Don't Mock Types You Can't Change

When we use third-party code we often do not have a deep understanding of how it works. Even if we have the source available, we rarely have time to read it thoroughly enough to explore all its quirks. We can read its documentation, which is often incomplete or incorrect. The software may also have bugs that we will need to work around. So, although we know how we want our abstraction to behave, we don't know if it really does so until we test it in combination with the third-party code.

We also prefer not to change third-party code, even when we have the sources. It's usually too much trouble to apply private patches every time there's a new version. If we can't change an API, then we can't respond to any design feedback we get from writing unit tests that touch it. Whatever alarm bells the unit tests

69

might be ringing about the awkwardness of an external API, we have to live with it as it stands.

This means that providing mock implementations of third-party types is of limited use when unit-testing the objects that call them. We find that tests that mock external libraries often need to be complex to get the code into the right state for the functionality we need to exercise. The mess in such tests is telling us that the design isn't right but, instead of fixing the problem by improving the code, we have to carry the extra complexity in both code and test.

A second risk is that we have to be sure that the behavior we stub or mock matches what the external library will actually do. How difficult this is depends on the quality of the library—whether it's specified (and implemented) well enough for us to be certain that our unit tests are valid. Even if we get it right once, we have to make sure that the tests remain valid when we upgrade the libraries.

Write an Adapter Layer

If we don't want to mock an external API, how can we test the code that drives it? We will have used TDD to design interfaces for the services our objects need—which will be defined in terms of our objects' domain, not the external library.

We write a layer of *adapter objects* (as described in [Gamma94]) that uses the third-party API to implement these interfaces, as in Figure 8.1. We keep this layer as thin as possible, to minimize the amount of potentially brittle and hard-to-test code. We test these adapters with focused integration tests to confirm our understanding of how the third-party API works. There will be relatively few integration tests compared to the number of unit tests, so they should not get in the way of the build even if they're not as fast as the in-memory unit tests.

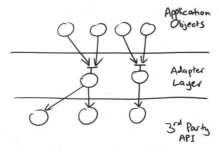

Figure 8.1 *Mockable adapters to third-party objects*

Following this approach consistently produces a set of interfaces that define the relationship between our application and the rest of the world *in our application's terms* and discourages low-level technical concepts from leaking into the application domain model. In Chapter 25, we discuss a common example where abstractions in the application's domain model are implemented using a persistence API.

There are *some* exceptions where mocking third-party libraries can be helpful. We might use mocks to simulate behavior that is hard to trigger with the real library, such as throwing exceptions. Similarly, we might use mocks to test a sequence of calls, for example making sure that a transaction is rolled back if there's a failure. There should not be many tests like this in a test suite.

This pattern does not apply to value types because, of course, we don't need to mock them. We still, however, have to make design decisions about how much to use third-party value types in our code. They might be so fundamental that we just use them directly. Often, however, we want to follow the same principles of isolation as for third-party services, and translate between value types appropriate to the application domain and to the external domain.

Mock Application Objects in Integration Tests

As described above, adapter objects are passive, reacting to calls from our code. Sometimes, adapter objects must call back to objects from the application. Event-based libraries, for example, usually expect the client to provide a callback object to be notified when an event happens. In this case, the application code will give the adapter its own event callback (defined in terms of the application domain). The adapter will then pass an adapter callback to the external library to receive external events and translate them for the application callback.

In these cases, we *do* use mock objects when testing objects that integrate with third-party code—but only to mock the callback interfaces defined in the application, to verify that the adapter translates events between domains correctly (Figure 8.2).

Multithreading adds more complication to integration tests. For example, third-party libraries may start background threads to deliver events to the application code, so synchronization is a vital aspect of the design effort of adapter layers; we discuss this further in Chapter 26.

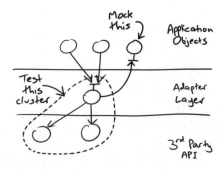

Figure 8.2 *Using mock objects in integration tests*

Part III

A Worked Example

One of our goals in writing this book was to convey the whole experience of test-driven software development. We want to show how the techniques fit together over a larger scale than the examples usually presented in books. We make a point of including external components, in this case Swing and messaging infrastructure, since the stress points of this kind of approach are usually at the boundaries between code that we own and code that we have to work with. The application that we build includes such complexities as event-based design, multiple threads, and distribution.

Another goal was to tell a realistic story, so we include episodes where we have to backtrack on decisions that turn out to be wrong. This happens in any software development that we've seen. Even the best people misunderstand requirements and technologies or, sometimes, just miss the point. A resilient process allows for mistakes and includes techniques for discovering and recovering from errors as early as possible. After all, the only alternative is to leave the problems in the code where, generally, they will cause more expensive damage later.

Finally, we wanted to emphasize our culture of very incremental development. Experienced teams can learn to make substantial changes to their code in small, safe steps. To those not used to it, incremental change can feel as if it takes too long. But we've been burned too often by large restructurings that lose their way and end up taking longer—unpredictably so. By keeping the system always clean and always working, we can focus on just the immediate change at hand (instead of having to maintain a mental model of all the code at once), and merging changes back in is never a crisis.

 On formatting

Some of the code and output layout in this example looks a bit odd. We've had to trim and wrap the long lines to make them fit on the printed page. In our development environments we use a longer line length, which (we think) makes for more readable layout of the code.

Chapter 9

Commissioning an Auction Sniper

To Begin at the Beginning

In which we are commissioned to build an application that automatically bids in auctions. We sketch out how it should work and what the major components should be. We put together a rough plan for the incremental steps in which we will grow the application.

We're a development team for Markup and Gouge, a company that buys antiques on the professional market to sell to clients "with the best possible taste." Markup and Gouge has been following the industry and now does a lot of its buying online, largely from Southabee's, a venerable auction house that is keen to grow online. The trouble is that our buyers are spending a lot of their time manually checking the state of an auction to decide whether or not to bid, and even missed a couple of attractive items because they could not respond quickly enough.

After intense discussion, the management decides to commission an *Auction Sniper*, an application that watches online auctions and automatically bids slightly higher whenever the price changes, until it reaches a stop-price or the auction closes. The buyers are keen to have this new application and some of them agree to help us clarify what to build.

We start by talking through their ideas with the buyers' group and find that, to avoid confusion, we need to agree on some basic terms:

- *Item* is something that can be identified and bought.

- *Bidder* is a person or organization that is interested in buying an item.

- *Bid* is a statement that a bidder will pay a given price for an item.

- *Current price* is the current highest bid for the item.

- *Stop price* is the most a bidder is prepared to pay for an item.

- *Auction* is a process for managing bids for an item.

- *Auction house* is an institution that hosts auctions.

75

The discussions generate a long list of requirements, such as being able to bid for related groups of items. There's no way anyone could deliver everything within a useful time, so we talk through the options and the buyers reluctantly agree that they'd rather get a basic application working first. Once that's in place, we can make it more powerful.

It turns out that in the online system there's an auction for every item, so we decide to use an item's identifier to refer to its auction. In practice, it also turns out that the Sniper application doesn't have to concern itself with managing any items we've bought, since other systems will handle payment and delivery.

We decide to build the Auction Sniper as a Java Swing application. It will run on a desktop and allow the user to bid for multiple items at a time. It will show the identifier, stop price, and the current auction price and status for each item it's sniping. Buyers will be able to add new items for sniping through the user interface, and the display values will change in response to events arriving from the auction house. The buyers are still working with our usability people, but we've agreed a rough version that looks like Figure 9.1.

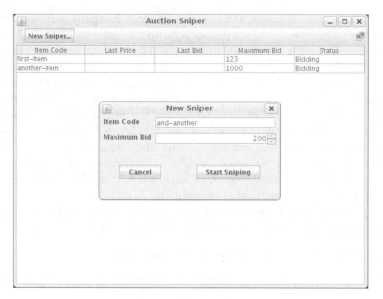

Figure 9.1 *A first user interface*

This is obviously incomplete and not pretty, but it's close enough to get us started.

While these discussions are taking place, we also talk to the technicians at Southabee's who support their online services. They send us a document that describes their protocol for bidding in auctions, which uses *XMPP* (Jabber) for its underlying communication layer. Figure 9.2 shows how it handles multiple bidders sending bids over XMPP to the auction house, our Sniper being one of them. As the auction progresses, Southabee's will send events to all the connected bidders to tell them when anyone's bid has raised the current price and when the auction closes.

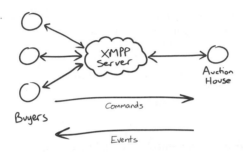

Figure 9.2   *Southabee's online auction system*

XMPP: the eXtensible Messaging and Presence Protocol

XMPP is a protocol for streaming XML elements across the network. It was originally designed for, and named after, the Jabber instant messaging system and was renamed to XMPP when submitted to the IETF for approval as an Internet standard. Because it is a generic framework for exchanging XML elements across the network, it can be used for a wide variety of applications that need to exchange structured data in close to real time.

XMPP has a decentralized, client/server architecture. There is no central server, in contrast with other chat services such as AOL Instant Messenger or MSN Messenger. Anyone may run an XMPP server that hosts users and lets them communicate among themselves and with users hosted by other XMPP servers on the network.

A user can log in to an XMPP server simultaneously from multiple devices or clients, known in XMPP terminology as *resources*. A user assigns each resource a priority. Unless addressed to a specific resource, messages sent to the user are delivered to this user's highest priority resource that is currently logged in.

Every user on the network has a unique Jabber ID (usually abbreviated as *JID*) that is rather like an e-mail address. A JID contains a username and a DNS address of the server where that user resides, separated by an at sign (@, for example, `username@example.com`), and can optionally be suffixed with a resource name after a forward slash (for example, `username@example.com/office`).

Communicating with an Auction

The Auction Protocol

The protocol for messages between a bidder and an auction house is simple. Bidders send *commands*, which can be:

Join

> A bidder joins an auction. The sender of the XMPP message identifies the bidder, and the name of the chat session identifies the item.

Bid

> A bidder sends a bidding price to the auction.

Auctions send *events*, which can be:

Price

> An auction reports the currently accepted price. This event also includes the minimum increment that the next bid must be raised by, and the name of bidder who bid this price. The auction will send this event to a bidder when it joins and to all bidders whenever a new bid has been accepted.

Close

> An auction announces that it has closed. The winner of the last price event has won the auction.

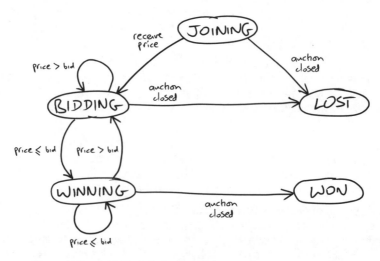

Figure 9.3 *A bidder's behavior represented as a state machine*

We spend some time working through the documentation and talking to Southabee's On-Line support people, and figure out a state machine that shows the transitions a Sniper can make. Essentially, a Sniper *joins* an auction, then there are some rounds of *bidding*, until the auction *closes*, at which point the Sniper will have *won* or *lost*; see Figure 9.3. We've left out the stop price for now to keep things simple; it'll turn up in Chapter 18.

The XMPP Messages

Southabee's On-Line has also sent us details of the formats they use within the XMPP messages. They're pretty simple, since they only involve a few names and values, and are serialized in a single line with key/value pairs. Each line starts with a version number for the protocol itself. The messages look like this:

```
SOLVersion: 1.1; Command: JOIN;
SOLVersion: 1.1; Event: PRICE; CurrentPrice: 192; Increment: 7; Bidder: Someone else;
SOLVersion: 1.1; Command: BID; Price: 199;
SOLVersion: 1.1; Event: CLOSE;
```

Southabee's On-Line uses login names to identify items for sale, so to bid for an item with identifier 12793, a client would start a chat with the "user" auction-12793 at the Southabee's server. The server can tell who is bidding from the identity of the caller, assuming the accounts have been set up beforehand.

Getting There Safely

Even a small application like this is too large to write in one go, so we need to figure out, roughly, the steps we might take to get there. A critical technique with incremental development is learning how to slice up the functionality so that it can be built a little at a time. Each slice should be significant and concrete enough that the team can tell when it's done, *and* small enough to be focused on one concept and achievable quickly. Dividing our work into small, coherent chunks also helps us manage the development risk. We get regular, concrete feedback on the progress we're making, so we can adjust our plan as the team discovers more about the domain and the technologies.

Our immediate task is to figure out a series of incremental development steps for the Sniper application. The first is absolutely the smallest feature we can build, the "walking skeleton" we described in "First, Test a Walking Skeleton" (page 32). Here, the skeleton will cut a minimum path through Swing, XMPP, and our application; it's just enough to show that we can plug these components together. Each subsequent step adds a single element of complexity to the existing application, building on the work that's done before. After some discussion, we come up with this sequence of features to build:

Single item: join, lose without bidding
  This is our starting case where we put together the core infrastructure; it is the subject of Chapter 10.

Single item: join, bid, and lose
  Add bidding to the basic connectivity.

Single item: join, bid, and win
  Distinguish who sent the winning bid.

Show price details
  Start to fill out the user interface.

Multiple items
  Support bidding for multiple items in the same application.

Add items through the user interface
  Implement input via the user interface.

Stop bidding at the stop price
  More intelligence in the Sniper algorithm.

Within the list, the buyers have prioritized the user interface over the stop price, partly because they want to make sure they'll feel comfortable with the application and partly because there won't be an easy way to add multiple items, each with its own stop price, without a user interface.

Once this is stable, we can work on more complicated scenarios, such as retrying if a bid failed or using different strategies for bidding. For now, implementing just these features should keep us busy.

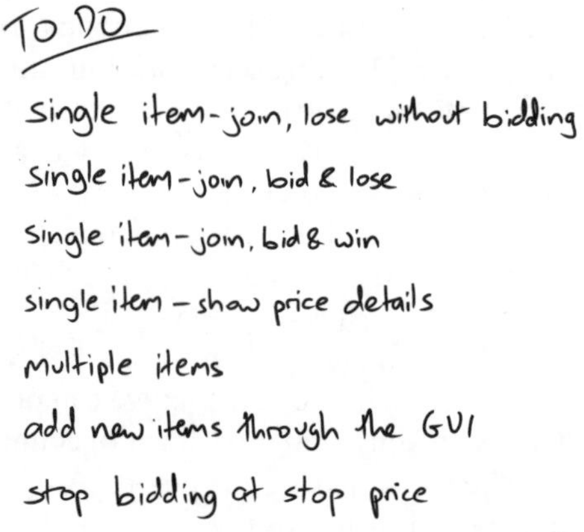

TO DO

single item - join, lose without bidding
single item - join, bid & lose
single item - join, bid & win
single item - show price details
multiple items
add new items through the GUI
stop bidding at stop price

Figure 9.4   *The initial plan*

We don't know if this is exactly the order of steps we'll take, but we believe we need all of this, and we can adjust as we go along. To keep ourselves focused, we've written the plan on an index card, as in Figure 9.4.

This Isn't Real

By now you may be raising objections about all the practicalities we've skipped over. We saw them too. We've taken shortcuts with the process and design to give you a feel of how a real project works while remaining within the limits of a book. In particular:

- *This isn't a realistic architecture:* XMPP is neither reliable nor secure, and so is unsuitable for transactions. Ensuring any of those qualities is outside our scope. That said, the fundamental techniques that we describe still apply whatever the underlying architecture may be. (In our defense, we see that major systems have been built on a protocol as inappropriate as HTTP, so perhaps we're not as unrealistic as we fear.)

- *This isn't Agile Planning:* We rushed through the planning of the project to produce a single to-do list. In a real project, we'd likely have a view of the whole deliverable (a *release plan*) before jumping in. There are good descriptions of how to do agile planning in other books, such as [Shore07] and [Cohn05].

- *This isn't realistic usability design:* Good user experience design investigates what the end user is really trying to achieve and uses that to create a consistent experience. The User Experience community has been engaging with the Agile Development community for some time on how to do this iteratively. This project is simple enough that we can draft a vision of what we want to achieve and work towards it.

Chapter 10

The Walking Skeleton

In which we set up our development environment and write our first end-to-end test. We make some infrastructure choices that allow us to get started, and construct a build. We're surprised, yet again, at how much effort this takes.

Get the Skeleton out of the Closet

So now we've got an idea of what to build, can we get on with it and write our first unit test?

Not yet.

Our first task is to create the "walking skeleton" we described in "First, Test a Walking Skeleton" (page 32). Again, the point of the walking skeleton is to help us understand the requirements well enough to propose *and validate* a broad-brush system structure. We can always change our minds later, when we learn more, but it's important to start with something that maps out the landscape of our solution. Also, it's very important to be able to assess the approach we've chosen and to test our decisions so we can make changes with confidence later.

For most projects, developing the walking skeleton takes a surprising amount of effort. First, because deciding what to do will flush out all sorts of questions about the application and its place in the world. Second, because the automation of building, packaging, and deploying into a production-like environment (once we know what that means) will flush out all sorts of technical and organizational questions.

 Iteration Zero

In most Agile projects, there's a first stage where the team is doing initial analysis, setting up its physical and technical environments, and otherwise getting started. The team isn't adding much visible functionality since almost all the work is infra-structure, so it might not make sense to count this as a conventional iteration for scheduling purposes. A common practice is to call this step *iteration zero*: "iteration" because the team still needs to time-box its activities and "zero" because it's before functional development starts in iteration one. One important task for iteration zero is to use the walking skeleton to test-drive the initial architecture.

Of course, we start our walking skeleton by writing a test.

Our Very First Test

The walking skeleton must cover all the components of our Auction Sniper system: the user interface, the sniping component, and the communication with an auction server. The thinnest slice we can imagine testing, the first item on our to-do list, is that the Auction Sniper can join an auction and then wait for it to close. This slice is so minimal that we're not even concerned with sending a bid; we just want to know that the two sides can communicate and that we can test the system from outside (through the client's GUI and by injecting events as if from the external auction server). Once that's working, we have a solid base on which to build the rest of the features that the clients want.

We like to start by writing a test as if its implementation already exists, and then filling in whatever is needed to make it work—what Abelson and Sussman call "programming by wishful thinking" [Abelson96]. Working backwards from the test helps us focus on *what* we want the system to do, instead of getting caught up in the complexity of *how* we will make it work. So, first we code up a test to describe our intentions as clearly as we can, given the expressive limits of a programming language. Then we build the infrastructure to support the way we want to test the system, instead of writing the tests to fit in with an existing infrastructure. This usually takes a large part of our initial effort because there is so much to get ready. With this infrastructure in place, we can implement the feature and make the test pass.

An outline of the test we want is:

1. When an auction is selling an item,

2. And an Auction Sniper has started to bid in that auction,

3. Then the auction will receive a Join request from the Auction Sniper.

4. When an auction announces that it is Closed,

5. Then the Auction Sniper will show that it lost the auction.

This describes one transition in the state machine (see Figure 10.1).

We need to translate this into something executable. We use JUnit as our test framework since it's familiar and widely supported. We also need mechanisms to control the application and the auction that the application is talking to.

Southabee's On-Line test services are not freely available. We have to book ahead and pay for each test session, which is not practical if we want to run tests all the time. We'll need a fake auction service that we can control from our tests to behave like the real thing—or at least like we *think* the real thing behaves until we get a chance to test against it for real. This fake auction, or *stub*, will be as simple as we can make it. It will connect to an XMPP message broker, receive commands from the Sniper to be checked by the test, and allow the test to send back events. We're not trying to reimplement all of Southabee's On-Line, just enough of it to support test scenarios.

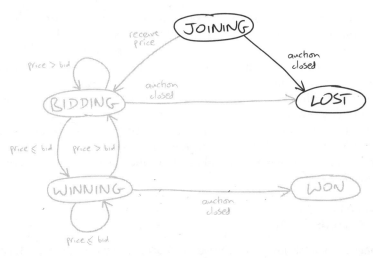

Figure 10.1 *A Sniper joins, then loses*

Controlling the Sniper application is more complicated. We want our skeleton test to exercise our application as close to end-to-end as possible, to show that the main() method initializes the application correctly and that the components really work together. This means that we should start by working through the publicly visible features of the application (in this case, its user interface) instead of directly invoking its domain objects. We also want our test to be clear about what is being checked, written in terms of the relationship between a Sniper and its auction, so we'll hide all the messy code for manipulating Swing in an ApplicationRunner class. We'll start by writing the test as if all the code it needs exists and will fill in the implementations afterwards.

```
public class AuctionSniperEndToEndTest {
  private final FakeAuctionServer auction = new FakeAuctionServer("item-54321");
  private final ApplicationRunner application = new ApplicationRunner();

  @Test public void sniperJoinsAuctionUntilAuctionCloses() throws Exception {
    auction.startSellingItem();                    // Step 1
    application.startBiddingIn(auction);           // Step 2
    auction.hasReceivedJoinRequestFromSniper();    // Step 3
    auction.announceClosed();                      // Step 4
    application.showsSniperHasLostAuction();        // Step 5
  }

  // Additional cleanup
  @After public void stopAuction() {
    auction.stop();
  }
  @After public void stopApplication() {
    application.stop();
  }
}
```

We've adopted certain naming conventions for the methods of the helper objects. If a method triggers an event to drive the test, its name will be a command, such as *start*BiddingIn(). If a method asserts that something should have happened, its name will be descriptive;[1] for example, *shows*SniperHasLostAuction() will throw an exception if the application is not showing the auction status as lost. JUnit will call the two stop() methods after the test has run, to clean up the runtime environment.

In writing the test, one of the assumptions we've made is that a FakeAuctionServer is tied to a given item. This matches the structure of our intended architecture, where Southabee's On-Line hosts multiple auctions, each selling a single item.

 One Domain at a Time

The language of this test is concerned with auctions and Snipers; there's nothing about messaging layers or components in the user interface—that's all incidental detail here. Keeping the language consistent helps us understand what's significant in this test, with a nice side effect of protecting us when the implementation inevitably changes.

Some Initial Choices

Now we have to make the test pass, which will require a lot of preparation. We need to find or write four components: an XMPP message broker, a stub auction that can communicate over XMPP, a GUI testing framework, and a test harness that can cope with our multithreaded, asynchronous architecture. We also have to get the project under version control with an automated build/deploy/test process. Compared to unit-testing a single class, there is a lot to do—but it's essential. Even at this high level, the exercise of writing tests drives the development of the system. Working through our first end-to-end test will force some of the structural decisions we need to make, such as packaging and deployment.

First the package selection, we will need an XMPP message broker to let the application talk to our stub auction house. After some investigation, we decide on an open source implementation called Openfire and its associated client library Smack. We also need a high-level test framework that can work with Swing and Smack, both of which are multithreaded and event-driven. Luckily for us, there are several frameworks for testing Swing applications and the way that they deal with Swing's multithreaded, event-driven architecture also works well with XMPP messaging. We pick WindowLicker which is open source and supports

---

1. For the grammatically pedantic, the names of methods that trigger events are in the *imperative* mood whereas the names of assertions are in the *indicative* mood.

the asynchronous approach that we need in our tests. When assembled, the infrastructure will look like Figure 10.2:

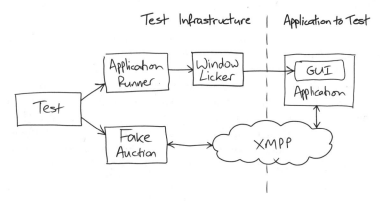

Figure 10.2 *The end-to-end test rig*

End-to-End Testing

End-to-end testing for event-based systems, such as our Sniper, has to cope with asynchrony. The tests run in parallel with the application and do not know precisely when the application is or isn't ready. This is unlike unit testing, where a test drives an object directly in the same thread and so can make direct assertions about its state and behavior.

An end-to-end test can't peek inside the target application, so it must wait to detect some visible effect, such as a user interface change or an entry in a log. The usual technique is to poll for the effect and fail if it doesn't happen within a given time limit. There's a further complexity in that the target application has to stabilize after the triggering event long enough for the test to catch the result. An asynchronous test waiting for a value that just flashes on the screen will be too unreliable for an automated build, so a common technique is to control the application and step through the scenario. At each stage, the test waits for an assertion to pass, then sends an event to wake the application for the next step. See Chapter 14 for a full discussion of testing asynchronous behavior.

All this makes end-to-end testing slower and more brittle (perhaps the test network is just busy today), so failures might need interpretation. We've heard of teams where timing-related tests have to fail several times in a row before they're reported. This is unlike unit tests which must all pass every time.

In our case, both Swing and the messaging infrastructure are asynchronous, so using WindowLicker (which polls for values) to drive the Sniper covers the natural asynchrony of our end-to-end testing.

Ready to Start

You might have noticed that we skipped over one point: this first test is not really end-to-end. It doesn't include the real auction service because that is not easily available. An important part of the test-driven development skills is judging where to set the boundaries of what to test and how to eventually cover everything. In this case, we have to start with a fake auction service based on the documentation from Southabee's On-Line. The documentation might or might not be correct, so we will record that as a known risk in the project plan and schedule time to test against the real server as soon as we have enough functionality to complete a meaningful transaction—even if we end up buying a hideous (but cheap) pair of candlesticks in a real auction. The sooner we find a discrepancy, the less code we will have based on that misunderstanding and the more time to fix it.

We'd better get on with it.

Chapter 11

Passing the First Test

In which we write test infrastructure to drive our non-existent applica-
tion, so that we can make the first test fail. We repeatedly fail the test
and fix symptoms, until we have a minimal working application that
passes the first test. We step through this very slowly to show how the
process works.

Building the Test Rig

At the start of every test run, our test script starts up the Openfire server, creates accounts for the Sniper and the auction, and then runs the tests. Each test will start instances of the application and the fake auction, and then test their communication through the server. At first, we'll run everything on the same host. Later, as the infrastructure stabilizes, we can consider running different components on different machines, which will be a better match to the real deployment.

This leaves us with two components to write for the test infrastructure: `ApplicationRunner` and `FakeAuctionServer`.

Setting Up the Openfire Server

At the time of writing, we were using version 3.6 of Openfire. For these end-to-end tests, we set up our local server with three user accounts and passwords:

sniper
> *sniper*

auction-item-54321
> *auction*

auction-item-65432
> *auction*

For desktop development, we usually started the server by hand and left it running. We set it up to not store offline messages, which meant there was no persistent state. In the System Manager, we edited the "System Name" property to be `localhost`, so the tests would run consistently. Finally, we set the resource policy to "Never kick," which will not allow a new resource to log in if there's a conflict.

The Application Runner

An ApplicationRunner is an object that wraps up all management and communicating with the Swing application we're building. It runs the application as if from the command line, obtaining and holding a reference to its main window for querying the state of the GUI and for shutting down the application at the end of the test.

   We don't have to do much here, because we can rely on WindowLicker to do the hard work: find and control Swing GUI components, synchronize with Swing's threads and event queue, and wrap that all up behind a simple API.[1] WindowLicker has the concept of a *ComponentDriver*: an object that can manipulate a feature in a Swing user interface. If a ComponentDriver can't find the Swing component it refers to, it will time out with an error. For this test, we're looking for a label component that shows a given string; if our application doesn't produce this label, we'll get an exception. Here's the implementation (with the constants left out for clarity) and some explanation:

```
public class ApplicationRunner {
  public static final String SNIPER_ID = "sniper";
  public static final String SNIPER_PASSWORD = "sniper";
  private AuctionSniperDriver driver;

  public void startBiddingIn(final FakeAuctionServer auction) {
    Thread thread = new Thread("Test Application") {
      @Override public void run() { ❶
        try {
          Main.main(XMPP_HOSTNAME, SNIPER_ID, SNIPER_PASSWORD, auction.getItemId()); ❷
        } catch (Exception e) {
          e.printStackTrace(); ❸
        }
      }
    };
    thread.setDaemon(true);
    thread.start();
    driver = new AuctionSniperDriver(1000); ❹
    driver.showsSniperStatus(Main.STATUS_JOINING); ❺
  }
  public void showsSniperHasLostAuction() {
    driver.showsSniperStatus(Main.STATUS_LOST);   ❻
  }
  public void stop() {
    if (driver != null) {
      driver.dispose(); ❼
    }
  }
}
```

---

1. We're assuming that you know how Swing works; there are many other books that do a good job of describing it. The essential point here is that it's an event-driven framework that creates its own internal threads to dispatch events, so we can't be precise about when things will happen.

❶ We call the application through its main() function to make sure we've assembled the pieces correctly. We're following the convention that the entry point to the application is a Main class in the top-level package. WindowLicker can control Swing components if they're in the same JVM, so we start the Sniper in a new thread. Ideally, the test would start the Sniper in a new process, but that would be much harder to test; we think this is a reasonable compromise.

❷ To keep things simple at this stage, we'll assume that we're only bidding for one item and pass the identifier to main().

❸ If main() throws an exception, we just print it out. Whatever test we're running will fail and we can look for the stack trace in the output. Later, we'll handle exceptions properly.

❹ We turn down the timeout period for finding frames and components. The default values are longer than we need for a simple application like this one and will slow down the tests when they fail. We use one second, which is enough to smooth over minor runtime delays.

❺ We wait for the status to change to Joining so we know that the application has attempted to connect. This assertion says that somewhere in the user interface there's a label that describes the Sniper's state.

❻ When the Sniper loses the auction, we expect it to show a Lost status. If this doesn't happen, the driver will throw an exception.

❼ After the test, we tell the driver to dispose of the window to make sure it won't be picked up in another test before being garbage-collected.

The AuctionSniperDriver is simply an extension of a WindowLicker JFrameDriver specialized for our tests:

```
public class AuctionSniperDriver extends JFrameDriver {
  public AuctionSniperDriver(int timeoutMillis) {
    super(new GesturePerformer(),
        JFrameDriver.topLevelFrame(
          named(MainWindow.MAIN_WINDOW_NAME),
          showingOnScreen()),
        new AWTEventQueueProber(timeoutMillis, 100));
  }

  public void showsSniperStatus(String statusText) {
    new JLabelDriver(
      this, named(Main.SNIPER_STATUS_NAME)).hasText(equalTo(statusText));
  }
}
```

On construction, it attempts to find a visible top-level window for the Auction Sniper within the given timeout. The method `showsSniperStatus()` looks for the relevant label in the user interface and confirms that it shows the given status. If the driver cannot find a feature it expects, it will throw an exception and fail the test.

The Fake Auction

A `FakeAuctionServer` is a substitute server that allows the test to check how the Auction Sniper interacts with an auction using XMPP messages. It has three responsibilities: it must connect to the XMPP broker and accept a request to join the chat from the Sniper; it must receive chat messages from the Sniper or fail if no message arrives within some timeout; and, it must allow the test to send messages back to the Sniper as specified by Southabee's On-Line.

Smack (the XMPP client library) is event-driven, so the fake auction has to register listener objects for it to call back. There are two levels of events: events *about* a chat, such as people joining, and events *within* a chat, such as messages being received. We need to listen for both.

We'll start by implementing the `startSellingItem()` method. First, it connects to the XMPP broker, using the item identifier to construct the login name; then it registers a `ChatManagerListener`. Smack will call this listener with a `Chat` object that represents the session when a Sniper connects in. The fake auction holds on to the chat so it can exchange messages with the Sniper.

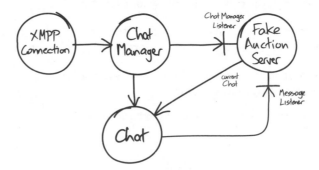

Figure 11.1 *Smack objects and callbacks*

So far, we have:

```
public class FakeAuctionServer {
  public static final String ITEM_ID_AS_LOGIN = "auction-%s";
  public static final String AUCTION_RESOURCE = "Auction";
  public static final String XMPP_HOSTNAME = "localhost";
  private static final String AUCTION_PASSWORD = "auction";

  private final String itemId;
  private final XMPPConnection connection;
  private Chat currentChat;

  public FakeAuctionServer(String itemId) {
    this.itemId = itemId;
    this.connection = new XMPPConnection(XMPP_HOSTNAME);
  }

  public void startSellingItem() throws XMPPException {
    connection.connect();
    connection.login(String.format(ITEM_ID_AS_LOGIN, itemId),
                     AUCTION_PASSWORD, AUCTION_RESOURCE);
    connection.getChatManager().addChatListener(
      new ChatManagerListener() {
        public void chatCreated(Chat chat, boolean createdLocally) {
          currentChat = chat;
        }
      });
  }

  public String getItemId() {
    return itemId;
  }
}
```

 A Minimal Fake Implementation

We want to emphasize again that this fake is a minimal implementation just to
support testing. For example, we use a single instance variable to hold the chat
object. A real auction server would manage multiple chats for all the bidders—but
this is a fake; its only purpose is to support the test, so it only needs one chat.

Next, we have to add a MessageListener to the chat to accept messages from
the Sniper. This means that we need to coordinate between the thread that
runs the test and the Smack thread that feeds messages to the listener—the test
has to wait for messages to arrive and time out if they don't—so we'll use a
single-element BlockingQueue from the java.util.concurrent package. Just as
we only have one chat in the test, we expect to process only one message at a
time. To make our intentions clearer, we wrap the queue in a helper class
SingleMessageListener. Here's the rest of FakeAuctionServer:

```java
public class FakeAuctionServer {
  private final SingleMessageListener messageListener = new SingleMessageListener();

  public void startSellingItem() throws XMPPException {
    connection.connect();
    connection.login(format(ITEM_ID_AS_LOGIN, itemId),
                     AUCTION_PASSWORD, AUCTION_RESOURCE);
    connection.getChatManager().addChatListener(
      new ChatManagerListener() {
        public void chatCreated(Chat chat, boolean createdLocally) {
          currentChat = chat;
          chat.addMessageListener(messageListener);
        }
      });
  }

  public void hasReceivedJoinRequestFromSniper() throws InterruptedException {
    messageListener.receivesAMessage(); ❶
  }

  public void announceClosed() throws XMPPException {
    currentChat.sendMessage(new Message()); ❷
  }

  public void stop() {
    connection.disconnect(); ❸
  }
}

public class SingleMessageListener implements MessageListener {
  private final ArrayBlockingQueue<Message> messages =
                          new ArrayBlockingQueue<Message>(1);

  public void processMessage(Chat chat, Message message) {
    messages.add(message);
  }

  public void receivesAMessage() throws InterruptedException {
    assertThat("Message", messages.poll(5, TimeUnit.SECONDS), is(notNullValue())); ❹
  }
}
```

❶ The test needs to know when a Join message has arrived. We just check whether *any* message has arrived, since the Sniper will only be sending Join messages to start with; we'll fill in more detail as we grow the application. This implementation will fail if no message is received within 5 seconds.

❷ The test needs to be able to simulate the auction announcing when it closes, which is why we held onto the currentChat when it opened. As with the Join request, the fake auction just sends an empty message, since this is the only event we support so far.

❸ stop() closes the connection.

④ The clause is(notNullValue()) uses the Hamcrest *matcher* syntax. We describe Matchers in "Methods" (page 339); for now, it's enough to know that this checks that the Listener has received a message within the timeout period.

The Message Broker

There's one more component to mention which doesn't involve any coding—the installation of an XMPP message broker. We set up an instance of Openfire on our local host. The Sniper and fake auction in our end-to-end tests, even though they're running in the same process, will communicate through this server. We also set up logins to match the small number of item identifiers that we'll be using in our tests.

A Working Compromise

As we wrote before, we are cheating a little at this stage to keep development moving. We want all the developers to have their own environments so they don't interfere with each other when running their tests. For example, we've seen teams make their lives very complicated because they didn't want to create a database instance for each developer. In a professional organization, we would also expect to see at least one test rig that represents the production environment, including the distribution of processing across a network and a build cycle that uses it to make sure the system works.

Failing and Passing the Test

We have enough infrastructure in place to run the test and watch it fail. For the rest of this chapter we'll add functionality, a tiny slice at a time, until eventually we make the test pass. When we first started using this technique, it felt too fussy: "Just write the code, we know what to do!" Over time, we realized that it didn't take any longer and that our progress was much more predictable. Focusing on just one aspect at a time helps us to make sure we understand it; as a rule, when we get something working, it stays working. Where there's no need to discuss the solution, many of these steps take hardly any time at all—they take longer to explain than to implement.

We start by writing a build script for *ant*. We'll skip over the details of its content, since it's standard practice these days, but the important point is that we always have a single command that reliably compiles, builds, deploys, and tests the application, and that we run it repeatedly. We only start coding once we have an automated build and test working.

At this stage, we'll describe each step, discussing each test failure in turn. Later we'll speed up the pace.

First User Interface

Test Failure

The test can't find a user interface component with the name "Auction Sniper Main".

```
java.lang.AssertionError:
Tried to look for...
    exactly 1 JFrame (with name "Auction Sniper Main" and showing on screen)
    in all top level windows
but...
    all top level windows
    contained 0 JFrame (with name "Auction Sniper Main" and showing on screen)
  [...]
  at auctionsniper.ApplicationRunner.stop()
  at auctionsniper.AuctionSniperEndToEndTest.stopApplication()
  [...]
```

WindowLicker is verbose in its error reporting, trying to make failures easy to understand. In this case, we couldn't even find the top-level frame so JUnit failed before even starting the test. The stack trace comes from the @After method that stops the application.

Implementation

We need a top-level window for our application. We write a MainWindow class in the auctionsniper.ui package that extends Swing's JFrame, and call it from main(). All it will do is create a window with the right name.

```java
public class Main {
  private MainWindow ui;

  public Main() throws Exception {
    startUserInterface()
  }

  public static void main(String... args) throws Exception {
    Main main = new Main();
  }

  private void startUserInterface() throws Exception {
    SwingUtilities.invokeAndWait(new Runnable() {
      public void run() {
        ui = new MainWindow();
      }
    });
  }
}
```

```
public class MainWindow extends JFrame {
  public MainWindow() {
    super("Auction Sniper");
    setName(MAIN_WINDOW_NAME);
    setDefaultCloseOperation(JFrame.EXIT_ON_CLOSE);
    setVisible(true);
  }
}
```

Unfortunately, this is a little messy because Swing requires us to create the user interface on its event dispatch thread. We've further complicated the implementation so we can hang on to the main window object in our code. It's not strictly necessary here but we thought we'd get it over with.

Notes

The user interface in Figure 11.2 really is minimal. It does not look like much but it confirms that we can start up an application window and connect to it.

Our test still fails, but we've moved on a step. Now we know that our harness is working, which is one less thing to worry about as we move on to more interesting functionality.

Figure 11.2   *Just a top-level window*

Showing the Sniper State

Test Failure

The test finds a top-level window, but no display of the current state of the Sniper. To start with, the Sniper should show Joining while waiting for the auction to respond.

```
java.lang.AssertionError:
Tried to look for...
    exactly 1 JLabel (with name "sniper status")
    in exactly 1 JFrame (with name "Auction Sniper Main" and showing on screen)
    in all top level windows
and check that its label text is "Joining"
but...
    all top level windows
    contained 1 JFrame (with name "Auction Sniper Main" and showing on screen)
    contained 0 JLabel (with name "sniper status")
  at com.objogate.wl.AWTEventQueueProber.check()
  [...]
  at AuctionSniperDriver.showsSniperStatus()
  at ApplicationRunner.startBiddingIn()
  at AuctionSniperEndToEndTest.sniperJoinsAuctionUntilAuctionCloses()
  [...]
```

Implementation

We add a label representing the Sniper's state to `MainWindow`.

```
public class MainWindow extends JFrame {
  public static final String SNIPER_STATUS_NAME = "sniper status";
  private final JLabel sniperStatus = createLabel(STATUS_JOINING);

  public MainWindow() {
    super("Auction Sniper");
    setName(MAIN_WINDOW_NAME);
    add(sniperStatus);
    pack();
    setDefaultCloseOperation(JFrame.EXIT_ON_CLOSE);
    setVisible(true);
  }

  private static JLabel createLabel(String initialText) {
    JLabel result = new JLabel(initialText);
    result.setName(SNIPER_STATUS_NAME);
    result.setBorder(new LineBorder(Color.BLACK));
    return result;
  }
}
```

Notes

Another minimal change, but now we can show some content in our application, as in Figure 11.3.

Figure 11.3 *Showing* Joining *status*

Connecting to the Auction

Test Failure

Our user interface is working, but the auction does not receive a `Join` request from the Sniper.

```
java.lang.AssertionError:
Expected: is not null
    got: null
  at org.junit.Assert.assertThat()
  at SingleMessageListener.receivesAMessage()
  at FakeAuctionServer.hasReceivedJoinRequestFromSniper()
  at AuctionSniperEndToEndTest.sniperJoinsAuctionUntilAuctionCloses()
  [...]
```

This failure message is a bit cryptic, but the names in the stack trace tell us what's wrong.

Implementation

We write a simplistic implementation to get us past this failure. It connects to the chat in Main and sends an empty message. We create a null MessageListener to allow us to create a Chat for sending the empty initial message, since we don't yet care about receiving messages.

```java
public class Main {
  private static final int ARG_HOSTNAME = 0;
  private static final int ARG_USERNAME = 1;
  private static final int ARG_PASSWORD = 2;
  private static final int ARG_ITEM_ID  = 3;

  public static final String AUCTION_RESOURCE = "Auction";
  public static final String ITEM_ID_AS_LOGIN = "auction-%s";
  public static final String AUCTION_ID_FORMAT =
                            ITEM_ID_AS_LOGIN + "@%s/" + AUCTION_RESOURCE;

  [...]

  public static void main(String... args) throws Exception {
    Main main = new Main();
    XMPPConnection connection = connectTo(args[ARG_HOSTNAME],
                                          args[ARG_USERNAME],
                                          args[ARG_PASSWORD]);
    Chat chat = connection.getChatManager().createChat(
        auctionId(args[ARG_ITEM_ID], connection),
        new MessageListener() {
          public void processMessage(Chat aChat, Message message) {
            // nothing yet
          }
        });
    chat.sendMessage(new Message());
  }

  private static XMPPConnection
  connectTo(String hostname, String username, String password)
      throws XMPPException
  {
    XMPPConnection connection = new XMPPConnection(hostname);
    connection.connect();
    connection.login(username, password, AUCTION_RESOURCE);

    return connection;
  }

  private static String auctionId(String itemId, XMPPConnection connection) {
    return String.format(AUCTION_ID_FORMAT, itemId,
                         connection.getServiceName());
  }
  [...]
}
```

Notes

This shows that we can establish a connection from the Sniper to the auction, which means we had to sort out details such as interpreting the item and user credentials from the command-line arguments and using the Smack library. We're leaving the message contents until later because we only have one message type, so sending an empty value is enough to prove the connection.

This implementation may seem gratuitously naive—after all, we should be able to design a structure for something as simple as this, but we've often found it worth writing a *small* amount of ugly code and seeing how it falls out. It helps us to test our ideas before we've gone too far, and sometimes the results can be surprising. The important point is to make sure we don't leave it ugly.

We make a point of keeping the connection code out of the Swing invokeAndWait() call that creates the MainWindow, because we want the user interface to settle before we try anything more complicated.

Receiving a Response from the Auction

Test Failure

With a connection established, the Sniper should receive and display the Lost response from the auction. It doesn't yet:

```
java.lang.AssertionError:
Tried to look for...
    exactly 1 JLabel (with name "sniper status")
    in exactly 1 JFrame (with name "Auction Sniper Main" and showing on screen)
    in all top level windows
and check that its label text is "Lost"
but...
    all top level windows
    contained 1 JFrame (with name "Auction Sniper Main" and showing on screen)
    contained 1 JLabel (with name "sniper status")
    label text was "Joining"
  [...]
  at AuctionSniperDriver.showsSniperStatus()
  at ApplicationRunner.showsSniperHasLostAuction()
  at AuctionSniperEndToEndTest.sniperJoinsAuctionUntilAuctionCloses()
  [...]
```

Implementation

We need to attach the user interface to the chat so it can receive the response from the auction, so we create a connection and pass it to Main to create the Chat object. joinAuction() creates a MessageListener that sets the status label, using an invokeLater() call to avoid blocking the Smack library. As with the Join message, we don't bother with the contents of the incoming message since there's only one possible response the auction can send at the moment. While we're at it, we rename connectTo() to connection() to make the code read better.

```
public class Main {
  @SuppressWarnings("unused") private Chat notToBeGCd;
  [...]
  public static void main(String... args) throws Exception {
    Main main = new Main();
    main.joinAuction(
      connection(args[ARG_HOSTNAME], args[ARG_USERNAME], args[ARG_PASSWORD]),
      args[ARG_ITEM_ID]);
  }

  private void joinAuction(XMPPConnection connection, String itemId)
    throws XMPPException
  {
    final Chat chat = connection.getChatManager().createChat(
        auctionId(itemId, connection),
        new MessageListener() {
          public void processMessage(Chat aChat, Message message) {
            SwingUtilities.invokeLater(new Runnable() {
              public void run() {
                ui.showStatus(MainWindow.STATUS_LOST);
              }
            });
          }
        });
    this.notToBeGCd = chat;

    chat.sendMessage(new Message());
  }
```

 ## Why the Chat Field?

You'll notice that we've assigned the chat that we create to the field notToBeGCd in Main. This is to make sure that the chat is not garbage-collected by the Java runtime. There's a note at the top of the ChatManager documentation that says:

> The chat manager keeps track of references to all current chats. It will not hold any references in memory on its own so it is necessary to keep a reference to the chat object itself.

If the chat is garbage-collected, the Smack runtime will hand the message to a new Chat which it will create for the purpose. In an interactive application, we would listen for and show these new chats, but our needs are different, so we add this quirk to stop it from happening.

We made this reference clumsy on purpose—to highlight in the code why we're doing it. We also know that we're likely to come up with a better solution in a while.

We implement the display method in the user interface and, finally, the whole test passes.

```
public class MainWindow extends JFrame {
  [...]
  public void showStatus(String status) {
    sniperStatus.setText(status);
  }
}
```

Notes

Figure 11.4 is visible confirmation that the code works.

Figure 11.4 *Showing* Lost *status*

It may not look like much, but it confirms that a Sniper can establish a connection with an auction, accept a response, and display the result.

The Necessary Minimum

In one of his school reports, Steve was noted as "a fine judge of the necessary minimum." It seems he's found his calling in writing software since this is a critical skill during iteration zero.

What we hope you've seen in this chapter is the degree of focus that's required to put together your first walking skeleton. The point is to design and validate the initial structure of the end-to-end system—where *end-to-end* includes deployment to a working environment—to prove that our choices of packages, libraries, and tooling will actually work. A sense of urgency will help the team to strip the functionality down to the absolute minimum sufficient to test their assumptions. That's why we didn't put any content in our Sniper messages; it would be a diversion from making sure that the communication and event handling work. We didn't sweat too hard over the detailed code design, partly because there isn't much but mainly because we're just getting the pieces in place; that effort will come soon enough.

Of course, all you see in this chapter are edited highlights. We've left out many diversions and discussions as we figured out which pieces to use and how to make them work, trawling through product documentation and discussion lists. We've also left out some of our discussions about what this project is *for*. Iteration zero usually brings up project chartering issues as the team looks for criteria to guide its decisions, so the project's sponsors should expect to field some deep questions about its purpose.

We have something visible we can present as a sign of progress, so we can cross off the first item on our list, as in Figure 11.5.

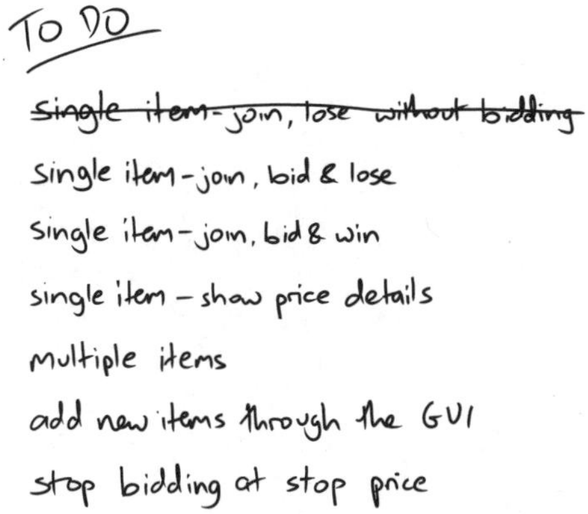

TO DO

~~single item - join, lose without bidding~~
Single item - join, bid & lose
Single item - join, bid & win
single item - show price details
multiple items
add new items through the GUI
stop bidding at stop price

Figure 11.5 *First item done*

The next step is to start building out real functionality.

Chapter 12

Getting Ready to Bid

In which we write an end-to-end test so that we can make the Sniper bid in an auction. We start to interpret the messages in the auction protocol and discover some new classes in the process. We write our first unit tests and then refactor out a helper class. We describe every last detail of this effort to show what we were thinking at the time.

An Introduction to the Market

Now, to continue with the skeleton metaphor, we start to flesh out the application. The core behavior of a Sniper is that it makes a higher bid on an item in an auction when there's a change in price. Going back to our to-do list, we revisit the next couple of items:

- *Single item: join, bid, and lose.* When a price comes in, send a bid raised by the minimum increment defined by the auction. This amount will be included in the price update information.

- *Single item: join, bid, and win.* Distinguish which bidder is currently winning the auction and don't bid against ourselves.

We know there'll be more coming, but this is a coherent slice of functionality that will allow us to explore the design and show concrete progress.

In any distributed system similar to this one there are lots of interesting failure and timing issues, but our application only has to deal with the client side of the protocol. We rely on the underlying XMPP protocol to deal with many common distributed programming problems; in particular, we expect it to ensure that messages between a bidder and an auction arrive in the same order in which they were sent.

As we described in Chapter 5, we start the next feature with an acceptance test. We used our first test in the previous chapter to help flush out the structure of our application. From now on, we can use acceptance tests to show incremental progress.

A Test for Bidding

Starting with a Test

Each acceptance test we write should have just enough new requirements to force
a manageable increase in functionality, so we decide that the next one will add
some price information. The steps are:

1. Tell the auction to send a price to the Sniper.

2. Check the Sniper has received and responded to the price.

3. Check the auction has received an incremented bid from Sniper.

To make this pass, the Sniper will have to distinguish between `Price` and `Close`
events from the auction, display the current price, and generate a new bid. We'll
also have to extend our stub auction to handle bids. We've deferred implementing
other functionality that will also be required, such as displaying when the Sniper
has won the auction; we'll get to that later. Here's the new test:

```
public class AuctionSniperEndToEndTest {
  @Test public void
  sniperMakesAHigherBidButLoses() throws Exception {
    auction.startSellingItem();

    application.startBiddingIn(auction);
    auction.hasReceivedJoinRequestFromSniper(); ❶

    auction.reportPrice(1000, 98, "other bidder"); ❷
    application.hasShownSniperIsBidding(); ❸

    auction.hasReceivedBid(1098, ApplicationRunner.SNIPER_XMPP_ID); ❹

    auction.announceClosed(); ❺
    application.showsSniperHasLostAuction();
  }
}
```

We have three new methods to implement as part of this test.

❶   We have to wait for the stub auction to receive the `Join` request before con-
     tinuing with the test. We use this assertion to synchronize the Sniper with
     the auction.

❷   This method tells the stub auction to send a message back to the Sniper with
     the news that at the moment the price of the item is 1000, the increment for
     the next bid is 98, and the winning bidder is "other bidder."

❸   This method asks the `ApplicationRunner` to check that the Sniper shows that
     it's now bidding after it's received the price update message from the auction.

➍ This method asks the stub auction to check that it has received a bid from the Sniper that is equal to the last price plus the minimum increment. We have to do a fraction more work because the XMPP layer constructs a longer name from the basic identifier, so we define a constant SNIPER_XMPP_ID which in practice is sniper@localhost/Auction.

➎ We reuse the closing logic from the first test, as the Sniper still loses the auction.

 Unrealistic Money

We're using integers to represent value (imagine that auctions are conducted in Japanese Yen). In a real system, we would define a domain type to represent monetary values, using a fixed decimal implementation. Here, we simplify the representation to make the example code easier to fit onto a printed page.

Extending the Fake Auction

We have two methods to write in the FakeAuctionServer to support the end-to-end test: reportPrice() has to send a Price message through the chat; hasReceivedBid() is a little more complex—it has to check that the auction received the right values from the Sniper. Instead of parsing the incoming message, we construct the expected message and just compare strings. We also pull up the Matcher clause from the SingleMessageListener to give the FakeAuctionServer more flexibility in defining what it will accept as a message. Here's a first cut:

```
public class FakeAuctionServer { [...]
  public void reportPrice(int price, int increment, String bidder)
    throws XMPPException
  {
    currentChat.sendMessage(
        String.format("SOLVersion: 1.1; Event: PRICE; "
                    + "CurrentPrice: %d; Increment: %d; Bidder: %s;",
                    price, increment, bidder));
  }
  public void hasReceivedJoinRequestFromSniper() throws InterruptedException {
    messageListener.receivesAMessage(is(anything()));
  }
  public void hasReceivedBid(int bid, String sniperId)
    throws InterruptedException
  {
    assertThat(currentChat.getParticipant(), equalTo(sniperId));
    messageListener.receivesAMessage(
      equalTo(
        String.format("SOLVersion: 1.1; Command: BID; Price: %d;", bid)));
  }
}
```

```java
public class SingleMessageListener implements MessageListener { [...]
  @SuppressWarnings("unchecked")
  public void receivesAMessage(Matcher<? super String> messageMatcher)
    throws InterruptedException
  {
    final Message message = messages.poll(5, TimeUnit.SECONDS);
    assertThat("Message", message, is(notNullValue()));
    assertThat(message.getBody(), messageMatcher);
  }
}
```

Looking again, there's an imbalance between the two "receives" methods. The Join method is much more lax than the bid message, in terms of both the contents of the message and the sender; we will have to remember to come back later and fix it. We defer a great many decisions when developing incrementally, but sometimes consistency and symmetry make more sense. We decide to retrofit more detail into hasReceivedJoinRequestFromSniper() while we have the code cracked open. We also extract the message formats and move them to Main because we'll need them to construct raw messages in the Sniper.

```java
public class FakeAuctionServer { [...]
  public void hasReceivedJoinRequestFrom(String sniperId)
    throws InterruptedException
  {
    receivesAMessageMatching(sniperId, equalTo(Main.JOIN_COMMAND_FORMAT));
  }

  public void hasReceivedBid(int bid, String sniperId)
    throws InterruptedException
  {
    receivesAMessageMatching(sniperId,
                        equalTo(format(Main.BID_COMMAND_FORMAT, bid)));
  }

  private void receivesAMessageMatching(String sniperId,
                                  Matcher<? super String> messageMatcher)
    throws InterruptedException
  {
    messageListener.receivesAMessage(messageMatcher);
    assertThat(currentChat.getParticipant(), equalTo(sniperId));
  }
}
```

Notice that we check the Sniper's identifier *after* we check the contents of the message. This forces the server to wait until the message has arrived, which means that it must have accepted a connection and set up currentChat. Otherwise the test would fail by checking the Sniper's identifier prematurely.

Double-Entry Values

We're using the same constant to both create a `Join` message and check its contents. By using the same construct, we're removing duplication and expressing in the code a link between the two sides of the system. On the other hand, we're making ourselves vulnerable to getting them *both* wrong and not having a test to catch the invalid content. In this case, the code is so simple that pretty much any implementation would do, but the answers become less certain when developing something more complex, such as a persistence layer. Do we use the same framework to write and read our values? Can we be sure that it's not just caching the results, or that the values are persisted correctly? Should we just write some straight database queries to be sure?

The critical question is, what do we think we're testing? Here, we think that the communication features are more important, that the messages are simple enough so we can rely on string constants, and that we'd like to be able to find code related to message formats in the IDE. Other developers might come to a different conclusion and be right for their project.

We adjust the end-to-end tests to match the new API, watch the test fail, and then add the extra detail to the Sniper to make the test pass.

```
public class AuctionSniperEndToEndTest {
  @Test public void
  sniperMakesAHigherBidButLoses() throws Exception {
    auction.startSellingItem();

    application.startBiddingIn(auction);
    auction.hasReceivedJoinRequestFrom(ApplicationRunner.SNIPER_XMPP_ID);

    auction.reportPrice(1000, 98, "other bidder");
    application.hasShownSniperIsBidding();

    auction.hasReceivedBid(1098, ApplicationRunner.SNIPER_XMPP_ID);

    auction.announceClosed();
    application.showsSniperHasLostAuction();
  }
}
```

```
public class Main { [...]
  private void joinAuction(XMPPConnection connection, String itemId)
    throws XMPPException
  {
    Chat chat = connection.getChatManager().createChat(
        auctionId(itemId, connection),
        new MessageListener() {
          public void processMessage(Chat aChat, Message message) {
            SwingUtilities.invokeLater(new Runnable() {
              public void run() {
                ui.showStatus(MainWindow.STATUS_LOST);
              }
            });
          }
        });
    this.notToBeGCd = chat;
    chat.sendMessage(JOIN_COMMAND_FORMAT);
  }
}
```

A Surprise Failure

Finally we write the "checking" method on the `ApplicationRunner` to give us our first failure. The implementation is simple: we just add another status constant and copy the existing method.

```
public class ApplicationRunner { [...]
  public void hasShownSniperIsBidding() {
    driver.showsSniperStatus(MainWindow.STATUS_BIDDING);
  }

  public void showsSniperHasLostAuction() {
    driver.showsSniperStatus(MainWindow.STATUS_LOST);
  }
}
```

We're expecting to see something about a missing label text but instead we get this:

```
java.lang.AssertionError:
Expected: is not null
     got: null
  [...]
  at auctionsniper.SingleMessageListener.receivesAMessage()
  at auctionsniper.FakeAuctionServer.hasReceivedJoinRequestFromSniper()
  at auctionsniper.AuctionSniperEndToEndTest.sniperMakesAHigherBid()
  [...]
```

and this on the error stream:

```
conflict(409)
  at jivesoftware.smack.SASLAuthentication.bindResourceAndEstablishSession()
  at jivesoftware.smack.SASLAuthentication.authenticate()
  at jivesoftware.smack.XMPPConnection.login()
  at jivesoftware.smack.XMPPConnection.login()
  at auctionsniper.Main.connection()
  at auctionsniper.Main.main()
```

After some investigation we realize what's happened. We've introduced a second test which tries to connect using the same account and resource name as the first. The server is configured, like Southabee's On-Line, to reject multiple open connections, so the second test fails because the server thinks that the first is still connected. In production, our application would work because we'd stop the whole process when closing, which would break the connection. Our little compromise (of starting the application in a new thread) has caught us out. The Right Thing to do here is to add a callback to disconnect the client when we close the window so that the application will clean up after itself:

```
public class Main { […]
  private void joinAuction(XMPPConnection connection, String itemId)
    throws XMPPException
  {
    disconnectWhenUICloses(connection);
    Chat chat = connection.getChatManager().createChat(
    […]
    chat.sendMessage(JOIN_COMMAND_FORMAT);
  }
  private void disconnectWhenUICloses(final XMPPConnection connection) {
    ui.addWindowListener(new WindowAdapter() {
      @Override public void windowClosed(WindowEvent e) {
        connection.disconnect();
      }
    });
  }
}
```

Now we get the failure we expected, because the Sniper has no way to start bidding.

```
java.lang.AssertionError:
Tried to look for...
    exactly 1 JLabel (with name "sniper status")
    in exactly 1 JFrame (with name "Auction Sniper Main" and showing on screen)
    in all top level windows
and check that its label text is "Bidding"
but...
    all top level windows
    contained 1 JFrame (with name "Auction Sniper Main" and showing on screen)
    contained 1 JLabel (with name "sniper status")
    label text was "Lost"
    […]
  at auctionsniper.AuctionSniperDriver.showsSniperStatus()
  at auctionsniper.ApplicationRunner.hasShownSniperIsBidding()
  at auctionsniper.AuctionSniperEndToEndTest.sniperMakesAHigherBidButLoses()
```

Outside-In Development

This failure defines the target for our next coding episode. It tells us, at a high level, what we're aiming for—we just have to fill in implementation until it passes.

Our approach to test-driven development is to start with the outside event that triggers the behavior we want to implement and work our way into the code an object at a time, until we reach a visible effect (such as a sent message or log entry) indicating that we've achieved our goal. The end-to-end test shows us the end points of that process, so we can explore our way through the space in the middle.

In the following sections, we build up the types we need to implement our Auction Sniper. We'll take it slowly, strictly by the TDD rules, to show how the process works. In real projects, we sometimes design a bit further ahead to get a sense of the bigger picture, but much of the time this is what we actually do. It produces the right results and forces us to ask the right questions.

Infinite Attention to Detail?

We caught the resource clash because, by luck or insight, our server configuration matched that of Southabee's On-Line. We might have used an alternative setting which allows new connections to kick off existing ones, which would have resulted in the tests passing but with a confusing conflict message from the Smack library on the error stream. This would have worked fine in development, but with a risk of Snipers starting to fail in production.

How can we hope to catch all the configuration options in an entire system? At some level we can't, and this is at the heart of what professional testers do. What we *can* do is push to exercise as much as possible of the system as early as possible, and to do so repeatedly. We can also help ourselves cope with total system complexity by keeping the quality of its components high and by constantly pushing to simplify. If that sounds expensive, consider the cost of finding and fixing a transient bug like this one in a busy production system.

The AuctionMessageTranslator

Teasing Out a New Class

Our entry point to the Sniper is where we receive a message from the auction through the Smack library: it's the event that triggers the next round of behavior we want to make work. In practice, this means that we need a class implementing MessageListener to attach to the Chat. When this class receives a raw message from the auction, it will translate it into something that represents an auction event within our code which, eventually, will prompt a Sniper action and a change in the user interface.

We already have such a class in `Main`—it's anonymous and its responsibilities aren't very obvious:

```
new MessageListener() {
  public void processMessage(Chat aChat, Message message) {
    SwingUtilities.invokeLater(new Runnable() {
      public void run() {
        ui.showStatus(MainWindow.STATUS_LOST);
      }
    });
  }
}
```

This code implicitly accepts a `Close` message (the only kind of message we have so far) and implements the Sniper's response. We'd like to make this situation explicit before we add more features. We start by promoting the anonymous class to a top-level class in its own right, which means it needs a name. From our description in the paragraph above, we pick up the word "translate" and call it an `AuctionMessageTranslator`, because it will *translate messages* from the *auction*.

The catch is that the current anonymous class picks up the `ui` field from `Main`. We'll have to attach something to our newly promoted class so that it can respond to a message. The most obvious thing to do is pass it the `MainWindow` but we're unhappy about creating a dependency on a user interface component. That would make it hard to unit-test, because we'd have to query the state of a component that's running in the Swing event thread.

More significantly, such a dependency would break the "single responsibility" principle which says that unpacking raw messages from the auction is quite enough for one class to do, without also having to know how to present the Sniper status. As we wrote in "Designing for Maintainability" (page 47), we want to maintain a *separation of concerns*.

Given these constraints, we decide that our new `AuctionMessageTranslator` will delegate the handling of an interpreted event to a collaborator, which we will represent with an `AuctionEventListener` interface; we can pass an object that implements it into the translator on construction. We don't yet know what's in this interface and we haven't yet begun to think about its implementation. Our immediate concern is to get the message translation to work; the rest can wait. So far the design looks like Figure 12.1 (types that belong to external frameworks, such as `Chat`, are shaded):

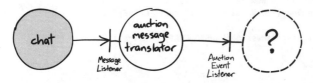

Figure 12.1 *The* `AuctionMessageTranslator`

The First Unit Test

We start with the simpler event type. As we've seen, a Close event has no values—it's a simple trigger. When the translator receives one, we want it to call its listener appropriately.

As this is our first unit test, we'll build it up very slowly to show the process (later, we will move faster). We start with the test method name. JUnit picks up test methods by reflection, so we can make their names as long and descriptive as we like because we never have to include them in code. The first test says that the translator will tell anything that's listening that the auction has closed when it receives a raw Close message.

```
package test.auctionsniper;

public class AuctionMessageTranslatorTest {
  @Test public void
  notifiesAuctionClosedWhenCloseMessageReceived() {
    // nothing yet
  }
}
```

Put Tests in a Different Package

We've adopted a habit of putting tests in a different package from the code they're exercising. We want to make sure we're driving the code through its public interfaces, like any other client, rather than opening up a package-scoped back door for testing. We also find that, as the application and test code grows, separate packages make navigation in modern IDEs easier.

The next step is to add the action that will trigger the behavior we want to test—in this case, sending a Close message. We already know what this will look like since it's a call to the Smack MessageListener interface.

```
public class AuctionMessageTranslatorTest {
  public static final Chat UNUSED_CHAT = null;
  private final AuctionMessageTranslator translator =
                                    new AuctionMessageTranslator();
  @Test public void
  notfiesAuctionClosedWhenCloseMessageReceived() {
    Message message = new Message();
    message.setBody("SOLVersion: 1.1; Event: CLOSE;");

    translator.processMessage(UNUSED_CHAT, message);
  }
}
```

Use null When an Argument Doesn't Matter

UNUSED_CHAT is a meaningful name for a constant that is defined as null. We pass it into processMessage() instead of a real Chat object because the Chat class is difficult to instantiate—its constructor is package-scoped and we'd have to fill in a chain of dependencies to create one. As it happens, we don't need one anyway for the current functionality, so we just pass in a null value to satisfy the compiler but use a named constant to make clear its significance.

To be clear, this null is not a *null object* [Woolf98] which may be called and will do nothing in response. This null is just a placeholder and will fail if called during the test.

We generate a skeleton implementation from the MessageListener interface.

```
package auctionsniper;

public class AuctionMessageTranslator implements MessageListener {
  public void processMessage(Chat chat, Message message) {
    // TODO Fill in here
  }
}
```

Next, we want a check that shows whether the translation has taken place—which should fail since we haven't implemented anything yet. We've already decided that we want our translator to notify its listener when the Close event occurs, so we'll describe that expected behavior in our test.

```
@RunWith(JMock.class)
public class AuctionMessageTranslatorTest {
  private final Mockery context = new Mockery();
  private final AuctionEventListener listener =
                          context.mock(AuctionEventListener.class);
  private final AuctionMessageTranslator translator =
                          new AuctionMessageTranslator();

  @Test public void
  notfiesAuctionClosedWhenCloseMessageReceived() {
    context.checking(new Expectations() {{
      oneOf(listener).auctionClosed();
    }});

    Message message = new Message();
    message.setBody("SOLVersion: 1.1; Event: CLOSE;");

    translator.processMessage(UNUSED_CHAT, message);
  }
}
```

This is more or less the kind of unit test we described at the end of Chapter 2, so we won't go over its structure again here except to emphasize the highlighted expectation line. This is the most significant line in the test, our declaration of what matters about the translator's effect on its environment. It says that when we send an appropriate message to the translator, we expect it to call the listener's `auctionClosed()` method exactly once.

We get a failure that shows that we haven't implemented the behavior we need:

```
not all expectations were satisfied
expectations:
  ! expected once, never invoked: auctionEventListener.auctionClosed()
what happened before this: nothing!
  at org.jmock.Mockery.assertIsSatisfied(Mockery.java:199)
  [...]
  at org.junit.internal.runners.JUnit4ClassRunner.run()
```

The critical phrase is this one:

```
expected once, never invoked: auctionEventListener.auctionClosed()
```

which tells us that we haven't called the listener as we should have.

We need to do two things to make the test pass. First, we need to connect the translator and listener so that they can communicate. We decide to pass the listener into the translator's constructor; it's simple and ensures that the translator is always set up correctly with a listener—the Java type system won't let us forget. The test setup looks like this:

```
public class AuctionMessageTranslatorTest {
  private final Mockery context = new Mockery();
  private final AuctionEventListener listener =
                          context.mock(AuctionEventListener.class);
  private final AuctionMessageTranslator translator =
                          new AuctionMessageTranslator(listener);
```

The second thing we need to do is call the `auctionClosed()` method. Actually, that's *all* we need to do to make this test pass, since we haven't defined any other behavior.

```
public void processMessage(Chat chat, Message message) {
   listener.auctionClosed();
 }
```

The test passes. This might feel like cheating since we haven't actually unpacked a message. What we *have* done is figured out where the pieces are and got them into a test harness—and locked down *one* piece of functionality that should continue to work as we add more features.

Simplified Test Setup

You might have noticed that all the fields in the test class are `final`. As we described in Chapter 3, JUnit creates a new instance of the test class for each test method, so the fields are recreated for each test method. We exploit this by declaring as many fields as possible as `final` and initializing them during construction, which flushes out any circular dependencies. Steve likes to think of this visually as creating a lattice of objects that acts a frame to support the test.

Sometimes, as you'll see later in this example, we can't lock everything down and have to attach a dependency directly, but most of the time we can. Any exceptions will attract our attention and highlight a possible dependency loop. NUnit, on the other hand, reuses the same instance of the test class, so in that case we'd have to renew any supporting test values and objects explicitly.

Closing the User Interface Loop

Now we have the beginnings of our new component, we can retrofit it into the Sniper to make sure we don't drift too far from working code. Previously, Main updated the Sniper user interface, so now we make it implement AuctionEventListener and move the functionality to the new auctionClosed() method.

```
public class Main implements AuctionEventListener { […]

  private void joinAuction(XMPPConnection connection, String itemId)
    throws XMPPException
  {
    disconnectWhenUICloses(connection);

    Chat chat = connection.getChatManager().createChat(
        auctionId(itemId, connection),
        new AuctionMessageTranslator(this));
    chat.sendMessage(JOIN_COMMAND_FORMAT);
    notToBeGCd = chat;
  }

  public void auctionClosed() {
    SwingUtilities.invokeLater(new Runnable() {
      public void run() {
        ui.showStatus(MainWindow.STATUS_LOST);
      }
    });
  }
}
```

The structure now looks like Figure 12.2.

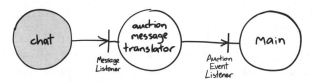

Figure 12.2 *Introducing the* AuctionMessageTranslator

What Have We Achieved?

In this baby step, we've extracted a single feature of our application into a separate class, which means the functionality now has a name and can be unit-tested. We've also made Main a little simpler, now that it's no longer concerned with interpreting the text of messages from the auction. This is not yet a big deal but we will show, as the Sniper application grows, how this approach helps us keep code clean and flexible, with clear responsibilities and relationships between its components.

Unpacking a Price Message

Introducing Message Event Types

We're about to introduce a second auction message type, the current price update. The Sniper needs to distinguish between the two, so we take another look at the message formats in Chapter 9 that Southabee's On-Line have sent us. They're simple—just a single line with a few name/value pairs. Here are examples for the formats again:

```
SOLVersion: 1.1; Event: PRICE; CurrentPrice: 192; Increment: 7; Bidder: Someone else;
SOLVersion: 1.1; Event: CLOSE;
```

At first, being object-oriented enthusiasts, we try to model these messages as types, but we're not clear enough about the behavior to justify any meaningful structure, so we back off the idea. We decide to start with a simplistic solution and adapt from there.

The Second Test

The introduction of a different Price event in our second test will force us to parse the incoming message. This test has the same structure as the first one but gets a different input string and expects us to call a different method on the listener. A Price message includes details of the last bid, which we need to unpack and pass to the listener, so we include them in the signature of the new method currentPrice(). Here's the test:

```
@Test public void
notifiesBidDetailsWhenCurrentPriceMessageReceived() {
```

```
context.checking(new Expectations() {{
  exactly(1).of(listener).currentPrice(192, 7);
}});

Message message = new Message();
  message.setBody(
"SOLVersion: 1.1; Event: PRICE; CurrentPrice: 192; Increment: 7; Bidder: Someone else;"
                );

translator.processMessage(UNUSED_CHAT, message);
}
```

To get through the compiler, we add a method to the listener; this takes just a keystroke in the IDE:[1]

```
public interface AuctionEventListener {
  void auctionClosed();
  void currentPrice(int price, int increment);
}
```

The test fails.

```
unexpected invocation: auctionEventListener.auctionClosed()
expectations:
  ! expected once, never invoked: auctionEventListener.currentPrice(<192>, <7>)
what happened before this: nothing!
  [...]
  at $Proxy6.auctionClosed()
  at auctionsniper.AuctionMessageTranslator.processMessage()
  at AuctionMessageTranslatorTest.translatesPriceMessagesAsAuctionPriceEvents()
  [...]
  at JUnit4ClassRunner.run(JUnit4ClassRunner.java:42)
```

This time the critical phrase is:

```
unexpected invocation: auctionEventListener.auctionClosed()
```

which means that the code called the wrong method, auctionClosed(), during the test. The Mockery isn't expecting this call so it fails immediately, showing us in the stack trace the line that triggered the failure (you can see the workings of the Mockery in the line $Proxy6.auctionClosed() which is the runtime substitute for a real AuctionEventListener). Here, the place where the code failed is obvious, so we can just fix it.

Our first version is rough, but it passes the test.

---

1. Modern development environments, such as Eclipse and IDEA, will fill in a missing method on request. This means that we can write the call we'd like to make and ask the tool to fill in the declaration for us.

```
public class AuctionMessageTranslator implements MessageListener {
  private final AuctionEventListener listener;

  public AuctionMessageTranslator(AuctionEventListener listener) {
    this.listener = listener;
  }

  public void processMessage(Chat chat, Message message) {
    HashMap<String, String> event = unpackEventFrom(message);

    String type = event.get("Event");
    if ("CLOSE".equals(type)) {
      listener.auctionClosed();
    } else if ("PRICE".equals(type)) {
      listener.currentPrice(Integer.parseInt(event.get("CurrentPrice")),
                            Integer.parseInt(event.get("Increment")));
    }
  }

  private HashMap<String, String> unpackEventFrom(Message message) {
    HashMap<String, String> event = new HashMap<String, String>();
    for (String element : message.getBody().split(";")) {
      String[] pair = element.split(":");
      event.put(pair[0].trim(), pair[1].trim());
    }
    return event;
  }
}
```

This implementation breaks the message body into a set of key/value pairs, which it interprets as an auction event so it can notify the `AuctionEventListener`. We also have to fix the `FakeAuctionServer` to send a real `Close` event rather than the current empty message, otherwise the end-to-end tests will fail incorrectly.

```
public void announceClosed() throws XMPPException {
  currentChat.sendMessage("SOLVersion: 1.1; Event: CLOSE;");
}
```

Running our end-to-end test again reminds us that we're still working on the bidding feature. The test shows that the Sniper status label still displays `Joining` rather than `Bidding`.

Discovering Further Work

This code passes the unit test, but there's something missing. It assumes that the message is correctly structured and has the right version. Given that the message will be coming from an outside system, this feels risky, so we need to add some error handling. We don't want to break the flow of getting features to work, so we add error handling to the to-do list to come back to it later (Figure 12.3).

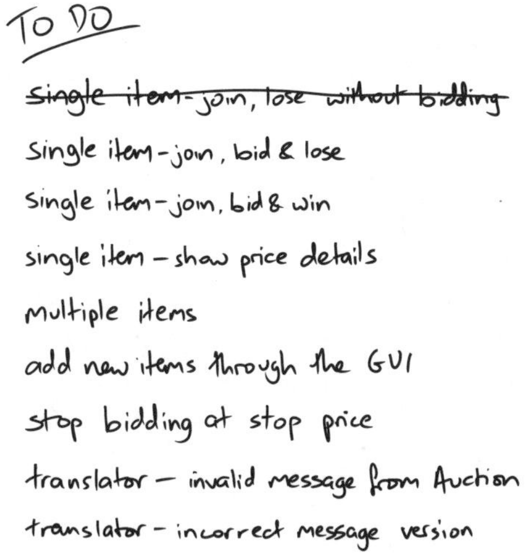

TO DO

~~single item - join, lose without bidding~~

single item - join, bid & lose

single item - join, bid & win

single item - show price details

multiple items

add new items through the GUI

stop bidding at stop price

translator - invalid message from Auction

translator - incorrect message version

Figure 12.3 *Added tasks for handling errors*

We're also concerned that the translator is not as clear as it could be about what it's doing, with its parsing and the dispatching activities mixed together. We make a note to address this class as soon as we've passed the acceptance test, which isn't far off.

Finish the Job

Most of the work in this chapter has been trying to decide what we want to say and how to say it: we write a high-level end-to-end test to describe what the Sniper should implement; we write long unit test names to tell us what a class does; we extract new classes to tease apart fine-grained aspects of the functionality; and we write lots of little methods to keep each layer of code at a consistent level of abstraction. But first, we write a rough implementation to prove that we know how to make the code do what's required *and then we refactor*—which we'll do in the next chapter.

We cannot emphasize strongly enough that "first-cut" code is not finished. It's good enough to sort out our ideas and make sure we have everything in place, but it's unlikely to express its intentions cleanly. That will make it a drag on productivity as it's read repeatedly over the lifetime of the code. It's like carpentry without sanding—eventually someone ends up with a nasty splinter.

Chapter 13

The Sniper Makes a Bid

In which we extract an AuctionSniper *class and tease out its dependencies. We plug our new class into the rest of the application, using an empty implementation of auction until we're ready to start sending commands. We close the loop back to the auction house with an* XMPPAuction *class. We continue to carve new types out of the code.*

Introducing AuctionSniper

A New Class, with Dependencies

Our application accepts Price events from the auction, but cannot interpret them yet. We need code that will perform two actions when the currentPrice() method is called: send a higher bid to the auction and update the status in the user interface. We could extend Main, but that class is looking rather messy—it's already doing too many things at once. It feels like this is a good time to introduce what we should call an "Auction Sniper," the component at the heart of our application, so we create an AuctionSniper class. Some of its intended behavior is currently buried in Main, and a good start would be to extract it into our new class—although, as we'll see in a moment, it will take a little effort.

Given that an AuctionSniper should respond to Price events, we decide to make *it* implement AuctionEventListener rather than Main. The question is what to do about the user interface. If we consider moving this method:

```
public void auctionClosed() {
  SwingUtilities.invokeLater(new Runnable() {
    public void run() {
      ui.showStatus(MainWindow.STATUS_LOST);
    }
  });
}
```

does it really make sense for an AuctionSniper to know about the implementation details of the user interface, such as the use of the Swing thread? We'd be at risk of breaking the "single responsibility" principle again. Surely an AuctionSniper ought to be concerned with bidding policy and only notify status changes in *its* terms?

Our solution is to insulate the `AuctionSniper` by introducing a new relationship: it will notify a `SniperListener` of changes in its status. The interface and the first unit test look like this:

```
public interface SniperListener extends EventListener {
  void sniperLost();
}

@RunWith(JMock.class)
public class AuctionSniperTest {
  private final Mockery context = new Mockery();
  private final SniperListener sniperListener =
                                context.mock(SniperListener.class);
  private final AuctionSniper sniper = new AuctionSniper(sniperListener);

  @Test public void
  reportsLostWhenAuctionCloses() {
    context.checking(new Expectations() {{
      one(sniperListener).sniperLost();
    }});

    sniper.auctionClosed();
  }
}
```

which says that Sniper should report that it has lost if it receives a `Close` event from the auction.

The failure report says:

```
not all expectations were satisfied
expectations:
! expected exactly 1 time, never invoked: SniperListener.sniperLost();
```

which we can make pass with a simple implementation:

```
public class AuctionSniper implements AuctionEventListener {
  private final SniperListener sniperListener;

  public AuctionSniper(SniperListener sniperListener) {
    this.sniperListener = sniperListener;
  }

  public void auctionClosed() {
    sniperListener.sniperLost();
  }

  public void currentPrice(int price, int increment) {
    // TODO Auto-generated method stub
  }
}
```

Finally, we retrofit the new `AuctionSniper` by having `Main` implement `SniperListener`.

```
public class Main implements SniperListener { […]
  private void joinAuction(XMPPConnection connection, String itemId)
    throws XMPPException
  {
    disconnectWhenUICloses(connection);

    Chat chat = connection.getChatManager().createChat(
        auctionId(itemId, connection),
        new AuctionMessageTranslator(new AuctionSniper(this)));
    this.notToBeGCd = chat;
    chat.sendMessage(JOIN_COMMAND_FORMAT);
  }

  public void sniperLost() {
    SwingUtilities.invokeLater(new Runnable() {
      public void run() {
        ui.showStatus(MainWindow.STATUS_LOST);
      }
    });
  }
}
```

Our working end-to-end test still passes and our broken one still fails at the same place, so we haven't made things worse. The new structure looks like Figure 13.1.

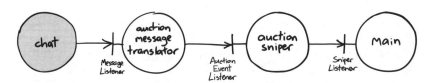

Figure 13.1 *Plugging in the* AuctionSniper

Focus, Focus, Focus

Once again, we've noticed complexity in a class and used that to tease out a new concept from our initial skeleton implementation. Now we have a Sniper to re-spond to events from the translator. As you'll see shortly, this is a better structure for expressing what the code does and for unit testing. We also think that the sniperLost() method is clearer than its previous incarnation, auctionClosed(), since there's now a closer match between its name and what it does—that is, reports a lost auction.

Isn't this wasteful fiddling, gold-plating the code while time slips by? Obviously we don't think so, especially when we're sorting out our ideas this early in the project. There are teams that overdo their design effort, but our experience is that most teams spend too little time clarifying the code and pay for it in mainte-nance overhead. As we've shown a couple of times now, the "single responsibil-ity" principle is a very effective heuristic for breaking up complexity, and developers shouldn't be shy about creating new types. We think Main still does too much, but we're not yet sure how best to break it up. We decide to push on and see where the code takes us.

Sending a Bid

An Auction Interface

The next step is to have the Sniper send a bid to the auction, so who should the Sniper talk to? Extending the SniperListener feels wrong because that relationship is about tracking what's happening in the Sniper, not about making external commitments. In the terms defined in "Object Peer Stereotypes" (page 52), SniperListener is a *notification*, not a *dependency*.

After the usual discussion, we decide to introduce a new collaborator, an Auction. Auction and SniperListener represent two different domains in the application: Auction is about financial transactions, it accepts bids for items in the market; and SniperListener is about feedback to the application, it reports changes to the current state of the Sniper. The Auction is a *dependency*, for a Sniper cannot function without one, whereas the SniperListener, as we discussed above, is not. Introducing the new interface makes the design look like Figure 13.2.

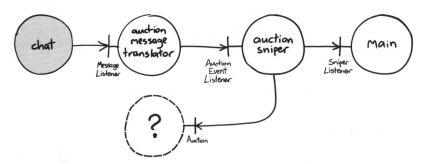

Figure 13.2   *Introducing* Auction

The AuctionSniper Bids

Now we're ready to start bidding. The first step is to implement the response to a Price event, so we start by adding a new unit test for the AuctionSniper. It says that the Sniper, when it receives a Price update, sends an incremented bid to the auction. It also notifies its listener that it's now bidding, so we add a sniperBidding() method. We're making an implicit assumption that the Auction knows which bidder the Sniper represents, so the Sniper does not have to pass in that information with the bid.

```java
public class AuctionSniperTest {
  private final Auction auction = context.mock(Auction.class);
  private final AuctionSniper sniper =
                  new AuctionSniper(auction, sniperListener);
  [...]

  @Test public void
  bidsHigherAndReportsBiddingWhenNewPriceArrives() {
    final int price = 1001;
    final int increment = 25;
    context.checking(new Expectations() {{
      one(auction).bid(price + increment);
      atLeast(1).of(sniperListener).sniperBidding();
    }});

    sniper.currentPrice(price, increment);
  }
}
```

The failure report is:

```
not all expectations were satisfied
expectations:
  ! expected once, never invoked: auction.bid(<1026>)
  ! expected at least 1 time, never invoked: sniperListener.sniperBidding()
what happened before this: nothing!
```

When writing the test, we realized that we don't actually care if the Sniper notifies the listener more than once that it's bidding; it's just a status update, so we use an atLeast(1) clause for the listener's expectation. On the other hand, we do care that we send a bid exactly once, so we use a one() clause for *its* expectation. In practice, of course, we'll probably only call the listener once, but this loosening of the conditions in the test expresses our intent about the two relationships. The test says that the listener is a more forgiving collaborator, in terms of how it's called, than the Auction. We also retrofit the atLeast(1) clause to the other test method.

How Should We Describe Expected Values?

We've specified the expected bid value by adding the price and increment. There are different opinions about whether test values should just be literals with "obvious" values, or expressed in terms of the calculation they represent. Writing out the calculation may make the test more readable but risks reimplementing the target code in the test, and in some cases the calculation will be too complicated to reproduce. Here, we decide that the calculation is so trivial that we can just write it into the test.

---

jMock Expectations Don't Need to Be Matched in Order

This is our first test with more than one expectation, so we'll point out that the order in which expectations are declared does not have to match the order in which the methods are called in the code. If the calling order does matter, the expectations should include a *sequence* clause, which is described in Appendix A.

The implementation to make the test pass is simple.

```
public interface Auction {
  void bid(int amount);
}

public class AuctionSniper implements AuctionEventListener { [...]
  private final SniperListener sniperListener;
  private final Auction auction;

  public AuctionSniper(Auction auction, SniperListener sniperListener) {
    this.auction = auction;
    this.sniperListener = sniperListener;
  }

  public void currentPrice(int price, int increment) {
    auction.bid(price + increment);
    sniperListener.sniperBidding();
  }
}
```

Successfully Bidding with the AuctionSniper

Now we have to fold our new AuctionSniper back into the application. The easy part is displaying the bidding status, the (slightly) harder part is sending the bid back to the auction. Our first job is to get the code through the compiler. We implement the new sniperBidding() method on Main and, to avoid having code that doesn't compile for too long, we pass the AuctionSniper a null implementation of Auction.

```
public class Main implements SniperListener { [...]
  private void joinAuction(XMPPConnection connection, String itemId)
    throws XMPPException
  {
    Auction nullAuction = new Auction() {
      public void bid(int amount) {}
    };
    disconnectWhenUICloses(connection);

    Chat chat = connection.getChatManager().createChat(
        auctionId(itemId, connection),
        new AuctionMessageTranslator(new AuctionSniper(nullAuction, this)));
    this.notToBeGCd = chat;
    chat.sendMessage(JOIN_COMMAND_FORMAT);
  }
  public void sniperBidding() {
    SwingUtilities.invokeLater(new Runnable() {
      public void run() {
        ui.showStatus(MainWindow.STATUS_BIDDING);
      }
    });
  }
}
```

So, what goes in the `Auction` implementation? It needs access to the chat so it
can send a bid message. To create the chat we need a translator, the translator
needs a Sniper, and the Sniper needs an auction. We have a dependency loop
which we need to break.

Looking again at our design, there are a couple of places we could intervene,
but it turns out that the `ChatManager` API is misleading. It does not *require* a
`MessageListener` to create a `Chat`, even though the `createChat()` methods imply
that it does. In our terms, the `MessageListener` is a notification; we can pass in
`null` when we create the `Chat` and add a `MessageListener` later.

Expressing Intent in API

We were only able to discover that we could pass `null` as a `MessageListener`
because we have the source code to the Smack library. This isn't clear from the
API because, presumably, the authors wanted to enforce the right behavior and
it's not clear why anyone would want a `Chat` without a listener. An alternative would
have been to provide equivalent creation methods that don't take a listener, but
that would lead to API bloat. There isn't an obvious best approach here, except to
note that including well-structured source code with the distribution makes libraries
much easier to work with.

Now we can restructure our connection code and use the Chat to send back a bid.

```java
public class Main implements SniperListener { [...]
  private void joinAuction(XMPPConnection connection, String itemId)
    throws XMPPException
  {
    disconnectWhenUICloses(connection);

    final Chat chat =
      connection.getChatManager().createChat(auctionId(itemId, connection), null);
    this.notToBeGCd = chat;

    Auction auction = new Auction() {
      public void bid(int amount) {
        try {
          chat.sendMessage(String.format(BID_COMMAND_FORMAT, amount));
        } catch (XMPPException e) {
          e.printStackTrace();
        }
      }
    };
    chat.addMessageListener(
          new AuctionMessageTranslator(new AuctionSniper(auction, this)));
    chat.sendMessage(JOIN_COMMAND_FORMAT);
  }
}
```

Null Implementation

A *null implementation* is similar to a *null object* [Woolf98]: both are implementations that respond to a protocol by not doing anything—but the intention is different. A null object is usually one implementation amongst many, introduced to reduce complexity in the code that calls the protocol. We define a null implementation as a temporary empty implementation that allows the programmer to make progress by deferring effort. It will be replaced be a real implementation before we ship.

The End-to-End Tests Pass

Now the end-to-end tests pass: the Sniper can lose without making a bid, and lose after making a bid. We can cross off another item on the to-do list, but that includes just catching and printing the XMPPException. Normally, we regard this as a *very* bad practice but we wanted to see the tests pass and get some structure into the code—and we know that the end-to-end tests will fail anyway if there's a problem sending a message. To make sure we don't forget, we add another to-do item to find a better solution, Figure 13.3.

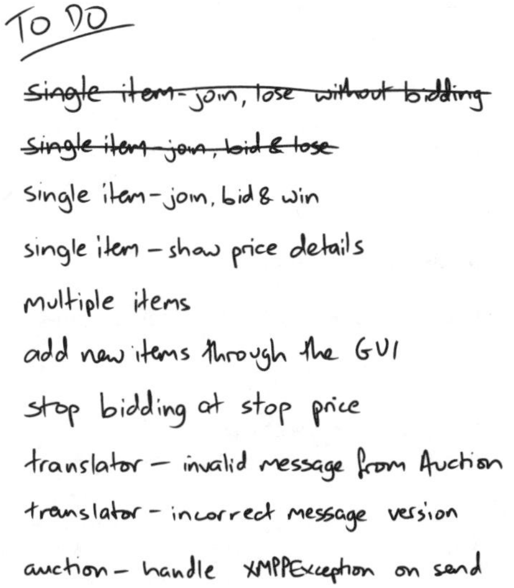

TO DO

~~single item-join, lose without bidding~~

~~single item-join, bid & lose~~

single item - join, bid & win

single item - show price details

multiple items

add new items through the GUI

stop bidding at stop price

translator - invalid message from Auction

translator - incorrect message version

auction - handle XMPPException on send

Figure 13.3 *One step forward*

Tidying Up the Implementation

Extracting XMPPAuction

Our end-to-end test passes, but we haven't finished because our new implementation feels messy. We notice that the activity in joinAuction() crosses multiple domains: managing chats, sending bids, creating snipers, and so on. We need to clean up. To start, we notice that we're sending auction commands from two different levels, at the top and from within the Auction. Sending commands to an auction sounds like the sort of thing that our Auction object should do, so it makes sense to package that up together. We add a new method to the interface, extend our anonymous implementation, and then extract it to a (temporarily) nested class—for which we need a name. The distinguishing feature of this implementation of Auction is that it's based on the messaging infrastructure, so we call our new class XMPPAuction.

```
public class Main implements SniperListener { [...]
  private void joinAuction(XMPPConnection connection, String itemId) {
    disconnectWhenUICloses(connection);

    final Chat chat =
      connection.getChatManager().createChat(auctionId(itemId, connection),
                                             null);
    this.notToBeGCd = chat;

    Auction auction = new XMPPAuction(chat);
    chat.addMessageListener(
        new AuctionMessageTranslator(new AuctionSniper(auction, this)));
    auction.join();
  }

  public static class XMPPAuction implements Auction {
    private final Chat chat;

    public XMPPAuction(Chat chat) {
      this.chat = chat;
    }

    public void bid(int amount) {
      sendMessage(format(BID_COMMAND_FORMAT, amount));
    }

    public void join() {
      sendMessage(JOIN_COMMAND_FORMAT);
    }

    private void sendMessage(final String message) {
      try {
        chat.sendMessage(message);
      } catch (XMPPException e) {
        e.printStackTrace();
      }
    }
  }
}
```

We're starting to see a clearer model of the domain. The line auction.join() expresses our intent more clearly than the previous detailed implementation of sending a string to a chat. The new design looks like Figure 13.4 and we promote XMPPAuction to be a top-level class.

We still think joinAuction() is unclear, and we'd like to pull the XMPP-related detail out of Main, but we're not ready to do that yet. Another point to keep in mind.

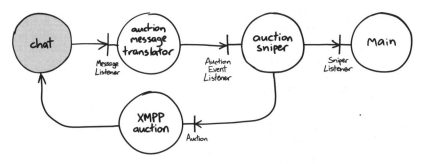

Figure 13.4   *Closing the loop with an* XMPPAuction

Extracting the User Interface

The other activity in Main is implementing the user interface and showing the current state in response to events from the Sniper. We're not really happy that Main implements SniperListener; again, it feels like mixing different responsibilities (starting the application and responding to events). We decide to extract the SniperListener behavior into a nested helper class, for which the best name we can find is SniperStateDisplayer. This new class is our bridge between two domains: it translates Sniper events into a representation that Swing can display, which includes dealing with Swing threading. We plug an instance of the new class into the AuctionSniper.

```
public class Main { // doesn't implement SniperListener
  private MainWindow ui;

  private void joinAuction(XMPPConnection connection, String itemId) {
    disconnectWhenUICloses(connection);
    final Chat chat =
      connection.getChatManager().createChat(auctionId(itemId, connection), null);
    this.notToBeGCd = chat;

    Auction auction = new XMPPAuction(chat);
    chat.addMessageListener(
        new AuctionMessageTranslator(
            connection.getUser(),
            new AuctionSniper(auction, new SniperStateDisplayer())));
    auction.join();
  }

  [...]
```

```java
public class SniperStateDisplayer implements SniperListener {
  public void sniperBidding() {
    showStatus(MainWindow.STATUS_BIDDING);
  }

  public void sniperLost() {
    showStatus(MainWindow.STATUS_LOST);
  }

  public void sniperWinning() {
    showStatus(MainWindow.STATUS_WINNING);
  }

  private void showStatus(final String status) {
    SwingUtilities.invokeLater(new Runnable() {
      public void run() { ui.showStatus(status); }
    });
  }
}
```

Figure 13.5 shows how we've reduced Main so much that it no longer participates in the running application (for clarity, we've left out the WindowAdapter that closes the connection). It has one job which is to create the various components and introduce them to each other. We've marked MainWindow as external, even though it's one of ours, to represent the Swing framework.

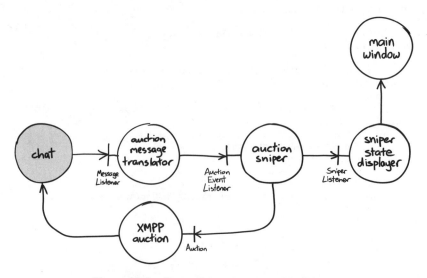

Figure 13.5   *Extracting* SniperStateDisplayer

Tidying Up the Translator

Finally, we fulfill our promise to ourselves and return to the AuctionMessageTranslator. We start trying to reduce the noise by adding constants and static imports, with some helper methods to reduce duplication. Then we realize that much of the code is about manipulating the map of name/value pairs and is rather procedural. We can do a better job by extracting an inner class, AuctionEvent, to encapsulate the unpacking of the message contents. We have confidence that we can refactor the class safely because it's protected by its unit tests.

```java
public class AuctionMessageTranslator implements MessageListener {
  private final AuctionEventListener listener;

  public AuctionMessageTranslator(AuctionEventListener listener) {
    this.listener = listener;
  }
  public void processMessage(Chat chat, Message message) {
    AuctionEvent event = AuctionEvent.from(message.getBody());

    String eventType = event.type();
    if ("CLOSE".equals(eventType)) {
      listener.auctionClosed();
    } if ("PRICE".equals(eventType)) {
      listener.currentPrice(event.currentPrice(), event.increment());
    }
  }
  private static class AuctionEvent {
    private final Map<String, String> fields = new HashMap<String, String>();
    public String type() { return get("Event"); }
    public int currentPrice() { return getInt("CurrentPrice"); }
    public int increment() { return getInt("Increment"); }

    private int getInt(String fieldName) {
      return Integer.parseInt(get(fieldName));
    }
    private String get(String fieldName) { return fields.get(fieldName); }

    private void addField(String field) {
      String[] pair = field.split(":");
      fields.put(pair[0].trim(), pair[1].trim());
    }
    static AuctionEvent from(String messageBody) {
      AuctionEvent event = new AuctionEvent();
      for (String field : fieldsIn(messageBody)) {
        event.addField(field);
      }
      return event;
    }
    static String[] fieldsIn(String messageBody) {
      return messageBody.split(";");
    }
  }
}
```

This is an example of "breaking out" that we described in "Value Types" (page 59). It may not be obvious, but AuctionEvent is a value: it's immutable and there are no interesting differences between two instances with the same contents. This refactoring separates the concerns within AuctionMessageTranslator: the top level deals with events and listeners, and the inner object deals with parsing strings.

Encapsulate Collections

We've developed a habit of packaging up common types, such as collections, in our own classes, even though Java generics avoid the need to cast objects. We're trying to use the language of the problem we're working on, rather than the language of Java constructs. In our two versions of processMessage(), the first has lots of incidental noise about looking up and parsing values. The second is written in terms of auction events, so there's less of a conceptual gap between the domain and the code.

Our rule of thumb is that we try to limit passing around types with generics (the types enclosed in angle brackets). Particularly when applied to collections, we view it as a form of duplication. It's a hint that there's a domain concept that should be extracted into a type.

Defer Decisions

There's a technique we've used a couple of times now, which is to introduce a null implementation of a method (or even a type) to get us through the next step. This helps us focus on the immediate task without getting dragged into thinking about the next significant chunk of functionality. The null Auction, for example, allowed us to plug in a new relationship we'd discovered in a unit test without getting pulled into messaging issues. That, in turn, meant we could stop and think about the dependencies between our objects without the pressure of having a broken compilation.

Keep the Code Compiling

We try to minimize the time when we have code that does not compile by keeping changes incremental. When we have compilation failures, we can't be quite sure where the boundaries of our changes are, since the compiler can't tell us. This, in turn, means that we can't check in to our source repository, which we like to do *often*. The more code we have open, the more we have to keep in our heads which, ironically, usually means we move more slowly. One of the great discoveries of test-driven development is just how fine-grained our development steps can be.

Emergent Design

What we hope is becoming clear from this chapter is how we're growing a design from what looks like an unpromising start. We alternate, more or less, between adding features and reflecting on—and cleaning up—the code that results. The cleaning up stage is essential, since without it we would end up with an unmaintainable mess. We're prepared to defer refactoring code if we're not yet clear what to do, confident that we will take the time when we're ready. In the meantime, we keep our code as clean as possible, moving in small increments and using techniques such as null implementation to minimize the time when it's broken.

Figure 13.5 shows that we're building up a layer around our core implementation that "protects" it from its external dependencies. We think this is just good practice, but what's interesting is that we're getting there incrementally, by looking for features in classes that either go together or don't. Of course we're influenced by our experience of working on similar codebases, but we're trying hard to follow what the code is telling us instead of imposing our preconceptions. Sometimes, when we do this, we find that the domain takes us in the most surprising directions.

Chapter 14

The Sniper Wins the Auction

In which we add another feature to our Sniper and let it win an auction. We introduce the concept of state to the Sniper which we test by listening to its callbacks. We find that even this early, one of our refactorings has paid off.

First, a Failing Test

We have a Sniper that can respond to price changes by bidding more, but it doesn't yet know when it's successful. Our next feature on the to-do list is to win an auction. This involves an extra state transition, as you can see in Figure 14.1:

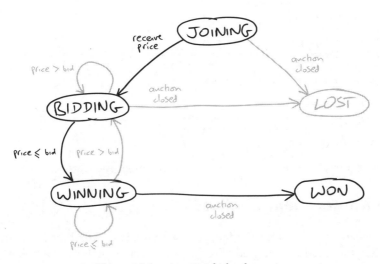

Figure 14.1 *A sniper bids, then wins*

To represent this, we add an end-to-end test based on `sniperMakesAHigherBid-ButLoses()` with a different conclusion—`sniperWinsAnAuctionByBiddingHigher()`. Here's the test, with the new features highlighted:

```
public class AuctionSniperEndToEndTest { [...]
  @Test public void
  sniperWinsAnAuctionByBiddingHigher() throws Exception {
    auction.startSellingItem();

    application.startBiddingIn(auction);
    auction.hasReceivedJoinRequestFrom(ApplicationRunner.SNIPER_XMPP_ID);

    auction.reportPrice(1000, 98, "other bidder");
    application.hasShownSniperIsBidding();

    auction.hasReceivedBid(1098, ApplicationRunner.SNIPER_XMPP_ID);

    auction.reportPrice(1098, 97, ApplicationRunner.SNIPER_XMPP_ID);
    application.hasShownSniperIsWinning();

    auction.announceClosed();
    application.showsSniperHasWonAuction();
  }
}
```

In our test infrastructure we add the two methods to check that the user interface shows the two new states to the ApplicationRunner.

This generates a new failure message:

```
java.lang.AssertionError:
Tried to look for...
  exactly 1 JLabel (with name "sniper status")
  in exactly 1 JFrame (with name "Auction Sniper Main" and showing on screen)
  in all top level windows
and check that its label text is "Winning"
but...
  all top level windows
  contained 1 JFrame (with name "Auction Sniper Main" and showing on screen)
  contained 1 JLabel (with name "sniper status")
  label text was "Bidding"
```

Now we know where we're going, we can implement the feature.

Who Knows about Bidders?

The application knows that the Sniper is winning if it's the bidder for the last price that the auction accepted. We have to decide where to put that logic. Looking again at Figure 13.5 on page 134, one choice would be that the translator could pass the bidder through to the Sniper and let the Sniper decide. That would mean that the Sniper would have to know something about how bidders are identified by the auction, with a risk of pulling in XMPP details that we've been careful to keep separate. To decide whether it's winning, the only thing the Sniper needs to know when a price arrives is, did this price come from *me*? This is a choice, not an identifier, so we'll represent it with an enumeration PriceSource which we include in AuctionEventListener.[1]

Incidentally, PriceSource is an example of a *value type*. We want code that describes the domain of Sniping—not, say, a boolean which we would have to interpret every time we read it; there's more discussion in "Value Types" (page 59).

```java
public interface AuctionEventListener extends EventListener {
  enum PriceSource {
    FromSniper, FromOtherBidder;
  };
  [...]
```

We take the view that determining whether this is our price or not is part of the translator's role. We extend currentPrice() with a new parameter and change the translator's unit tests; note that we change the name of the existing test to include the extra feature. We also take the opportunity to pass the Sniper identifier to the translator in SNIPER_ID. This ties the setup of the translator to the input message in the second test.

```java
public class AuctionMessageTranslatorTest { [...]
  private final AuctionMessageTranslator translator =
                  new AuctionMessageTranslator(SNIPER_ID, listener);

  @Test public void
  notifiesBidDetailsWhenCurrentPriceMessageReceivedFromOtherBidder() {
    context.checking(new Expectations() {{
      exactly(1).of(listener).currentPrice(192, 7, PriceSource.FromOtherBidder);
    }});
    Message message = new Message();
    message.setBody(
"SOLVersion: 1.1; Event: PRICE; CurrentPrice: 192; Increment: 7; Bidder: Someone else;"
                );
    translator.processMessage(UNUSED_CHAT, message);
  }

  @Test public void
  notifiesBidDetailsWhenCurrentPriceMessageReceivedFromSniper() {
    context.checking(new Expectations() {{
      exactly(1).of(listener).currentPrice(234, 5, PriceSource.FromSniper);
    }});
    Message message = new Message();
    message.setBody(
      "SOLVersion: 1.1; Event: PRICE; CurrentPrice: 234; Increment: 5; Bidder: "
      + SNIPER_ID + ";");
    translator.processMessage(UNUSED_CHAT, message);
  }
}
```

---

1. Some developers we know have an allergic reaction to nested types. In Java, we use them as a form of fine-grained scoping. In this case, PriceSource is always used together with AuctionEventListener, so it makes sense to bind the two together.

The new test fails:

```
unexpected invocation:
  auctionEventListener.currentPrice(<192>, <7>, <FromOtherBidder>)
expectations:
! expected once, never invoked:
    auctionEventListener.currentPrice(<192>, <7>, <FromSniper>)
      parameter 0 matched: <192>
      parameter 1 matched: <7>
      parameter 2 did not match: <FromSniper>, because was <FromOtherBidder>
what happened before this: nothing!
```

The fix is to compare the Sniper identifier to the bidder from the event message.

```
public class AuctionMessageTranslator implements MessageListener {  [...]
  private final String sniperId;

  public void processMessage(Chat chat, Message message) {
    [...]
    } else if (EVENT_TYPE_PRICE.equals(type)) {
      listener.currentPrice(event.currentPrice(),
                            event.increment(),
                            event.isFrom(sniperId));
    }
  }

  public static class AuctionEvent {  [...]
    public PriceSource isFrom(String sniperId) {
      return sniperId.equals(bidder()) ? FromSniper : FromOtherBidder;
    }
    private String bidder() { return get("Bidder"); }
  }
}
```

The work we did in "Tidying Up the Translator" (page 135) to separate the different responsibilities within the translator has paid off here. All we had to do was add a couple of extra methods to AuctionEvent to get a very readable solution.

Finally, to get all the code through the compiler, we fix joinAuction() in Main to pass in the new constructor parameter for the translator. We can get a correctly structured identifier from connection.

```
private void joinAuction(XMPPConnection connection, String itemId) {
  [...]
  Auction auction = new XMPPAuction(chat);
  chat.addMessageListener(
      new AuctionMessageTranslator(
              connection.getUser(),
              new AuctionSniper(auction, new SniperStateDisplayer())));
  auction.join();
}
```

The Sniper Has More to Say

Our immediate end-to-end test failure tells us that we should make the user interface show when the Sniper is winning. Our next implementation step is to follow through by fixing the `AuctionSniper` to interpret the `isFromSniper` parameter we've just added. Once again we start with a unit test.

```
public class AuctionSniperTest { […]
  @Test public void
  reportsIsWinningWhenCurrentPriceComesFromSniper() {
    context.checking(new Expectations() {{
      atLeast(1).of(sniperListener).sniperWinning();
    }});

    sniper.currentPrice(123, 45, PriceSource.FromSniper);
  }
}
```

To get through the compiler, we add the new `sniperWinning()` method to `SniperListener` which, in turn, means that we add an empty implementation to `SniperStateDisplayer`.

The test fails:

```
unexpected invocation: auction.bid(<168>)
expectations:
! expected at least 1 time, never invoked: sniperListener.sniperWinning()
what happened before this: nothing!
```

This failure is a nice example of trapping a method that we didn't expect. We set no expectations on the `auction`, so calls to any of its methods will fail the test. If you compare this test to `bidsHigherAndReportsBiddingWhenNewPriceArrives()` in "The AuctionSniper Bids" (page 126) you'll also see that we drop the `price` and `increment` variables and just feed in numbers. That's because, in this test, there's no calculation to do, so we don't need to reference them in an expectation. They're just details to get us to the interesting behavior.

The fix is straightforward:

```
public class AuctionSniper implements AuctionEventListener { […]
  public void currentPrice(int price, int increment, PriceSource priceSource) {
    switch (priceSource) {
    case FromSniper:
      sniperListener.sniperWinning();
      break;
    case FromOtherBidder:
      auction.bid(price + increment);
      sniperListener.sniperBidding();
      break;
    }
  }
}
```

Running the end-to-end tests again shows that we've fixed the failure that started this chapter (showing Bidding rather than Winning). Now we have to make the Sniper win:

```
java.lang.AssertionError:
Tried to look for...
  exactly 1 JLabel (with name "sniper status")
  in exactly 1 JFrame (with name "Auction Sniper Main" and showing on screen)
  in all top level windows
and check that its label text is "Won"
but...
  all top level windows
  contained 1 JFrame (with name "Auction Sniper Main" and showing on screen)
  contained 1 JLabel (with name "sniper status")
  label text was "Lost"
```

The Sniper Acquires Some State

We're about to introduce a step change in the complexity of the Sniper, if only a small one. When the auction closes, we want the Sniper to announce whether it has won or lost, which means that it must know whether it was bidding or winning at the time. This implies that the Sniper will have to maintain some state, which it hasn't had to so far.

To get to the functionality we want, we'll start with the simpler cases where the Sniper loses. As Figure 14.2 shows, we're starting with one- and two-step transitions, before adding the additional step that takes the Sniper to the Won state:

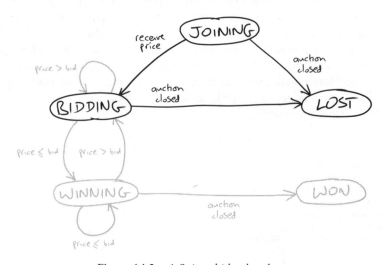

Figure 14.2   *A Sniper bids, then loses*

We start by revisiting an existing unit test and adding a new one. These tests will pass with the current implementation; they're there to ensure that we don't break the behavior when we add further transitions.

This introduces some new jMock syntax, *states*. The idea is to allow us to make assertions about the internal state of the object under test. We'll come back to this idea in a moment.

```
public class AuctionSniperTest { [...]
  private final States sniperState = context.states("sniper"); ❶

  @Test public void
  reportsLostIfAuctionClosesImmediately() { ❷
    context.checking(new Expectations() {{
      atLeast(1).of(sniperListener).sniperLost();
    }});

    sniper.auctionClosed();
  }

  @Test public void
  reportsLostIfAuctionClosesWhenBidding() {
    context.checking(new Expectations() {{
      ignoring(auction); ❸
      allowing(sniperListener).sniperBidding();
                            then(sniperState.is("bidding")); ❹

      atLeast(1).of(sniperListener).sniperLost();
                            when(sniperState.is("bidding")); ❺
    }});

    sniper.currentPrice(123, 45, PriceSource.FromOtherBidder); ❻
    sniper.auctionClosed();
  }
}
```

❶ We want to keep track of the Sniper's current state, as signaled by the events it sends out, so we ask context for a placeholder. The default state is null.

❷ We keep our original test, but now it will apply where there are no price updates.

❸ The Sniper will call auction but we really don't care about that *in this test*, so we tell the test to ignore this collaborator completely.

❹ When the Sniper sends out a bidding event, it's telling us that it's in a bidding state, which we record here. We use the allowing() clause to communicate that this is a supporting part of the test, not the part we really care about; see the note below.

❺ This is the phrase that matters, the expectation that we want to assert. If the Sniper isn't bidding when it makes this call, the test will fail.

⑥   This is our first test where we need a sequence of events to get the Sniper into the state we want to test. We just call its methods in order.

 Allowances

jMock distinguishes between *allowed* and *expected* invocations. An `allowing()` clause says that the object might make this call, but it doesn't have to—unlike an expectation which will fail the test if the call isn't made. We make the distinction to help express what is important in a test (the underlying implementation is actually the same): expectations are what we want to confirm to have happened; allowances are supporting infrastructure that helps get the tested objects into the right state, or they're side effects we don't care about. We return to this topic in "Allowances and Expectations" (page 277) and we describe the API in Appendix A.

 Representing Object State

In cases like this, we want to make assertions about an object's behavior depending on its state, but we don't want to break encapsulation by exposing how that state is implemented. Instead, the test can listen to the notification events that the Sniper provides to tell interested collaborators about its state *in their terms*. jMock provides `States` objects, so that tests can record and make assertions about the state of an object when something significant happens, i.e. when it calls its neighbors; see Appendix A for the syntax.

This is a "logical" representation of what's going on inside the object, in this case the Sniper. It allows the test to describe what it finds relevant about the Sniper, regardless of how the Sniper is actually implemented. As you'll see shortly, this separation will allow us to make radical changes to the implementation of the Sniper without changing the tests.

The unit test name `reportsLostIfAuctionClosesWhenBidding` is very similar to the expectation it enforces:

```
atLeast(1).of(sniperListener).sniperLost(); when(sniperState.is("bidding"));
```

That's not an accident. We put a lot of effort into figuring out which abstractions jMock should support and developing a style that expresses the essential intent of a unit test.

The Sniper Wins

Finally, we can close the loop and have the Sniper win a bid. The next test introduces the `Won` event.

```
@Test public void
reportsWonIfAuctionClosesWhenWinning() {
  context.checking(new Expectations() {{
    ignoring(auction);
    allowing(sniperListener).sniperWinning();  then(sniperState.is("winning"));

    atLeast(1).of(sniperListener).sniperWon(); when(sniperState.is("winning"));
  }});
  sniper.currentPrice(123, 45, PriceSource.FromSniper);
  sniper.auctionClosed();
}
```

It has the same structure but represents when the Sniper has won. The test fails because the Sniper called sniperLost().

```
unexpected invocation: sniperListener.sniperLost()
expectations:
  allowed, never invoked:
    auction.<any method>(<any parameters>) was[];
  allowed, already invoked 1 time: sniperListener.sniperWinning();
                                    then sniper is winning
  expected at least 1 time, never invoked: sniperListener.sniperWon();
                                    when sniper is winning
states:
  sniper is winning
what happened before this:
  sniperListener.sniperWinning()
```

We add a flag to represent the Sniper's state, and implement the new sniperWon() method in the SniperStateDisplayer.

```
public class AuctionSniper implements AuctionEventListener { [...]
  private boolean isWinning = false;

  public void auctionClosed() {
    if (isWinning) {
      sniperListener.sniperWon();
    } else {
      sniperListener.sniperLost();
    }
  }
  public void currentPrice(int price, int increment, PriceSource priceSource) {
    isWinning = priceSource == PriceSource.FromSniper;
    if (isWinning) {
      sniperListener.sniperWinning();
    } else {
      auction.bid(price + increment);
      sniperListener.sniperBidding();
    }
  }
}
public class SniperStateDisplayer implements SniperListener { [...]
  public void sniperWon() {
    showStatus(MainWindow.STATUS_WON);
  }
}
```

Having previously made a fuss about `PriceSource`, are we being inconsistent here by using a boolean for `isWinning`? Our excuse is that we did try an enum for the Sniper state, but it just looked too complicated. The field is private to `AuctionSniper`, which is small enough so it's easy to change later and the code reads well.

The unit and end-to-end tests all pass now, so we can cross off another item from the to-do list in Figure 14.3.

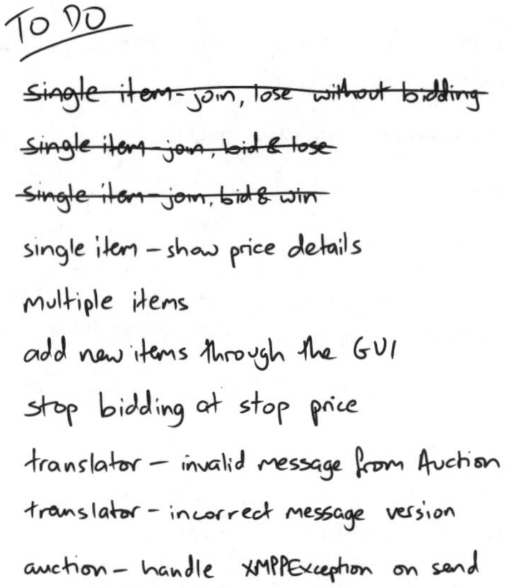

TO DO

~~single item – join, lose without bidding~~

~~single item – join, bid & lose~~

~~single item – join, bid & win~~

single item – show price details

multiple items

add new items through the GUI

stop bidding at stop price

translator – invalid message from Auction

translator – incorrect message version

auction – handle XMPPException on send

Figure 14.3   *The Sniper wins*

There are more tests we could write—for example, to describe the transitions from bidding to winning and back again, but we'll leave those as an exercise for you, Dear Reader. Instead, we'll move on to the next significant change in functionality.

Making Steady Progress

As always, we made steady progress by adding little slices of functionality. First we made the Sniper show when it's winning, then when it has won. We used empty implementations to get us through the compiler when we weren't ready to fill in the code, and we stayed focused on the immediate task.

One of the pleasant surprises is that, now the code is growing a little, we're starting to see some of our earlier effort pay off as new features just fit into the existing structure. The next tasks we have to implement will shake this up.

Chapter 15

Towards a Real User Interface

In which we grow the user interface from a label to a table. We achieve this by adding a feature at a time, instead of taking the risk of replacing the whole thing in one go. We discover that some of the choices we made are no longer valid, so we dare to change existing code. We continue to refactor and sense that a more interesting structure is starting to appear.

A More Realistic Implementation

What Do We Have to Do Next?

So far, we've been making do with a simple label in the user interface. That's been effective for helping us clarify the structure of the application and prove that our ideas work, but the next tasks coming up will need more, and the client wants to see something that looks closer to Figure 9.1. We will need to show more price details from the auction and handle multiple items.

The simplest option would be just to add more text into the label, but we think this is the right time to introduce more structure into the user interface. We deferred putting effort into this part of the application, and we think we should catch up now to be ready for the more complex requirements we're about to implement. We decide to make the obvious choice, given our use of Swing, and replace the label with a table component. This decision gives us a clear direction for where our design should go next.

The Swing pattern for using a `JTable` is to associate it with a `TableModel`. The table component queries the model for values to present, and the model notifies the table when those values change. In our application, the relationships will look like Figure 15.1. We call the new class `SnipersTableModel` because we want it to support multiple Snipers. It will accept updates from the Snipers and provide a representation of those values to its `JTable`.

The question is how to get there from here.

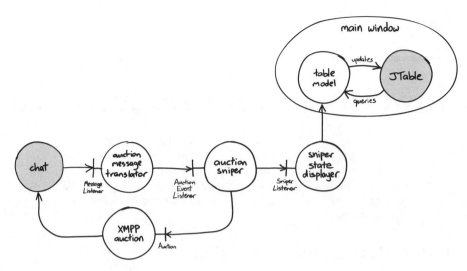

Figure 15.1 *Swing table model for the* AuctionSniper

Replacing JLabel

We want to get the pieces into place with a minimum of change, without tearing the whole application apart. The smallest step we can think of is to replace the existing implementation (a JLabel) with a single-cell JTable, from which we can then grow the additional functionality. We start, of course, with the test, changing our harness to look for a cell in a table, rather than a label.

```
public class AuctionSniperDriver extends JFrameDriver { [...]

  public void showsSniperStatus(String statusText) {
    new JTableDriver(this).hasCell(withLabelText(equalTo(statusText)));
  }
}
```

This generates a failure message because we don't yet have a table.

```
[...] but...
    all top level windows
    contained 1 JFrame (with name "Auction Sniper Main" and showing on screen)
    contained 0 JTable ()
```

We fix this test by retrofitting a minimal JTable implementation. From now on, we want to speed up our narrative, so we'll just show the end result. If we were feeling cautious we would first add an empty table, to fix the immediate failure, and then add its contents. It turns out that we don't have to change any existing classes outside MainWindow because it encapsulates the act of updating the status. Here's the new code:

```java
public class MainWindow extends JFrame { [...]
  private final SnipersTableModel snipers = new SnipersTableModel();

  public MainWindow() {
    super(APPLICATION_TITLE);
    setName(MainWindow.MAIN_WINDOW_NAME);
    fillContentPane(makeSnipersTable());
    pack();
    setDefaultCloseOperation(JFrame.EXIT_ON_CLOSE);
    setVisible(true);
  }

  private void fillContentPane(JTable snipersTable) {
    final Container contentPane = getContentPane();
    contentPane.setLayout(new BorderLayout());

    contentPane.add(new JScrollPane(snipersTable), BorderLayout.CENTER);
  }

  private JTable makeSnipersTable() {
    final JTable snipersTable = new JTable(snipers);
    snipersTable.setName(SNIPERS_TABLE_NAME);
    return snipersTable;
  }

  public void showStatusText(String statusText) {
    snipers.setStatusText(statusText);
  }
}

public class SnipersTableModel extends AbstractTableModel {
  private String statusText = STATUS_JOINING;

  public int getColumnCount() { return 1; }
  public int getRowCount() { return 1; }
  public Object getValueAt(int rowIndex, int columnIndex) { return statusText; }

  public void setStatusText(String newStatusText) {
    statusText = newStatusText;
    fireTableRowsUpdated(0, 0);
  }
}
```

Still Ugly

As you can see, the `SnipersTableModel` really is a minimal implementation; the only value that can vary is the `statusText`. It inherits most of its behavior from the Swing `AbstractTableModel`, including the infrastructure for notifying the `JTable` of data changes. The result is as ugly as our previous version, except that now the `JTable` adds a default column title "A", as in Figure 15.2. We'll work on the presentation in a moment.

Figure 15.2   *Sniper with a single-cell table*

Displaying Price Details

First, a Failing Test

Our next task is to display information about the Sniper's position in the auction: item identifier, last auction price, last bid, status. These values come from updates from the auction and the state held within the application. We need to pass them through from their source to the table model and then render them in the display. Of course, we start with the test. Given that this feature should be part of the basic functionality of the application, not separate from what we already have, we update our existing acceptance tests—starting with just one test so we don't break everything at once. Here's the new version:

```
public class AuctionSniperEndToEndTest {
  @Test public void
  sniperWinsAnAuctionByBiddingHigher() throws Exception {
    auction.startSellingItem();

    application.startBiddingIn(auction);
    auction.hasReceivedJoinRequestFrom(ApplicationRunner.SNIPER_XMPP_ID);

    auction.reportPrice(1000, 98, "other bidder");
    application.hasShownSniperIsBidding(1000, 1098); // last price, last bid

    auction.hasReceivedBid(1098, ApplicationRunner.SNIPER_XMPP_ID);

    auction.reportPrice(1098, 97, ApplicationRunner.SNIPER_XMPP_ID);
    application.hasShownSniperIsWinning(1098); // winning bid

    auction.announceClosed();
    application.showsSniperHasWonAuction(1098); // last price
  }
}
```

```
public class ApplicationRunner {
  private String itemId;

  public void startBiddingIn(final FakeAuctionServer auction) {
    itemId = auction.getItemId();
    [...]
  }

  [...]
  public void hasShownSniperIsBidding(int lastPrice, int lastBid) {
    driver.showsSniperStatus(itemId, lastPrice, lastBid,
                             MainWindow.STATUS_BIDDING);
  }

  public void hasShownSniperIsWinning(int winningBid) {
    driver.showsSniperStatus(itemId, winningBid, winningBid,
                             MainWindow.STATUS_WINNING);
  }

  public void showsSniperHasWonAuction(int lastPrice) {
    driver.showsSniperStatus(itemId, lastPrice, lastPrice,
                             MainWindow.STATUS_WON);
  }
}

public class AuctionSniperDriver extends JFrameDriver {
  [...]
  public void showsSniperStatus(String itemId, int lastPrice, int lastBid,
                                String statusText)
  {
    JTableDriver table = new JTableDriver(this);
    table.hasRow(
      matching(withLabelText(itemId), withLabelText(valueOf(lastPrice)),
               withLabelText(valueOf(lastBid)), withLabelText(statusText)));
  }
}
```

We need the item identifier so the test can look for it in the row, so we make the ApplicationRunner hold on it when connecting to an auction. We extend the AuctionSniperDriver to look for a table row that shows the item identifier, last price, last bid, and sniper status.

The test fails because the row has no details, only the status text:

```
[...] but...
    all top level windows
    contained 1 JFrame (with name "Auction Sniper Main" and showing on screen)
    contained 1 JTable ()
it is not with row with cells
  <label with text "item-54321">, <label with text "1000">,
  <label with text "1098">, <label with text "Bidding">
because
    in row 0: component 0 text was "Bidding"
```

Sending the State out of the Sniper

With an acceptance test to show us where we want to get to, we can fill in the steps along the way. As usual, we work "outside-in," from the event that triggers the behavior; in this case it's a price update from Southabee's On-Line. Following along the sequence of method calls, we don't have to change `AuctionMessageTranslator`, so we start by looking at `AuctionSniper` and its unit tests.

`AuctionSniper` notifies changes in its state to neighbors that implement the `SniperListener` interface which, as you might remember, has four callback methods, one for each state of the Sniper. Now we also need to pass in the current state of the Sniper when we notify a listener. We could add the same set of arguments to each method, but that would be duplication; so, we introduce a value type to carry the Sniper's state. This is an example of "bundling up" that we described in "Value Types" (page 59). Here's a first cut:

```java
public class SniperState {
  public final String itemId;
  public final int lastPrice;
  public final int lastBid;

  public SniperState(String itemId, int lastPrice, int lastBid) {
    this.itemId = itemId;
    this.lastPrice = lastPrice;
    this.lastBid = lastBid;
  }
}
```

To save effort, we use the reflective builders from the Apache `commons.lang` library to implement `equals()`, `hashCode()`, and `toString()` in the new class. We could argue that we're being premature with these features, but in practice we'll need them in a moment when we write our unit tests.

 ### Public Final Fields

We've adopted a habit of using public final fields in value types, at least while we're in the process of sorting out what the type should do. It makes it obvious that the value is immutable and reduces the overhead of maintaining getters when the class isn't yet stable. Our ambition, which we might not achieve, is to replace all field access with meaningful action methods on the type. We'll see how that pans out.

We don't want to break all the tests at once, so we start with an easy one. In this test there's no history, all we have to do in the Sniper is construct a `SniperState` from information available at the time and pass it to the listener.

```
public class AuctionSniperTest { [...]
  @Test public void
  bidsHigherAndReportsBiddingWhenNewPriceArrives() {
    final int price = 1001;
    final int increment = 25;
    final int bid = price + increment;

    context.checking(new Expectations() {{
      one(auction).bid(bid);
      atLeast(1).of(sniperListener).sniperBidding(
                                new SniperState(ITEM_ID, price, bid));
    }});

    sniper.currentPrice(price, increment, PriceSource.FromOtherBidder);
  }
}
```

Then we make the test pass:

```
public class AuctionSniper implements AuctionEventListener { [...]
  public void currentPrice(int price, int increment, PriceSource priceSource) {
    isWinning = priceSource == PriceSource.FromSniper;
    if (isWinning) {
      sniperListener.sniperWinning();
    } else {
      int bid = price + increment;
      auction.bid(bid);
      sniperListener.sniperBidding(new SniperState(itemId, price, bid));
    }
  }
}
```

To get the code to compile, we also add the state argument to the
sniperBidding() method in SniperStateDisplayer, which implements
SniperListener, but don't yet do anything with it.

The one significant change is that the Sniper needs access to the item identifier
so it can construct a SniperState. Given that the Sniper doesn't need this value
for any other reason, we could have kept it in the SniperStateDisplayer and
added it in when an event passes through, but we think it's reasonable that the
Sniper has access to this information. We decide to pass the identifier into the
AuctionSniper constructor; it's available at the time, and we don't want to get
it from the Auction object which may have its own form of identifier for an item.

We have one other test that refers to the sniperBidding() method, but only
as an "allowance." We use a matcher that says that, since it's only supporting
the interesting part of the test, we don't care about the contents of the state object.

```
allowing(sniperListener).sniperBidding(with(any(SniperState.class)));
```

Showing a Bidding Sniper

We'll take larger steps for the next task—presenting the state in the user
interface—as there are some new moving parts, including a new unit test. The

first version of the code will be clumsier than we would like but, as you'll soon see, there'll be interesting opportunities for cleaning up.

Our very first step is to pass the new state parameter, which we've been ignoring, through MainWindow to a new method in SnipersTableModel. While we're at it, we notice that just passing events through MainWindow isn't adding much value, so we make a note to deal with that later.

```
public class SniperStateDisplayer implements SniperListener { [...]
  public void sniperBidding(final SniperState state) {
    SwingUtilities.invokeLater(new Runnable() {
      public void run() {
        ui.sniperStatusChanged(state, MainWindow.STATUS_BIDDING);
      }
    });
  }
}

public class MainWindow extends JFrame { [...]
  public void sniperStatusChanged(SniperState sniperState, String statusText) {
    snipers.sniperStatusChanged(sniperState, statusText);
  }
}
```

To get the new values visible on screen, we need to fix SnipersTableModel so that it makes them available to its JTable, starting with a unit test. We take a small design leap by introducing a Java enum to represent the columns in the table—it's more meaningful than just using integers.

```
public enum Column {
  ITEM_IDENTIFIER,
  LAST_PRICE,
  LAST_BID,
  SNIPER_STATUS;

  public static Column at(int offset) { return values()[offset]; }
}
```

The table model needs to do two things when its state changes: hold onto the new values and notify the table that they've changed. Here's the test:

```
@RunWith(JMock.class)
public class SnipersTableModelTest {
  private final Mockery context = new Mockery();
  private TableModelListener listener = context.mock(TableModelListener.class);
  private final SnipersTableModel model = new SnipersTableModel();

  @Before public void attachModelListener() {  ❶
    model.addTableModelListener(listener);
  }

  @Test public void
  hasEnoughColumns() {  ❷
    assertThat(model.getColumnCount(), equalTo(Column.values().length));
  }
```

```
@Test public void
setsSniperValuesInColumns() {
  context.checking(new Expectations() {{
    one(listener).tableChanged(with(aRowChangedEvent())));   ❸
  }});

  model.sniperStatusChanged(new SniperState("item id", 555, 666),   ❹
                            MainWindow.STATUS_BIDDING);

  assertColumnEquals(Column.ITEM_IDENTIFIER, "item id"); ❺
  assertColumnEquals(Column.LAST_PRICE, 555);
  assertColumnEquals(Column.LAST_BID, 666);
  assertColumnEquals(Column.SNIPER_STATUS, MainWindow.STATUS_BIDDING);
}

private void assertColumnEquals(Column column, Object expected) {
  final int rowIndex = 0;
  final int columnIndex = column.ordinal();
  assertEquals(expected, model.getValueAt(rowIndex, columnIndex));
}

private Matcher<TableModelEvent> aRowChangedEvent() { ❻
  return samePropertyValuesAs(new TableModelEvent(model, 0));
}
}
```

❶   We attach a mock implementation of `TableModelListener` to the model. This is one of the few occasions where we break our rule "Only Mock Types That You Own" (page 69) because the table model design fits our design approach so well.

❷   We add a first test to make sure we're rendering the right number of columns. Later, we'll do something about the column titles.

❸   This expectation checks that we notify any attached `JTable` that the contents have changed.

❹   This is the event that triggers the behavior we want to test.

❺   We assert that the table model returns the right values in the right columns. We hard-code the row number because we're still assuming that there is only one.

❻   There's no specific `equals()` method on `TableModelEvent`, so we use a matcher that will reflectively compare the property values of any event it receives against an expected example. Again, we hard-code the row number.

After the usual red/green cycle, we end up with an implementation that looks like this:

```
public class SnipersTableModel extends AbstractTableModel {
  private final static SniperState STARTING_UP = new SniperState("", 0, 0);
  private String statusText = MainWindow.STATUS_JOINING;
  private SniperState sniperState = STARTING_UP; ❶
  [...]
  public int getColumnCount() { ❷
    return Column.values().length;
  }
  public int getRowCount() {
    return 1;
  }
  public Object getValueAt(int rowIndex, int columnIndex) { ❸
    switch (Column.at(columnIndex)) {
    case ITEM_IDENTIFIER:
      return sniperState.itemId;
    case LAST_PRICE:
      return sniperState.lastPrice;
    case LAST_BID:
      return sniperState.lastBid;
    case SNIPER_STATUS:
      return statusText;
    default:
      throw new IllegalArgumentException("No column at " + columnIndex);
    }
  }
  public void sniperStatusChanged(SniperState newSniperState, ❹
                                  String newStatusText)
  {
    sniperState = newSniperState;
    statusText = newStatusText;
    fireTableRowsUpdated(0, 0);
  }
}
```

❶ We provide an initial SniperState with "empty" values so that the table model will work before the Sniper has connected.

❷ For the dimensions, we just return the numbers of values in Column or a hard-coded row count.

❸ This method unpacks the value to return depending on the column that is specified. The advantage of using an enum is that the compiler will help with missing branches in the switch statement (although it still insists on a default case). We're not keen on using switch, as it's not object-oriented, so we'll keep an eye on this too.

❹ The Sniper-specific method. It sets the fields and then triggers its clients to update.

If we run our acceptance test again, we find we've made some progress. It's gone past the Bidding check and now fails because the last price column, "B", has not yet been updated. Interestingly, the status column shows Winning correctly, because that code is still working.

```
[…] but...
    all top level windows
    contained 1 JFrame (with name "Auction Sniper Main" and showing on screen)
    contained 1 JTable ()
  it is not with row with cells
    <label with text "item-54321">, <label with text "1098">,
    <label with text "1098">, <label with text "Winning">
    because
      in row 0: component 1 text was "1000"
```

and the proof is in Figure 15.3.

Figure 15.3 *Sniper showing a row of detail*

Simplifying Sniper Events

Listening to the Mood Music

We have one kind of Sniper event, `Bidding`, that we can handle all the way through our application. Now we have to do the same thing to `Winning`, `Lost`, and `Won`.

Frankly, that's just dull. There's too much repetitive work needed to make the other cases work—setting them up in the Sniper and passing them through the layers. Something's wrong with the design. We toss this one around for a while and eventually notice that we would have a subtle duplication in our code if we just carried on. We would be splitting the transmission of the Sniper state into two mechanisms: the choice of listener method and the state object. That's one mechanism too many.

We realize that we could collapse our events into one notification that includes the prices *and* the Sniper status. Of course we're transmitting the same information whichever mechanism we choose—but, looking at the chain of methods calls, it would be simpler to have just one method and pass everything through in `SniperState`.

Having made this choice, can we do it cleanly without ripping up the metaphorical floorboards? We believe we can—but first, one more clarification. We want to start by creating a type to represent the Sniper's status (winning, losing, etc.) in the auction, but the terms "status" and "state" are too close to distinguish easily. We kick around some vocabulary and eventually decide that a better term for what we now call `SniperState` would be `SniperSnapshot`: a description of the Sniper's relationship with the auction at this moment in time. This frees up the name `SniperState` to describe whether the Sniper is winning, losing, and so on, which matches the terminology of the state machine we drew in Figure 9.3 on page 78. Renaming the SniperState takes a moment, and we change the value in Column from SNIPER_STATUS to SNIPER_STATE.

 20/20 Hindsight

We've just gone through not one but two of those forehead-slapping moments that make us wonder why we didn't see it the first time around. Surely, if we'd spent more time on the design, we wouldn't have to change it now? Sometimes that's true. Our experience, however, is that nothing shakes out a design like trying to implement it, and between us we know just a handful of people who are smart enough to get their designs always right. Our coping mechanism is to get into the critical areas of the code early and to allow ourselves to change our collective mind when we could do better. We rely on our skills, on taking small steps, and on the tests to protect us when we make changes.

Repurposing sniperBidding()

Our first step is to take the method that does most of what we want, sniperBidding(), and rework it to fit our new scheme. We create an enum that takes the SniperState name we've just freed up and add it to SniperSnapshot; we take the sniperState field out of the method arguments; and, finally, we rename the method to sniperStateChanged() to match its intended new role. We push the changes through to get the following code:

```
public enum SniperState {
  JOINING,
  BIDDING,
  WINNING,
  LOST,
  WON;
}

public class AuctionSniper implements AuctionEventListener { […]
  public void currentPrice(int price, int increment, PriceSource priceSource) {
    isWinning = priceSource == PriceSource.FromSniper;
    if (isWinning) {
      sniperListener.sniperWinning();
    } else {
      final int bid = price + increment;
      auction.bid(bid);
      sniperListener.sniperStateChanged(
        new SniperSnapshot(itemId, price, bid, SniperState.BIDDING));
    }
  }
}
```

In the table model, we use simple indexing to translate the enum into displayable text.

```
public class SnipersTableModel extends AbstractTableModel { [...]

  private static String[] STATUS_TEXT = { MainWindow.STATUS_JOINING,
                                          MainWindow.STATUS_BIDDING };
  public void sniperStateChanged(SniperSnapshot newSnapshot) {
    this.snapshot = newSnapshot;
    this.state = STATUS_TEXT[newSnapshot.state.ordinal()];

    fireTableRowsUpdated(0, 0);
  }
}
```

We make some minor changes to the test code, to get it through the compiler, plus one more interesting adjustment. You might remember that we wrote an expectation clause that ignored the details of the SniperState:

```
allowing(sniperListener).sniperBidding(with(any(SniperState.class)));
```

We can no longer rely on the choice of method to distinguish between different events, so we have to dig into the new SniperSnapshot object to make sure we're matching the right one. We rewrite the expectation with a custom matcher that checks just the state:

```
public class AuctionSniperTest {
  [...]

  context.checking(new Expectations() {{
    ignoring(auction);
    allowing(sniperListener).sniperStateChanged(
                            with(aSniperThatIs(BIDDING)));
                                        then(sniperState.is("bidding"));

    atLeast(1).of(sniperListener).sniperLost(); when(sniperState.is("bidding"));
  }});

  [...]

  private Matcher<SniperSnapshot> aSniperThatIs(final SniperState state) {
    return new FeatureMatcher<SniperSnapshot, SniperState>(
            equalTo(state), "sniper that is ", "was")
    {
      @Override
      protected SniperState featureValueOf(SniperSnapshot actual) {
        return actual.state;
      }
    };
  }
}
```

Lightweight Extensions to jMock

We added a small helper method aSniperThatIs() to package up our specialization of FeatureMatcher behind a descriptive name. You'll see that the method name is intended to make the expectation code read well (or as well as we can manage in Java). We did the same earlier in the chapter with aRowChangedEvent(). As we discussed in "Different Levels of Language" on page 51, we're effectively writing extensions to a language that's embedded in Java. jMock was designed to be extensible in this way, so that programmers can plug in features described in terms of the code they're testing. You could think of these little helper methods as creating new nouns in jMock's expectation language.

Filling In the Numbers

Now we're in a position to feed the missing price to the user interface, which means changing the listener call from sniperWinning() to sniperStateChanged() so that the listener will receive the value in a SniperSnapshot. We start by changing the test to expect the different listener call, and to trigger the event by calling currentPrice() twice: once to force the Sniper to bid, and again to tell the Sniper that it's winning.

```java
public class AuctionSniperTest { […]
  @Test public void
  reportsIsWinningWhenCurrentPriceComesFromSniper() {
    context.checking(new Expectations() {{
      ignoring(auction);
      allowing(sniperListener).sniperStateChanged(
                          with(aSniperThatIs(BIDDING)));
                                        then(sniperState.is("bidding"));

      atLeast(1).of(sniperListener).sniperStateChanged(
                          new SniperSnapshot(ITEM_ID, 135, 135, WINNING));
                                        when(sniperState.is("bidding"));
    }});

    sniper.currentPrice(123, 12, PriceSource.FromOtherBidder);
    sniper.currentPrice(135, 45, PriceSource.FromSniper);
  }
}
```

We change AuctionSniper to retain its most recent values by holding on to the last snapshot. We also add some helper methods to SniperSnapshot, and find that our implementation starts to simplify.

```
public class AuctionSniper implements AuctionEventListener { […]
  private SniperSnapshot snapshot;

  public AuctionSniper(String itemId, Auction auction, SniperListener sniperListener)
  {
    this.auction = auction;
    this.sniperListener = sniperListener;
    this.snapshot = SniperSnapshot.joining(itemId);
  }

  public void currentPrice(int price, int increment, PriceSource priceSource) {
    isWinning = priceSource == PriceSource.FromSniper;
    if (isWinning) {
      snapshot = snapshot.winning(price);
    } else {
      final int bid = price + increment;
      auction.bid(bid);
      snapshot = snapshot.bidding(price, bid);
    }
    sniperListener.sniperStateChanged(snapshot);
  }
}

public class SniperSnapshot { […]
  public SniperSnapshot bidding(int newLastPrice, int newLastBid) {
    return new SniperSnapshot(itemId, newLastPrice, newLastBid, SniperState.BIDDING);
  }

  public SniperSnapshot winning(int newLastPrice) {
    return new SniperSnapshot(itemId, newLastPrice, lastBid, SniperState.WINNING);
  }

  public static SniperSnapshot joining(String itemId) {
    return new SniperSnapshot(itemId, 0, 0, SniperState.JOINING);
  }
}
```

Nearly a State Machine

We've added some constructor methods to `SniperSnapshot` that provide a clean mechanism for moving between snapshot states. It's not a full state machine, in that we don't enforce only "legal" transitions, but it's a hint, and it nicely packages up the getting and setting of fields.

We remove `sniperWinning()` from `SniperListener` and its implementations, and add a value for winning to `SnipersTableModel.STATUS_TEXT`.

Now, the end-to-end test passes.

Follow Through

Converting Won and Lost

This works, but we still have two notification methods in SniperListener left to convert before we can say we're done: sniperWon() and sniperLost(). Again, we replace these with sniperStateChanged() and add two new values to SniperState.

Plugging these changes in, we find that the code simplifies further. We drop the isWinning field from the Sniper and move some decision-making into SniperSnapshot, which will know whether the Sniper is winning or losing, and SniperState.

```
public class AuctionSniper implements AuctionEventListener { [...]
  public void auctionClosed() {
    snapshot = snapshot.closed();
    notifyChange();
  }

  public void currentPrice(int price, int increment, PriceSource priceSource) {
    switch(priceSource) {
    case FromSniper:
      snapshot = snapshot.winning(price);
      break;
    case FromOtherBidder:
      int bid = price + increment;
      auction.bid(bid);
      snapshot = snapshot.bidding(price, bid);
      break;
    }
    notifyChange();
  }

  private void notifyChange() {
    sniperListener.sniperStateChanged(snapshot);
  }
}
```

We note, with smug satisfaction, that AuctionSniper no longer refers to SniperState; it's hidden in SniperSnapshot.

```
public class SniperSnapshot { [...]
  public SniperSnapshot closed() {
    return new SniperSnapshot(itemId, lastPrice, lastBid, state.whenAuctionClosed());
  }
}
```

```
public enum SniperState {
  JOINING {
    @Override public SniperState whenAuctionClosed() { return LOST; }
  },
  BIDDING {
    @Override public SniperState whenAuctionClosed() { return LOST; }
  },
  WINNING {
    @Override public SniperState whenAuctionClosed() { return WON; }
  },
  LOST,
  WON;

  public SniperState whenAuctionClosed() {
    throw new Defect("Auction is already closed");
  }
}
```

We would have preferred to use a field to implement `whenAuctionClosed()`. It turns out that the compiler cannot handle an enum referring to one of its values which has not yet been defined, so we have to put up with the syntax noise of overridden methods.

 Not Too Small to Test

At first `SniperState` looked too simple to unit-test—after all, it's exercised through the `AuctionSniper` tests—but we thought we should keep ourselves honest. Writing the test showed that our simple implementation didn't handle re-closing an auction, which shouldn't happen, so we added an exception. It would be better to write the code so that this case is impossible, but we can't see how to do that right now.

 A Defect Exception

In most systems we build, we end up writing a runtime exception called something like `Defect` (or perhaps `StupidProgrammerMistakeException`). We throw this when the code reaches a condition that could only be caused by a programming error, rather than a failure in the runtime environment.

Trimming the Table Model

We remove the accessor setStatusText() that sets the state display string in
SnipersTableModel, as everything uses sniperStatusChanged() now. While we're
at it, we move the description string constants for the Sniper state over from
MainWindow.

```java
public class SnipersTableModel extends AbstractTableModel { [...]
  private final static String[] STATUS_TEXT = {
    "Joining", "Bidding", "Winning", "Lost", "Won"
  };

  public Object getValueAt(int rowIndex, int columnIndex) {
    switch (Column.at(columnIndex)) {
    case ITEM_IDENTIFIER:
      return snapshot.itemId;
    case LAST_PRICE:
      return snapshot.lastPrice;
    case LAST_BID:
      return snapshot.lastBid;
    case SNIPER_STATE:
      return textFor(snapshot.state);
    default:
      throw new IllegalArgumentException("No column at" + columnIndex);
    }
  }

  public void sniperStateChanged(SniperSnapshot newSnapshot) {
    this.snapshot = newSnapshot;
    fireTableRowsUpdated(0, 0);
  }

  public static String textFor(SniperState state) {
    return STATUS_TEXT[state.ordinal()];
  }
}
```

The helper method, textFor(), helps with readability, and we also use it to get
hold of the display strings in tests since the constants are no longer accessible
from MainWindow.

Object-Oriented Column

We still have a couple of things to do before we finish this task. We start by
removing all the old test code that didn't specify the price details, filling in the
expected values in the tests as required. The tests still run.

The next change is to replace the switch statement which is noisy, not very
object-oriented, and includes an unnecessary default: clause just to satisfy the
compiler. It's served its purpose, which was to get us through the previous coding
stage. We add a method to Column that will extract the appropriate field:

```
public enum Column {
  ITEM_IDENTIFIER {
    @Override public Object valueIn(SniperSnapshot snapshot) {
      return snapshot.itemId;
    }
  },

  LAST_PRICE {
    @Override public Object valueIn(SniperSnapshot snapshot) {
      return snapshot.lastPrice;
    }
  },

  LAST_BID{
    @Override public Object valueIn(SniperSnapshot snapshot) {
      return snapshot.lastBid;
    }
  },

  SNIPER_STATE {
    @Override public Object valueIn(SniperSnapshot snapshot) {
      return SnipersTableModel.textFor(snapshot.state);
    }
  };

  abstract public Object valueIn(SniperSnapshot snapshot);
  [...]
}
```

and the code in `SnipersTableModel` becomes negligible:

```
public class SnipersTableModel extends AbstractTableModel { [...]
  public Object getValueAt(int rowIndex, int columnIndex) {
    return Column.at(columnIndex).valueIn(snapshot);
  }
}
```

Of course, we write a unit test for `Column`. It may seem unnecessary now, but it will protect us when we make changes and forget to keep the column mapping up to date.

Shortening the Event Path

Finally, we see that we have some forwarding calls that we no longer need. `MainWindow` just forwards the update and `SniperStateDisplayer` has collapsed to almost nothing.

```
public class MainWindow extends JFrame { [...]
  public void sniperStateChanged(SniperSnapshot snapshot) {
    snipers.sniperStateChanged(snapshot);
  }
}
```

```
public class SniperStateDisplayer implements SniperListener { [...]
  public void sniperStateChanged(final SniperSnapshot snapshot) {
    SwingUtilities.invokeLater(new Runnable() {
      public void run() { mainWindow.sniperStateChanged(snapshot); }
    });
  }
}
```

SniperStateDisplayer still serves a useful purpose, which is to push updates onto the Swing event thread, but it no longer does any translation between domains in the code, and the call to MainWindow is unnecessary. We decide to simplify the connections by making SnipersTableModel implement SniperListener. We change SniperStateDisplayer to be a *Decorator* and rename it to SwingThreadSniperListener, and we rewire Main so that the Sniper connects to the table model rather than the window.

```
public class Main { [...]
  private final SnipersTableModel snipers = new SnipersTableModel();
  private MainWindow ui;

  public Main() throws Exception {
    SwingUtilities.invokeAndWait(new Runnable() {
      public void run() { ui = new MainWindow(snipers); }
    });
  }

  private void joinAuction(XMPPConnection connection, String itemId) {
    [...]
    Auction auction = new XMPPAuction(chat);
    chat.addMessageListener(
        new AuctionMessageTranslator(
            connection.getUser(),
            new AuctionSniper(itemId, auction,
                        new SwingThreadSniperListener(snipers))));
    auction.join();
  }
}
```

The new structure looks like Figure 15.4.

Final Polish

A Test for Column Titles

To make the user interface presentable, we need to fill in the column titles which, as we saw in Figure 15.3, are still missing. This isn't difficult, since most of the implementation is built into Swing's TableModel. As always, we start with the acceptance test. We add extra validation to AuctionSniperDriver that will be called by the method in ApplicationRunner that starts up the Sniper. For good measure, we throw in a check for the application's displayed title.

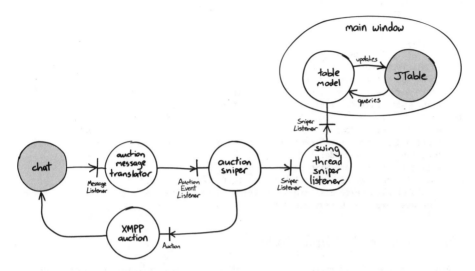

Figure 15.4   TableModel *as a* SniperListener

```
public class ApplicationRunner { [...]
  public void startBiddingIn(final FakeAuctionServer auction) {
    itemId = auction.getItemId();

    Thread thread = new Thread("Test Application") {
      [...]
    };
    thread.setDaemon(true);
    thread.start();

    driver = new AuctionSniperDriver(1000);
    driver.hasTitle(MainWindow.APPLICATION_TITLE);
    driver.hasColumnTitles();
    driver.showsSniperStatus(JOINING.itemId, JOINING.lastPrice,
                             JOINING.lastBid, textFor(SniperState.JOINING));
  }
}

public class AuctionSniperDriver extends JFrameDriver { [...]
  public void hasColumnTitles() {
    JTableHeaderDriver headers = new JTableHeaderDriver(this, JTableHeader.class);
    headers.hasHeaders(matching(withLabelText("Item"), withLabelText("Last Price"),
                                withLabelText("Last Bid"), withLabelText("State")));
  }
}
```

The test fails:

```
java.lang.AssertionError:
Tried to look for...
    exactly 1 JTableHeader ()
    in exactly 1 JFrame (with name "Auction Sniper Main" and showing on screen)
    in all top level windows
and check that it is with headers with cells
  <label  with text "Item">, <label with text "Last Price">,
    <label with text "Last Bid">, <label with text "State">
but...
    all top level windows
    contained 1 JFrame (with name "Auction Sniper Main" and showing on screen)
    contained 1 JTableHeader ()
  it is not with headers with cells
    <label with text "Item">, <label with text "Last Price">,
      <label with text "Last Bid">, <label with text "State">
    because component 0 text was "A"
```

Implementing the TableModel

Swing allows a JTable to query its TableModel for the column headers, which is the mechanism we've chosen to use. We already have Column to represent the columns, so we extend this enum by adding a field for the header text which we reference in SnipersTableModel.

```
public enum Column {
  ITEM_IDENTIFIER("Item") { […] }
  LAST_PRICE("Last Price") { […] }
  LAST_BID("Last Bid") { […] }
  SNIPER_STATE("State") { […] }
  public final String name;

  private Column(String name) {
    this.name = name;
  }
}
public class SnipersTableModel extends AbstractTableModel implements SniperListener
{ […]
  @Override public String getColumnName(int column) {
    return Column.at(column).name;
  }
}
```

All we really need to check in the unit test for SniperTablesModel is the link between a Column value and a column name, but it's so simple to iterate that we check them all:

```
public class SnipersTableModelTest { […]
  @Test public void
  setsUpColumnHeadings() {
    for (Column column: Column.values()) {
      assertEquals(column.name, model.getColumnName(column.ordinal()));
    }
  }
}
```

The acceptance test passes, and we can see the result in Figure 15.5.

Item	Last Price	Last Bid	State
item-54321	1098	1098	Won

Auction Sniper

Figure 15.5 *Sniper with column headers*

Enough for Now

There's more we should do, such as set up borders and text alignment, to tune the user interface. We might do that by associating `CellRenderers` with each `Column` value, or perhaps by introducing a `TableColumnModel`. We'll leave those as an exercise for the reader, since they don't add any more insight into our development process.

In the meantime, we can cross off one more task from our to-do list: Figure 15.6.

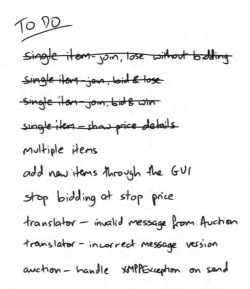

TO DO

~~Single item—join, lose without bidding~~

~~Single item—join, bid & lose~~

~~Single item—join, bid & win~~

~~single item—show price details~~

multiple items

add new items through the GUI

stop bidding at stop price

translator — invalid message from Auction

translator — incorrect message version

auction — handle XMPPException on send

Figure 15.6 *The Sniper shows price information*

Observations

Single Responsibilities

`SnipersTableModel` has one responsibility: to represent the state of our bidding in the user interface. It follows the heuristic we described in "No And's, Or's, or

But's" (page 51). We've seen too much user interface code that is brittle because it has business logic mixed in. In this case, we could also have made the model responsible for deciding whether to bid ("because that would be simpler"), but that would make it harder to respond when either the user interface or the bidding policy change. It would be harder to even *find* the bidding policy, which is why we isolated it in `AuctionSniper`.

Keyhole Surgery for Software

In this chapter we repeatedly used the practice of adding little slices of behavior all the way through the system: replace a label with a table, get that working; show the Sniper bidding, get that working; add the other values, get that working. In all of these cases, we've figured out where we want to get to (always allowing that we might discover a better alternative along the way), but we want to avoid ripping the application apart to get there. Once we start a major rework, we can't stop until it's finished, we can't check in without branching, and merging with rest of the team is harder. There's a reason that surgeons prefer keyhole surgery to opening up a patient—it's less invasive and cheaper.

Programmer Hyper-Sensitivity

We have a well-developed sense of the value of our own time. We keep an eye out for activities that don't seem to be making the best of our (doubtless significant) talents, such as boiler-plate copying and adapting code: if we had the right abstraction, we wouldn't have to bother. Sometimes this just has to be done, especially when working with existing code—but there are fewer excuses when it's our own. Deciding when to change the design requires a good sense for trade-offs, which implies both sensitivity and technical maturity: "I'm about to repeat this code with minor variations, that seems dull and wasteful" as against "This may not be the right time to rework this, I don't understand it yet."

We don't have a simple, reproducible technique here; it requires skill and experience. Developers should have a habit of reflecting on their activity, on the best way to invest their time for the rest of a coding session. This might mean carrying on exactly as before, but at least they'll have thought about it.

Celebrate Changing Your Mind

> *When the facts change, I change my mind. What do you do, sir?*
>
> —John Maynard Keynes

During this chapter, we renamed several features in the code. In many development cultures, this is viewed as a sign of weakness, as an inability to do a proper job. Instead, we think this is an essential part of our development process. Just as we learn more about what the structure should be by using the code we've written, we learn more about the names we've chosen when we work with them. We see how the type and method names fit together and whether the concepts are clear, which stimulates the discovery of new ideas. If the name of a feature isn't right, the only smart thing to do is change it and avoid countless hours of confusion for all who will read the code later.

This Isn't the Only Solution

Examples in books, such as this one, tend to read as if there was an inevitability about the solution. That's partly because we put effort into making the narrative flow, but it's also because presenting one solution tends to drive others out of the reader's consciousness. There are other variations we could have considered, some of which might even resurface as the example develops.

For example, we could argue that `AuctionSniper` doesn't need to know whether it's won or lost the auction—just whether it should bid or not. At present, the only part of the application that cares about winning is the user interface, and it would certainly simplify the `AuctionSniper` and `SniperSnapshot` if we moved that decision away from them. We won't do that now, because we don't yet know if it's the right choice, but we find that kicking around design options sometimes leads to much better solutions.

Chapter 16

Sniping for Multiple Items

In which we bid for multiple items, splitting the per-connection code from the per-auction code. We use the table model we just introduced to display the additional bids. We extend the user interface to allow users to add items dynamically. We're pleased to find that we don't have to change the tests, just their implementation. We tease out a "user request listener" concept, which means we can test some features more directly. We leave the code in a bit of a mess.

Testing for Multiple Items

A Tale of Two Items

The next task on our to-do list is to be able to snipe for multiple items at the same time. We already have much of the machinery we'll need in place, since our user interface is based on a table, so some minor structural changes are all we need to make this work. Looking ahead in the list, we could combine this change with adding items through the user interface, but we don't think we need to do that yet. Just focusing on this one task means we can clarify the distinction between those features that belong to the Sniper's connection to the auction house, and those that belong to an individual auction. So far we've specified the item on the command line, but we can extend that to pass multiple items in the argument list.

As always, we start with a test. We want our new test to show that the application can bid for and win two different items, so we start by looking at the tests we already have. Our current test for a successful bid, in "First, a Failing Test" (page 152), assumes that the application has only one auction—it's implicit in code such as:

```
application.hasShownSniperIsBidding(1000, 1098);
```

We prepare for multiple items by passing an auction into each of the `ApplicationRunner` calls, so the code now looks like:

```
application.hasShownSniperIsBidding(auction, 1000, 1098);
```

Within the `ApplicationRunner`, we remove the `itemId` field and instead extract the item identifier from the `auction` parameters.

175

```java
public void hasShownSniperIsBidding(FakeAuctionServer auction,
                                    int lastPrice, int lastBid)
{
  driver.showsSniperStatus(auction.getItemId(), lastPrice, lastBid,
                           textFor(SniperState.BIDDING));
}
```

The rest is similar, which means we can write a new test:

```java
public class AuctionSniperEndToEndTest {
  private final FakeAuctionServer auction = new FakeAuctionServer("item-54321");
  private final FakeAuctionServer auction2 = new FakeAuctionServer("item-65432");

  @Test public void
  sniperBidsForMultipleItems() throws Exception {
    auction.startSellingItem();
    auction2.startSellingItem();

    application.startBiddingIn(auction, auction2);
    auction.hasReceivedJoinRequestFrom(ApplicationRunner.SNIPER_XMPP_ID);
    auction2.hasReceivedJoinRequestFrom(ApplicationRunner.SNIPER_XMPP_ID);

    auction.reportPrice(1000, 98, "other bidder");
    auction.hasReceivedBid(1098, ApplicationRunner.SNIPER_XMPP_ID);

    auction2.reportPrice(500, 21, "other bidder");
    auction2.hasReceivedBid(521, ApplicationRunner.SNIPER_XMPP_ID);

    auction.reportPrice(1098, 97, ApplicationRunner.SNIPER_XMPP_ID);
    auction2.reportPrice(521, 22, ApplicationRunner.SNIPER_XMPP_ID);

    application.hasShownSniperIsWinning(auction, 1098);
    application.hasShownSniperIsWinning(auction2, 521);

    auction.announceClosed();
    auction2.announceClosed();

    application.showsSniperHasWonAuction(auction, 1098);
    application.showsSniperHasWonAuction(auction2, 521);
  }
}
```

Following the protocol convention, we also remember to add a new user, auction-item-65432, to the chat server to represent the new auction.

 ## Avoiding False Positives

We group the showsSniper methods together instead of pairing them with their associated auction triggers. This is to catch a problem that we found in an earlier version where each checking method would pick up the most recent change—the one we'd just triggered in the previous call. Grouping the checking methods together gives us confidence that they're both valid at the same time.

The ApplicationRunner

The one significant change we have to make in the `ApplicationRunner` is to the `startBiddingIn()` method. Now it needs to accept a variable number of auctions passed through to the Sniper's command line. The conversion is a bit messy since we have to unpack the item identifiers and append them to the end of the other command-line arguments—this is the best we can do with Java arrays:

```
public class ApplicationRunner { [...]s
  public void startBiddingIn(final FakeAuctionServer... auctions) {
    Thread thread = new Thread("Test Application") {
      @Override public void run() {
        try {
          Main.main(arguments(auctions));
        } catch (Throwable e) {
    [...]
    for (FakeAuctionServer auction : auctions) {
      driver.showsSniperStatus(auction.getItemId(), 0, 0, textFor(JOINING));
    }
  }

  protected static String[] arguments(FakeAuctionServer... auctions) {
    String[] arguments = new String[auctions.length + 3];
    arguments[0] = XMPP_HOSTNAME;
    arguments[1] = SNIPER_ID;
    arguments[2] = SNIPER_PASSWORD;
    for (int i = 0; i < auctions.length; i++) {
      arguments[i + 3] = auctions[i].getItemId();
    }
    return arguments;
  }
}
```

We run the test and watch it fail.

```
java.lang.AssertionError:
Expected: is not null
     got: null
  at auctionsniper.SingleMessageListener.receivesAMessage()
```

A Diversion, Fixing the Failure Message

We first saw this cryptic failure message in Chapter 11. It wasn't so bad then because it could only occur in one place and there wasn't much code to test anyway. Now it's more annoying because we have to find this method:

```
public void receivesAMessage(Matcher<? super String> messageMatcher)
  throws InterruptedException
{
  final Message message = messages.poll(5, TimeUnit.SECONDS);
  assertThat(message, is(notNullValue()));
  assertThat(message.getBody(), messageMatcher);
}
```

and figure out what we're missing. We'd like to combine these two assertions and provide a more meaningful failure. We could write a *custom matcher* for the message body but, given that the structure of Message is not going to change soon, we can use a PropertyMatcher, like this:

```
public void receivesAMessage(Matcher<? super String> messageMatcher)
  throws InterruptedException
{
  final Message message = messages.poll(5, TimeUnit.SECONDS);
  assertThat(message, hasProperty("body", messageMatcher));
}
```

which produces this more helpful failure report:

```
java.lang.AssertionError:
Expected: hasProperty("body", "SOLVersion: 1.1; Command: JOIN;")
     got: null
```

With slightly more effort, we could have extended a FeatureMatcher to extract the message body with a nicer failure report. There's not much difference, expect that it would be statically type-checked. Now back to business.

Restructuring Main

The test is failing because the Sniper is not sending a Join message for the second auction. We must change Main to interpret the additional arguments. Just to remind you, the current structure of the code is:

```
public class Main {
  public Main() throws Exception {
    SwingUtilities.invokeAndWait(new Runnable() {
      public void run() {
        ui = new MainWindow(snipers);
      }
    });
  }

  public static void main(String... args) throws Exception {
    Main main = new Main();
    main.joinAuction(
      connection(args[ARG_HOSTNAME], args[ARG_USERNAME], args[ARG_PASSWORD]),
      args[ARG_ITEM_ID]);
  }

  private void joinAuction(XMPPConnection connection, String itemId) {
    disconnectWhenUICloses(connection);
    Chat chat = connection.getChatManager()
                          .createChat(auctionId(itemId, connection), null);
    [...]
  }
}
```

To add multiple items, we need to distinguish between the code that establishes a connection to the auction server and the code that joins an auction. We start by holding on to connection so we can reuse it with multiple chats; the result is not very object-oriented but we want to wait and see how the structure develops. We also change notToBeGCd from a single value to a collection.

```java
public class Main {
  public static void main(String... args) throws Exception {
    Main main = new Main();
    XMPPConnection connection =
        connection(args[ARG_HOSTNAME], args[ARG_USERNAME], args[ARG_PASSWORD]);
    main.disconnectWhenUICloses(connection);
    main.joinAuction(connection, args[ARG_ITEM_ID]);
  }
  private void joinAuction(XMPPConnection connection, String itemId) {
    Chat chat = connection.getChatManager()
                          .createChat(auctionId(itemId, connection), null);
    notToBeGCd.add(chat);

    Auction auction = new XMPPAuction(chat);
    chat.addMessageListener(
        new AuctionMessageTranslator(
            connection.getUser(),
            new AuctionSniper(itemId, auction,
                             new SwingThreadSniperListener(snipers))));
    auction.join();
  }
}
```

We loop through each of the items that we've been given:

```java
public static void main(String... args) throws Exception {
  Main main = new Main();
  XMPPConnection connection =
    connection(args[ARG_HOSTNAME], args[ARG_USERNAME], args[ARG_PASSWORD]);
  main.disconnectWhenUICloses(connection);

  for (int i = 3; i < args.length; i++) {
    main.joinAuction(connection, args[i]);
  }
}
```

This is ugly, but it does show us a separation between the code for the single connection and multiple auctions. We have a hunch it'll be cleaned up before long.

The end-to-end test now shows us that display cannot handle the additional item we've just fed in. The table model is still hard-coded to support one row, so one of the items will be ignored:

```
[…] but...
  it is not table with row with cells
    <label with text "item-65432">, <label with text "521">,
    <label with text "521">, <label with text "Winning">
  because
    in row 0: component 0 text was "item-54321"
```

Incidentally, this result is a nice example of why we needed to be aware of timing in end-to-end tests. This test might fail when looking for auction1 *or* auction2. The asynchrony of the system means that we can't tell which will arrive first.

Extending the Table Model

The SnipersTableModel needs to know about multiple items, so we add a new method to tell it when the Sniper joins an auction. We'll call this method from Main.joinAuction() so we show that context first, writing an empty implementation in SnipersTableModel to satisfy the compiler:

```
private void
joinAuction(XMPPConnection connection, String itemId) throws Exception {
  safelyAddItemToModel(itemId);
  [...]
}
private void safelyAddItemToModel(final String itemId) throws Exception {
  SwingUtilities.invokeAndWait(new Runnable() {
    public void run() {
      snipers.addSniper(SniperSnapshot.joining(itemId));
    }
  });
}
```

We have to wrap the call in an invokeAndWait() because it's changing the state of the user interface from outside the Swing thread.

The implementation of SnipersTableModel itself is single-threaded, so we can write direct unit tests for it—starting with this one for adding a Sniper:

```
@Test public void
notifiesListenersWhenAddingASniper() {
    SniperSnapshot joining = SniperSnapshot.joining("item123");
    context.checking(new Expectations() { {
      one(listener).tableChanged(with(anInsertionAtRow(0)));
    }});

    assertEquals(0, model.getRowCount());

    model.addSniper(joining);

    assertEquals(1, model.getRowCount());
    assertRowMatchesSnapshot(0, joining);
}
```

This is similar to the test for updating the Sniper state that we wrote in "Showing a Bidding Sniper" (page 155), except that we're calling the new method and matching a different TableModelEvent. We also package up the comparison of the table row values into a helper method assertRowMatchesSnapshot().

We make this test pass by replacing the single SniperSnapshot field with a collection and triggering the extra table event. These changes break the existing Sniper update test, because there's no longer a default Sniper, so we fix it:

```
@Test public void
setsSniperValuesInColumns() {
  SniperSnapshot joining = SniperSnapshot.joining("item id");
  SniperSnapshot bidding = joining.bidding(555, 666);
  context.checking(new Expectations() {{
    allowing(listener).tableChanged(with(anyInsertionEvent()));

    one(listener).tableChanged(with(aChangeInRow(0)));
  }});

  model.addSniper(joining);
  model.sniperStateChanged(bidding);

  assertRowMatchesSnapshot(0, bidding);
}
```

We have to add a Sniper to the model. This triggers an insertion event which isn't relevant to this test—it's just supporting infrastructure—so we add an allowing() clause to let the insertion through. The clause uses a more forgiving matcher that checks only the type of the event, not its scope. We also change the matcher for the update event (the one we *do* care about) to be precise about which row it's checking.

Then we write more unit tests to drive out the rest of the functionality. For these, we're not interested in the TableModelEvents, so we ignore the listener altogether.

```
@Test public void
holdsSnipersInAdditionOrder() {
  context.checking(new Expectations() { {
    ignoring(listener);
  }});

  model.addSniper(SniperSnapshot.joining("item 0"));
  model.addSniper(SniperSnapshot.joining("item 1"));

  assertEquals("item 0", cellValue(0, Column.ITEM_IDENTIFIER));
  assertEquals("item 1", cellValue(1, Column.ITEM_IDENTIFIER));
}
updatesCorrectRowForSniper() { […] }
throwsDefectIfNoExistingSniperForAnUpdate() { […] }
```

The implementation is obvious. The only point of interest is that we add an isForSameItemAs() method to SniperSnapshot so that it can decide whether it's referring to the same item, instead of having the table model extract and compare identifiers.[1] It's a clearer division of responsibilities, with the advantage that we can change its implementation without changing the table model. We also decide that not finding a relevant entry is a programming error.

---

1. This avoids the "feature envy" code smell [Fowler99].

```
public void sniperStateChanged(SniperSnapshot newSnapshot) {
  int row = rowMatching(newSnapshot);
  snapshots.set(row, newSnapshot);
  fireTableRowsUpdated(row, row);
}
private int rowMatching(SniperSnapshot snapshot) {
  for (int i = 0; i < snapshots.size(); i++) {
    if (snapshot.isForSameItemAs(snapshots.get(i))) {
      return i;
    }
  }
  throw new Defect("Cannot find match for " + snapshot);
}
```

This makes the current end-to-end test pass—so we can cross off the task from our to-do list, Figure 16.1.

TO DO

~~single item—join, lose without bidding~~

~~single item—join, bid & lose~~

~~single item—join, bid & win~~

~~single item = show price details~~

~~multiple items~~

add new items through the GUI

stop bidding at stop price

translator — invalid message from Auction

translator — incorrect message version

auction — handle XMPPException on send

Figure 16.1 *The Sniper handles multiple items*

The End of Off-by-One Errors?

Interacting with the table model requires indexing into a logical grid of cells. We find that this is a case where TDD is particularly helpful. Getting indexing right can be tricky, except in the simplest cases, and writing tests first clarifies the boundary conditions and then checks that our implementation is correct. We've both lost too much time in the past searching for indexing bugs buried deep in the code.

Adding Items through the User Interface

A Simpler Design

The buyers and user interface designers are still working through their ideas, but they have managed to simplify their original design by moving the item entry into a top bar instead of a pop-up dialog. The current version of the design looks like Figure 16.2, so we need to add a text field and a button to the display.

Figure 16.2   *The Sniper with input fields in its bar*

 ### Making Progress While We Can

The design of user interfaces is outside the scope of this book. For a project of any size, a user experience professional will consider all sorts of macro- and micro-details to provide the user with a coherent experience, so one route that some teams take is to try to lock down the interface design before coding. Our experience, and that of others like Jeff Patton, is that we *can* make development progress whilst the design is being sorted out. We can build to the team's current understanding of the features and keep our code (and attitude) flexible to respond to design ideas as they firm up—and perhaps even feed our experience back into the process.

Update the Test

Looking back at `AuctionSniperEndToEndTest`, it already expresses everything we want the application to do: it describes how the Sniper connects to one or more auctions and bids. The change is that we want to describe a different implementation of some of that behavior (establishing the connection through the user interface rather than the command line) which happens in the `ApplicationRunner`. We need a restructuring similar to the one we just made in `Main`, splitting the connection from the individual auctions. We pull out a `startSniper()` method that starts up and checks the Sniper, and then start bidding for each auction in turn.

```
public class ApplicationRunner {
  public void startBiddingIn(final FakeAuctionServer... auctions) {
    startSniper();
    for (FakeAuctionServer auction : auctions) {
      final String itemId = auction.getItemId();
      driver.startBiddingFor(itemId);
      driver.showsSniperStatus(itemId, 0, 0, textFor(SniperState.JOINING));
    }
  }

  private void startSniper() {
    // as before without the call to showsSniperStatus()
  }
  [...]
}
```

The other change to the test infrastructure is implementing the new method startBiddingFor() in AuctionSniperDriver. This finds and fills in the text field for the item identifier, then finds and clicks on the Join Auction button.

```
public class AuctionSniperDriver extends JFrameDriver {
  @SuppressWarnings("unchecked")
  public void startBiddingFor(String itemId) {
    itemIdField().replaceAllText(itemId);
    bidButton().click();
  }

  private JTextFieldDriver itemIdField() {
    JTextFieldDriver newItemId =
      new JTextFieldDriver(this, JTextField.class, named(MainWindow.NEW_ITEM_ID_NAME));
    newItemId.focusWithMouse();
    return newItemId;
  }

  private JButtonDriver bidButton() {
    return new JButtonDriver(this, JButton.class, named(MainWindow.JOIN_BUTTON_NAME));
  }
  [...]
}
```

Neither of these components exist yet, so the test fails looking for the text field.

```
[...] but...
    all top level windows
    contained 1 JFrame (with name "Auction Sniper Main" and showing on screen)
    contained 0 JTextField (with name "item id")
```

Adding an Action Bar

We address this failure by adding a new panel across the top to contain the text field for the identifier and the Join Auction button, wrapping up the activity in a makeControls() method to help express our intent. We realize that this code isn't very exciting, but we want to show its structure now before we add any behavior.

```
public class MainWindow extends JFrame {
  public MainWindow(TableModel snipers) {
    super(APPLICATION_TITLE);
    setName(MainWindow.MAIN_WINDOW_NAME);
    fillContentPane(makeSnipersTable(snipers), makeControls());
    [...]
  }

  private JPanel makeControls() {
    JPanel controls = new JPanel(new FlowLayout());
    final JTextField itemIdField = new JTextField();
    itemIdField.setColumns(25);
    itemIdField.setName(NEW_ITEM_ID_NAME);
    controls.add(itemIdField);

    JButton joinAuctionButton = new JButton("Join Auction");
    joinAuctionButton.setName(JOIN_BUTTON_NAME);
    controls.add(joinAuctionButton);

    return controls;
  }
  [...]
}
```

With the action bar in place, our next test fails because we don't create the identified rows in the table model.

```
[...] but...
  all top level windows
  contained 1 JFrame (with name "Auction Sniper Main" and showing on screen)
  contained 1 JTable ()
it is not with row with cells
  <label with text "item-54321">, <label with text "0">,
  <label with text "0">, <label with text "Joining">
```

A Design Moment

Now what do we do? To review our position: we have a broken acceptance test pending, we have the user interface structure but no behavior, and the SnipersTableModel still handles only one Sniper at a time. Our goal is that, when we click on the Join Auction button, the application will attempt to join the auction specified in the item field and add a new row to the list of auctions to show that the request is being handled.

In practice, this means that we need a Swing ActionListener for the JButton that will use the text from the JTextField as an item identifier for the new session. Its implementation will add a row to the SnipersTableModel and create a new Chat to the Southabee's On-Line server. The catch is that everything to do with connections is in Main, whereas the button and the text field are in MainWindow. This is a distinction we'd like to maintain, since it keeps the responsibilities of the two classes focused.

We stop for a moment to think about the structure of the code, using the CRC cards we mentioned in "Roles, Responsibilities, Collaborators" on page 16 to help us visualize our ideas. After some discussion, we remind ourselves that the job of MainWindow is to manage our UI components and their interactions; it shouldn't also have to manage concepts such as "connection" or "chat." When a user interaction implies an action outside the user interface, MainWindow should delegate to a collaborating object.

To express this, we decide to add a listener to MainWindow to notify neighboring objects about such requests. We call the new collaborator a UserRequestListener since it will be responsible for handling requests made by the user:

```
public interface UserRequestListener extends EventListener {
  void joinAuction(String itemId);
}
```

Another Level of Testing

We want to write a test for our proposed new behavior, but we can't just write a simple unit test because of Swing threading. We can't be sure that the Swing code will have finished running by the time we check any assertions at the end of the test, so we need something that will wait until the tested code has stabilized—what we usually call an *integration test* because it's testing how our code works with a third-party library. We can use WindowLicker for this level of testing as well as for our end-to-end tests. Here's the new test:

```
public class MainWindowTest {
  private final SnipersTableModel tableModel = new SnipersTableModel();
  private final MainWindow mainWindow = new MainWindow(tableModel);
  private final AuctionSniperDriver driver = new AuctionSniperDriver(100);

  @Test public void
  makesUserRequestWhenJoinButtonClicked() {
    final ValueMatcherProbe<String> buttonProbe =
      new ValueMatcherProbe<String>(equalTo("an item-id"), "join request");

    mainWindow.addUserRequestListener(
        new UserRequestListener() {
          public void joinAuction(String itemId) {
            buttonProbe.setReceivedValue(itemId);
          }
        });

    driver.startBiddingFor("an item-id");
    driver.check(buttonProbe);
  }
}
```

WindowLicker Probes

In WindowLicker, a *probe* is an object that checks for a given state. A driver's `check()` method repeatedly fires the given probe until it's satisfied or times out. In this test, we use a `ValueMatcherProbe`, which compares a value against a Hamcrest matcher, to wait for the `UserRequestListener`'s `joinAuction()` to be called with the right auction identifier.

We create an empty implementation of `MainWindow.addUserRequestListener`, to get through the compiler, and the test fails:

```
Tried to look for...
    join request "an item-id"
but...
    join request "an item-id". Received nothing
```

To make this test pass, we fill in the request listener infrastructure in `MainWindow` using `Announcer`, a utility class that manages collections of listeners.[2] We add a Swing `ActionListener` that extracts the item identifier and announces it to the request listeners. The relevant parts of `MainWindow` look like this:

```
public class MainWindow extends JFrame {
  private final Announcer<UserRequestListener> userRequests =
                              Announcer.to(UserRequestListener.class);

  public void addUserRequestListener(UserRequestListener userRequestListener) {
    userRequests.addListener(userRequestListener);
  }

  [...]
  private JPanel makeControls(final SnipersTableModel snipers) {
    [...]
    joinAuctionButton.addActionListener(new ActionListener() {
      public void actionPerformed(ActionEvent e) {
        userRequests.announce().joinAuction(itemIdField.getText());
      }
    });
  [...]
  }
}
```

To emphasize the point here, we've converted an `ActionListener` event, which is internal to the user interface framework, to a `UserRequestListener` event, which is about users interacting with an auction. These are two separate domains and `MainWindow`'s job is to translate from one to the other. `MainWindow` is *not* concerned with how any implementation of `UserRequestListener` might work—that would be too much responsibility.

---

2. Announcer is included in the examples that ship with jMock.

Micro-Hubris

In case this level of testing seems like overkill, when we first wrote this example we managed to return the text field's *name*, not its *text*—one was item-id and the other was item id. This is just the sort of bug that's easy to let slip through and a nightmare to unpick in end-to-end tests—which is why we like to also write integration-level tests.

Implementing the UserRequestListener

We return to Main to see where we can plug in our new UserRequestListener. The changes are minor because we did most of the work when we restructured the class earlier in this chapter. We decide to preserve most of the existing code for now (even though it's not quite the right shape) until we've made more progress, so we just inline our previous joinAuction() method into the UserRequestListener's. We're also pleased to remove the safelyAddItemToModel() wrapper, since the UserRequestListener will be called on the Swing thread. This is not obvious from the code as it stands; we make a note to address that later.

```
public class Main {
  public static void main(String... args) throws Exception {
    Main main = new Main();
    XMPPConnection connection =
      connection(args[ARG_HOSTNAME], args[ARG_USERNAME], args[ARG_PASSWORD]);
    main.disconnectWhenUICloses(connection);
    main.addUserRequestListenerFor(connection);
  }

  private void addUserRequestListenerFor(final XMPPConnection connection) {
    ui.addUserRequestListener(new UserRequestListener() {
      public void joinAuction(String itemId) {
        snipers.addSniper(SniperSnapshot.joining(itemId));
        Chat chat = connection.getChatManager()
                            .createChat(auctionId(itemId, connection), null);
        notToBeGCd.add(chat);

        Auction auction = new XMPPAuction(chat);
        chat.addMessageListener(
            new AuctionMessageTranslator(connection.getUser(),
                new AuctionSniper(itemId, auction,
                              new SwingThreadSniperListener(snipers))));
        auction.join();
      }
    });
  }
}
```

We try our end-to-end tests again and find that they pass. Slightly stunned, we break for coffee.

Observations

Making Steady Progress

We're starting to see more payback from some of our restructuring work. It was pretty easy to convert the end-to-end test to handle multiple items, and most of the implementation consisted of teasing apart code that was already working. We've been careful to keep class responsibilities focused—except for the one place, Main, where we've put all our working compromises.

We made an effort to stay honest about writing enough tests, which has forced us to consider a couple of edge cases we might otherwise have left. We also introduced a new intermediate-level "integration" test to allow us to work out the implementation of the user interface without dragging in the rest of the system.

TDD Confidential

We don't write up everything that went into the development of our examples—that would be boring and waste paper—but we think it's worth a note about what happened with this one. It took us a couple of attempts to get this design pointing in the right direction because we were trying to allocate behavior to the wrong objects. What kept us honest was that for each attempt to write tests that were focused and made sense, the setup and our assertions kept drifting apart. Once we'd broken through our inadequacies as programmers, the tests became much clearer.

Ship It?

So now that everything works we can get on with more features, right? Wrong. We don't believe that "working" is the same thing as "finished." We've left quite a design mess in Main as we sorted out our ideas, with functionality from various slices of the application all jumbled into one, as in Figure 16.3. Apart from the confusion this leaves, most of this code is not really testable except through the end-to-end tests. We can get away with that now, while the code is still small, but it will be difficult to sustain as the application grows. More importantly, perhaps, we're not getting any unit-test feedback about the internal quality of the code.

We might put this code into production if we knew the code was never going to change or there was an emergency. We know that the first isn't true, because the application isn't finished yet, and being in a hurry is not really a crisis. We know we will be working in this code again soon, so we can either clean up now, while it's still fresh in our minds, or re-learn it every time we touch it. Given that we're trying to make an educational point here, you've probably guessed what we'll do next.

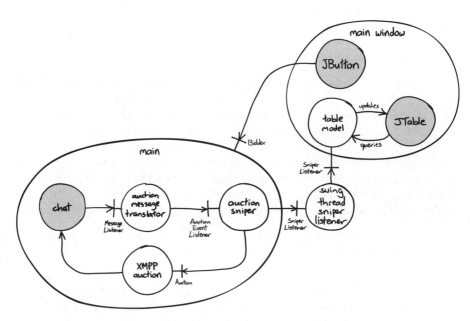

Figure 16.3   *Everything implemented in* Main

Chapter 17

Teasing Apart Main

In which we slice up our application, shuffling behavior around to isolate the XMPP and user interface code from the sniping logic. We achieve this incrementally, changing one concept at a time without breaking the whole application. We finally put a stake through the heart of notToBeGCd.

Finding a Role

We've convinced ourselves that we need to do some surgery on Main, but what do we want our improved Main to do?

For programs that are more than trivial, we like to think of our top-level class as a "matchmaker," finding components and introducing them to each other. Once that job is done it drops into the background and waits for the application to finish. On a larger scale, this what the current generation of application containers do, except that the relationships are often encoded in XML.

In its current form, Main acts as a matchmaker but it's *also* implementing some of the components, which means it has too many responsibilities. One clue is to look at its imports:

```
import java.awt.event.WindowAdapter;
import java.awt.event.WindowEvent;
import java.util.ArrayList;

import javax.swing.SwingUtilities;

import org.jivesoftware.smack.Chat;
import org.jivesoftware.smack.XMPPConnection;
import org.jivesoftware.smack.XMPPException;

import auctionsniper.ui.MainWindow;
import auctionsniper.ui.SnipersTableModel;
import auctionsniper.AuctionMessageTranslator;
import auctionsniper.XMPPAuction;
```

We're importing code from three unrelated packages, plus the auctionsniper package itself. In fact, we have a package loop in that the top-level and UI packages depend on each other. Java, unlike some other languages, tolerates package loops, but they're not something we should be pleased with.

191

We think we should extract some of this behavior from Main, and the XMPP features look like a good first candidate. The use of the Smack should be an implementation detail that is irrelevant to the rest of the application.

Extracting the Chat

Isolating the Chat

Most of the action happens in the implementation of UserRequestListener.joinAuction() within Main. We notice that we've interleaved different domain levels, auction sniping and chatting, in this one unit of code. We'd like to split them up. Here it is again:

```
public class Main { [...]
  private void addUserRequestListenerFor(final XMPPConnection connection) {
    ui.addUserRequestListener(new UserRequestListener() {
    public void joinAuction(String itemId) {
      snipers.addSniper(SniperSnapshot.joining(itemId));
      Chat chat = connection.getChatManager()
                                .createChat(auctionId(itemId, connection), null);
      notToBeGCd.add(chat);

      Auction auction = new XMPPAuction(chat);
      chat.addMessageListener(
            new AuctionMessageTranslator(connection.getUser(),
                new AuctionSniper(itemId, auction,
                    new SwingThreadSniperListener(snipers))));
      auction.join();
    }
  });
  }
}
```

The object that locks this code into Smack is the chat; we refer to it several times: to avoid garbage collection, to attach it to the Auction implementation, and to attach the message listener. If we can gather together the auction- and Sniper-related code, we can move the chat elsewhere, but that's tricky while there's still a dependency loop between the XMPPAuction, Chat, and AuctionSniper.

Looking again, the Sniper actually plugs in to the AuctionMessageTranslator as an AuctionEventListener. Perhaps using an Announcer to bind the two together, rather than a direct link, would give us the flexibility we need. It would also make sense to have the Sniper as a notification, as defined in "Object Peer Stereotypes" (page 52). The result is:

```
public class Main { […]
  private void addUserRequestListenerFor(final XMPPConnection connection) {
    ui.addUserRequestListener(new UserRequestListener() {
      public void joinAuction(String itemId) {
        Chat chat = connection.[…]
        Announcer<AuctionEventListener> auctionEventListeners =
          Announcer.to(AuctionEventListener.class);
        chat.addMessageListener(
          new AuctionMessageTranslator(
            connection.getUser(),
            auctionEventListeners.announce())));
        notToBeGCd.add(chat);

        Auction auction = new XMPPAuction(chat);
        auctionEventListeners.addListener(
          new AuctionSniper(itemId, auction, new SwingThreadSniperListener(snipers))));
        auction.join();
      }
    }
  }
}
```

This looks worse, but the interesting bit is the last three lines. If you squint, it looks like everything is described in terms of Auctions and Snipers (there's still the Swing thread issue, but we did tell you to squint).

Encapsulating the Chat

From here, we can push everything to do with chat, its setup, and the use of the Announcer, into XMPPAuction, adding management methods to the Auction interface for its AuctionEventListeners. We're just showing the end result here, but we changed the code incrementally so that nothing was broken for more than a few minutes.

```
public final class XMPPAuction implements Auction { […]
  private final Announcer<AuctionEventListener> auctionEventListeners = […]
  private final Chat chat;

  public XMPPAuction(XMPPConnection connection, String itemId) {
    chat = connection.getChatManager().createChat(
        auctionId(itemId, connection),
        new AuctionMessageTranslator(connection.getUser(),
                                     auctionEventListeners.announce())));
  }

  private static String auctionId(String itemId, XMPPConnection connection) {
    return String.format(AUCTION_ID_FORMAT, itemId, connection.getServiceName());
  }
}
```

Apart from the garbage collection "wart," this removes any references to Chat from Main.

```
public class Main { [...]
    private void addUserRequestListenerFor(final XMPPConnection connection) {
        ui.addUserRequestListener(new UserRequestListener() {
            public void joinAuction(String itemId) {
                snipers.addSniper(SniperSnapshot.joining(itemId));
                Auction auction = new XMPPAuction(connection, itemId);
                notToBeGCd.add(auction);
                auction.addAuctionEventListener(
                        new AuctionSniper(itemId, auction,
                                       new SwingThreadSniperListener(snipers)));
                auction.join();
            }
        });
    }
}
```

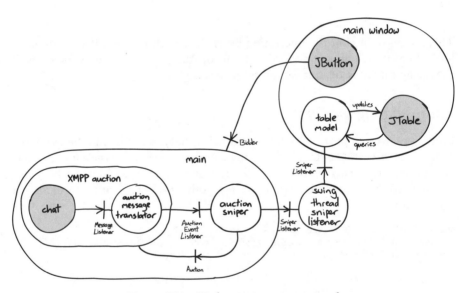

Figure 17.1 *With* XMPPAuction *extracted*

Writing a New Test

We also write a new integration test for the expanded XMPPAuction to show that it can create a Chat and attach a listener. We use some of our existing end-to-end test infrastructure, such as FakeAuctionServer, and a CountDownLatch from the Java concurrency libraries to wait for a response.

```
@Test public void
receivesEventsFromAuctionServerAfterJoining() throws Exception {
  CountDownLatch auctionWasClosed = new CountDownLatch(1);

  Auction auction =  new XMPPAuction(connection, auctionServer.getItemId());
  auction.addAuctionEventListener(auctionClosedListener(auctionWasClosed));

  auction.join();
  server.hasReceivedJoinRequestFrom(ApplicationRunner.SNIPER_XMPP_ID);
  server.announceClosed();

  assertTrue("should have been closed", auctionWasClosed.await(2, SECONDS));
}

private AuctionEventListener
auctionClosedListener(final CountDownLatch auctionWasClosed) {
  return new AuctionEventListener() {
    public void auctionClosed() { auctionWasClosed.countDown(); }
    public void currentPrice(int price, int increment, PriceSource priceSource) {
      // not implemented
    }
  };
}
```

Looking over the result, we can see that it makes sense for XMPPAuction to encapsulate a Chat as now it hides everything to do with communicating between a request listener and an auction service, including translating the messages. We can also see that the AuctionMessageTranslator is internal to this encapsulation, the Sniper doesn't need to see it. So, to recognize our new structure, we move XMPPAuction and AuctionMessageTranslator into a new auctionsniper.xmpp package, and the tests into equivalent xmpp test packages.

 Compromising on a Constructor

We have one doubt about this implementation: the constructor includes some real behavior. Our experience is that busy constructors enforce assumptions that one day we will want to break, especially when testing, so we prefer to keep them very simple—just setting the fields. For now, we convince ourselves that this is "veneer" code, a bridge to an external library, that can only be integration-tested because the Smack classes have just the kind of complicated constructors we try to avoid.

Extracting the Connection

The next thing to remove from Main is direct references to the XMPPConnection. We can wrap these up in a factory class that will create an instance of an Auction for a given item, so it will have a method like

```
Auction auction = <factory>.auctionFor(item id);
```

We struggle for a while over what to call this new type, since it should have a name that reflects the language of auctions. In the end, we decide that the concept that arranges auctions is an "auction house," so that's what we call our new type:

```java
public interface AuctionHouse {
  Auction auctionFor(String itemId);
}
```

The end result of this refactoring is:

```java
public class Main { [...]
  public static void main(String... args) throws Exception {
    Main main = new Main();
    XMPPAuctionHouse auctionHouse =
      XMPPAuctionHouse.connect(
        args[ARG_HOSTNAME], args[ARG_USERNAME], args[ARG_PASSWORD]);
    main.disconnectWhenUICloses(auctionHouse);
    main.addUserRequestListenerFor(auctionHouse);
  }
  private void addUserRequestListenerFor(final AuctionHouse auctionHouse) {
    ui.addUserRequestListener(new UserRequestListener() {
      public void joinAuction(String itemId) {
        snipers.addSniper(SniperSnapshot.joining(itemId));
        Auction auction = auctionHouse.auctionFor(itemId);
        notToBeGCd.add(auction);
        [...]
      }
    }
  }
}
```

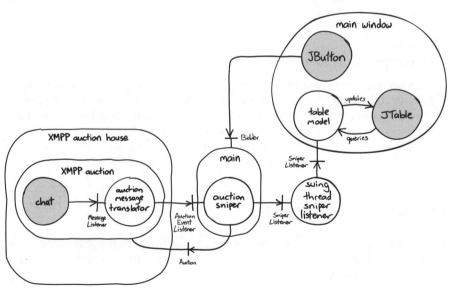

Figure 17.2   *With* XMPPAuctionHouse *extracted*

Implementing XMPPAuctionHouse is straightforward; we transfer there all the code related to connection, including the generation of the Jabber ID from the auction item ID. Main is now simpler, with just one import for all the XMPP code, auctionsniper.xmpp.XMPPAuctionHouse. The new version looks like Figure 17.2.

For consistency, we retrofit XMPPAuctionHouse to the integration test for XMPPAuction, instead of creating XMPPAuctions directly as it does now, and rename the test to XMPPAuctionHouseTest.

Our final touch is to move the relevant constants from Main where we'd left them: the message formats to XMPPAuction and the connection identifier format to XMPPAuctionHouse. This reassures us that we're moving in the right direction, since we're narrowing the scope of where these constants are used.

Extracting the SnipersTableModel

Sniper Launcher

Finally, we'd like to do something about the direct reference to the SnipersTableModel and the related SwingThreadSniperListener—and the awful notToBeGCd. We think we can get there, but it'll take a couple of steps.

The first step is to turn the anonymous implementation of UserRequestListener into a proper class so we can understand its dependencies. We decide to call the new class SniperLauncher, since it will respond to a request to join an auction by "launching" a Sniper. One nice effect is that we can make notToBeGCd local to the new class.

```
public class SniperLauncher implements UserRequestListener {
  private final ArrayList<Auction> notToBeGCd = new ArrayList<Auction>();
  private final AuctionHouse auctionHouse;
  private final SnipersTableModel snipers;

  public SniperLauncher(AuctionHouse auctionHouse, SnipersTableModel snipers) {
    // set the fields
  }

  public void joinAuction(String itemId) {
      snipers.addSniper(SniperSnapshot.joining(itemId));
      Auction auction = auctionHouse.auctionFor(itemId);
      notToBeGCd.add(auction);
      AuctionSniper sniper =
        new AuctionSniper(itemId, auction,
                          new SwingThreadSniperListener(snipers));
      auction.addAuctionEventListener(snipers);
      auction.join();
  }
}
```

With the SniperLauncher separated out, it becomes even clearer that the Swing features don't fit here. There's a clue in that our use of snipers, the

SnipersTableModel, is clumsy: we tell it about the new Sniper by giving it an initial SniperSnapshot, and we attach it to both the Sniper and the auction. There's also some hidden duplication in that we create an initial SniperSnaphot both here and in the AuctionSniper constructor.

Stepping back, we ought to simplify this class so that all it does is establish a new AuctionSniper. It can delegate the process of accepting the new Sniper into the application to a new role which we'll call a SniperCollector, implemented in the SnipersTableModel.

```
public static class SniperLauncher implements UserRequestListener {
  private final AuctionHouse auctionHouse;
  private final SniperCollector collector;
  [...]
  public void joinAuction(String itemId) {
    Auction auction = auctionHouse.auctionFor(itemId);
    AuctionSniper sniper = new AuctionSniper(itemId, auction);
    auction.addAuctionEventListener(sniper);
    collector.addSniper(sniper);
    auction.join();
  }
}
```

The one behavior that we want to confirm is that we only join the auction after everything else is set up. With the code now isolated, we can jMock a States to check the ordering.

```
public class SniperLauncherTest {
  private final States auctionState = context.states("auction state")
                                        .startsAs("not joined");
  [...]
  @Test public void
  addsNewSniperToCollectorAndThenJoinsAuction() {
    final String itemId = "item 123";
    context.checking(new Expectations() {{
      allowing(auctionHouse).auctionFor(itemId); will(returnValue(auction));

      oneOf(auction).addAuctionEventListener(with(sniperForItem(itemId)));
                                     when(auctionState.is("not joined"));
      oneOf(sniperCollector).addSniper(with(sniperForItem(item)));
                                     when(auctionState.is("not joined"));

      one(auction).join(); then(auctionState.is("joined"));
    }});

    launcher.joinAuction(itemId);
  }
}
```

where sniperForItem() returns a Matcher that matches any AuctionSniper associated with the given item identifier.

We extend SnipersTableModel to fulfill its new role: now it accepts AuctionSnipers rather than SniperSnapshots. To make this work, we have to convert a Sniper's listener from a dependency to a notification, so that we can add a listener after construction. We also change `SnipersTableModel` to use the new API and disallow adding `SniperSnapshots`.

```
public class SnipersTableModel extends AbstractTableModel
    implements SniperListener, SniperCollector
{
  private final ArrayList<AuctionSniper> notToBeGCd = […]

  public void addSniper(AuctionSniper sniper) {
    notToBeGCd.add(sniper);
    addSniperSnapshot(sniper.getSnapshot());
    sniper.addSniperListener(new SwingThreadSniperListener(this));
  }

  private void addSniperSnapshot(SniperSnapshot sniperSnapshot) {
    snapshots.add(sniperSnapshot);
    int row = snapshots.size() - 1;
    fireTableRowsInserted(row, row);
  }
}
```

One change that suggests that we're heading in the right direction is that the `SwingThreadSniperListener` is now packaged up in the Swing part of the code, not in the generic `SniperLauncher`.

Sniper Portfolio

As a next step, we realize that we don't yet have anything that represents all our sniping activity and that we might call our *portfolio*. At the moment, the `SnipersTableModel` is implicitly responsible for both maintaining a record of our sniping and displaying that record. It also pulls a Swing implementation detail into `Main`.

We want a clearer separation of concerns, so we extract a `SniperPortfolio` to maintain our Snipers, which we make our new implementer of `SniperCollector`. We push the creation of the `SnipersTableModel` into `MainWindow`, and make it a `PortfolioListener` so the portfolio can tell it when we add or remove a Sniper.

```
public interface PortfolioListener extends EventListener {
  void sniperAdded(AuctionSniper sniper);
}

public class MainWindow extends JFrame {
  private JTable makeSnipersTable(SniperPortfolio portfolio) {
    SnipersTableModel model = new SnipersTableModel();
    portfolio.addPortfolioListener(model);
    JTable snipersTable = new JTable(model);
    snipersTable.setName(SNIPERS_TABLE_NAME);
    return snipersTable;
  }
}
```

This makes our top-level code very simple—it just binds together the user interface and sniper creation through the portfolio:

```
public class Main {  [...]
  private final SniperPortfolio portfolio = new SniperPortfolio();

  public Main() throws Exception {
    SwingUtilities.invokeAndWait(new Runnable() {
      public void run() {
        ui = new MainWindow(portfolio);
      }
    });
  }

  private void addUserRequestListenerFor(final AuctionHouse auctionHouse) {
    ui.addUserRequestListener(new SniperLauncher(auctionHouse, portfolio));
  }
}
```

Even better, since SniperPortfolio maintains a list of all the Snipers, we can finally get rid of notToBeGCd.

This refactoring takes us to the structure shown in Figure 17.3. We've separated the code into three components: one for the core application, one for XMPP communication, and one for Swing display. We'll return to this in a moment.

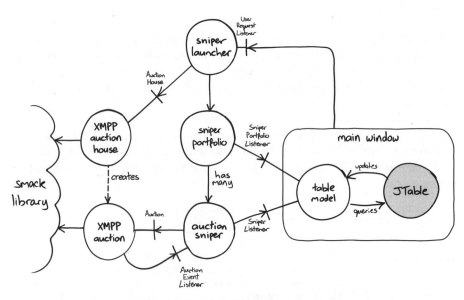

Figure 17.3   *With the* SniperPortfolio

Now that we've cleaned up, we can cross the next item off our list: Figure 17.4.

To DO

~~single item = join, lose without bidding~~
~~single item - join, bid & lose~~
~~single item - join, bid & win~~
~~single item = show price details~~
~~multiple items~~
~~add new items through the GUI~~
stop bidding at stop price
translator — invalid message from Auction
translator - incorrect message version
auction — handle XMPPException on send

Figure 17.4   *Adding items through the user interface*

Observations

Incremental Architecture

This restructuring of Main is a key moment in the development of the application.

As Figure 17.5 shows, we now have a structure that matches the "ports and adapters" architecture we described in "Designing for Maintainability" (page 47). There is core domain code (for example, AuctionSniper) which depends on bridging code (for example, SnipersTableModel) that drives or responds to technical code (for example, JTable). We've kept the domain code free of any reference to the external infrastructure. The contents of our auctionsniper package define a model of our auction sniping business, using a self-contained language. The exception is Main, which is our entry point and binds the domain model and infrastructure together.

What's important for the purposes of this example, is that we arrived at this design incrementally, by adding features and repeatedly following heuristics. Although we rely on our experience to guide our decisions, we reached this solution almost automatically by just following the code and taking care to keep it clean.

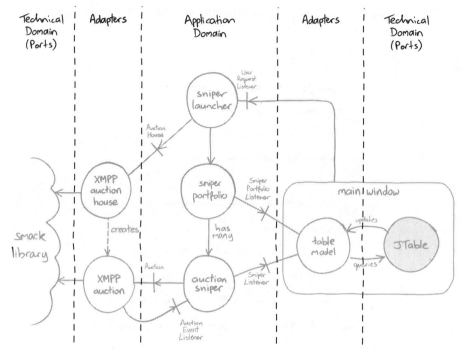

Figure 17.5   *The application now has a "ports and adapters" architecture*

Three-Point Contact

We wrote this refactoring up in detail because we wanted to make some points along the way and to show that we can do significant refactorings incrementally. When we're not sure what to do next or how to get there from here, one way of coping is to scale down the individual changes we make, as Kent Beck showed in [Beck02]. By repeatedly fixing local problems in the code, we find we can explore the design safely, never straying more than a few minutes from working code. Usually this is enough to lead us towards a better design, and we can always backtrack and take another path if it doesn't work out.

One way to think of this is the rock climbing rule of "three-point contact." Trained climbers only move one limb at a time (a hand or a foot), to minimize the risk of falling off. Each move is minimal and safe, but combining enough of them will get you to the top of the route.

In "elapsed time," this refactoring didn't take much longer than the time you spent reading it, which we think is a good return for the clearer separation of concerns. With experience, we've learned to recognize fault lines in code so we can often take a more direct route.

Dynamic as Well as Static Design

We did encounter one small bump whilst working on the code for this chapter. Steve was extracting the SniperPortfolio and got stuck trying to ensure that the sniperAdded() method was called within the Swing thread. Eventually he remembered that the event is triggered by a button click anyway, so he was already covered.

What we learn from this (apart from the need for pairing while writing book examples) is that we should consider more than one view when refactoring code. Refactoring is, after all, a design activity, which means we still need all the skills we were taught—except that now we need them all the time rather than periodically. Refactoring is so focused on static structure (classes and interfaces) that it's easy to lose sight of an application's dynamic structure (instances and threads). Sometimes we just need to step back and draw out, say, an interaction diagram like Figure 17.6:

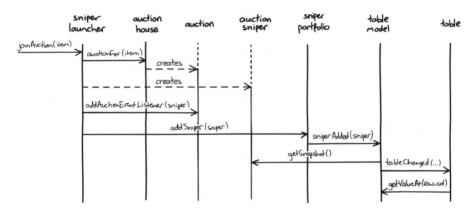

Figure 17.6   *An Interaction Diagram*

An Alternative Fix to notToBeGCd

Our chosen fix relies on the SniperPortfolio holding onto the reference. That's likely to be the case in practice, but if it ever changes we will get transient failures that are hard to track down. We're relying on a side effect of the application to fix an issue in the XMPP code.

An alternative would be to say that it's a Smack problem, so our XMPP layer should deal with it. We could make the XMPPAuctionHouse hang on to the XMPPAuctions it creates, in which case we'd to have to add a lifecycle listener of some sort to tell us when we're finished with an Auction and can release it. There is no obvious choice here; we just have to look at the circumstances and exercise some judgment.

Chapter 18

Filling In the Details

In which we introduce a stop price so we don't bid infinitely, which means we can now be losing an auction that hasn't yet closed. We add a new field to the user interface and push it through to the Sniper. We realize we should have created an Item *type much earlier.*

A More Useful Application

So far the functionality has been prioritized to attract potential customers by giving them a sense of what the application will look like. We can show items being added and some features of sniping. It's not a very useful application because, amongst other things, there's no upper limit for bidding on an item—it could be very expensive to deploy.

This is a common pattern when using Agile Development techniques to work on a new project. The team is flexible enough to respond to how the needs of the sponsors change over time: at the beginning, the emphasis might be on proving the concept to attract enough support to continue; later, the emphasis might be on implementing enough functionality to be ready to deploy; later still, the emphasis might change to providing more options to support a wider range of users.

This dynamic is very different from both a fixed design approach, where the structure of the development has to be approved before work can begin, and a code-and-fix approach, where the system might be initially successful but not resilient enough to adapt to its changing role.

Stop When We've Had Enough

Our next most pressing task (especially after recent crises in the financial markets) is to be able to set an upper limit, the "stop price," for our bid for an item.

Introducing a Losing State

With the introduction of a stop price, it's possible for a Sniper to be *losing* before the auction has closed. We could implement this by just marking the Sniper as Lost when it hits its stop price, but the users want to know the final price when the auction has finished after they've dropped out, so we model this as an extra state. Once a Sniper has been outbid at its stop price, it will never be able to win,

205

so the only option left is to wait for the auction to close, accepting updates of any new (higher) prices from other bidders.

We adapt the state machine we drew in Figure 9.3 to include the new transitions. The result is Figure 18.1.

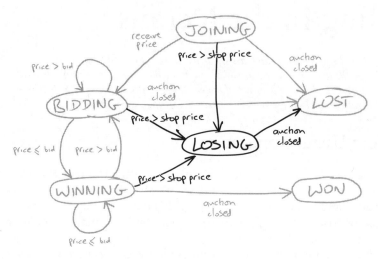

Figure 18.1   *A bidder may now be losing*

The First Failing Test

Of course we start with a failing test. We won't go through all the cases here, but this example will take us through the essentials. First, we write an end-to-end test to describe the new feature. It shows a scenario where our Sniper bids for an item but loses because it bumps into its stop price, and other bidders continue until the auction closes.

```
@Test public void sniperLosesAnAuctionWhenThePriceIsTooHigh() throws Exception {
    auction.startSellingItem();
    application.startBiddingWithStopPrice(auction, 1100);
    auction.hasReceivedJoinRequestFrom(ApplicationRunner.SNIPER_XMPP_ID);
    auction.reportPrice(1000, 98, "other bidder");
    application.hasShownSniperIsBidding(auction, 1000, 1098);

    auction.hasReceivedBid(1098, ApplicationRunner.SNIPER_XMPP_ID);

    auction.reportPrice(1197, 10, "third party");
    application.hasShownSniperIsLosing(auction, 1197, 1098);

    auction.reportPrice(1207, 10, "fourth party");
    application.hasShownSniperIsLosing(auction, 1207, 1098);

    auction.announceClosed();
    application.showsSniperHasLostAuction(auction, 1207, 1098);
}
```

This test introduces two new methods into our test infrastructure, which we need to fill in to get through the compiler. First, `startBiddingWithStopPrice()` passes the new stop price value through the `ApplicationRunner` to the `AuctionSniperDriver`.

```
public class AuctionSniperDriver extends JFrameDriver {
  public void startBiddingFor(String itemId, int stopPrice) {
    textField(NEW_ITEM_ID_NAME).replaceAllText(itemId);
    textField(NEW_ITEM_STOP_PRICE_NAME).replaceAllText(String.valueOf(stopPrice));
    bidButton().click();
  }
  [...]
}
```

This implies that we need a new input field in the user interface for the stop price, so we create a constant to identify it in `MainWindow` (we'll fill in the component itself soon). We also need to support our existing tests which do not have a stop price, so we change them to use `Integer.MAX_VALUE` to represent no stop price at all.

The other new method in `ApplicationRunner` is `hasShownSniperIsLosing()`, which is the same as the other checking methods, except that it uses a new `Losing` value in `SniperState`:

```
public enum SniperState {
  LOSING {
    @Override public SniperState whenAuctionClosed() { return LOST; }
  }, [...]
```

and, to complete the loop, we add a value to the display text in `SnipersTableModel`:

```
private final static String[] STATUS_TEXT = {
  "Joining", "Bidding", "Winning", "Losing", "Lost", "Won"
};
```

The failure message says that we have no stop price field:

```
[...] but...
  all top level windows
  contained 1 JFrame (with name "Auction Sniper Main" and showing on screen)
  contained 0 JTextField (with name "stop price")
```

Now we have a failing end-to-end test that describes our intentions for the feature, so we can implement it.

Typing In the Stop Price

To make any progress, we must add a component to the user interface that will accept a stop price. Our current design, which we saw in Figure 16.2, has only a field for the item identifier but we can easily adjust it to take a stop price in the top bar.

For our implementation, we will add a `JFormattedTextField` for the stop price that is constrained to accept only integer values, and a couple of labels. The new top bar looks like Figure 18.2.

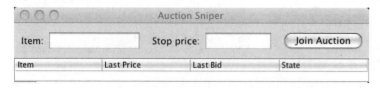

Figure 18.2   *The Sniper with a stop price field in its bar*

We get the test failure we expect, which is that the Sniper is not losing because it continues to bid:

```
[…] but...
    all top level windows
    contained 1 JFrame (with name "Auction Sniper Main" and showing on screen)
    contained 1 JTable ()
  it is not table with row with cells
    <label with text "item-54321">, <label with text "1098">,
    <label with text "1197">, <label with text "Losing">
  because
    in row 0: component 1 text was "1197"
```

Propagating the Stop Price

To make this feature work, we need to pass the stop price from the user interface to the `AuctionSniper`, which can then use it to limit further bidding. The chain starts when `MainWindow` notifies its `UserRequestListener` using:

```
void joinAuction(String itemId);
```

The obvious thing to do is to add a `stopPrice` argument to this method and to the rest of the chain of calls, until it reaches the `AuctionSniper` class. We want to make a point here, so we'll force a slightly different approach to propagating the new value.

Another way to look at it is that the user interface constructs a description of the user's "policy" for the Sniper's bidding on an item. So far this has only included the item's identifier ("bid on this item"), but now we're adding a stop price ("bid up to this amount on this item") so there's more structure.

We want to make this structure explicit, so we create a new class, Item. We start with a simple value that just carries the identifier and stop price as public immutable fields; we can move behavior into it later.

```
public class Item {
  public final String identifier;
  public final int stopPrice;

  public Item(String identifier, int stopPrice) {
    this.identifier = identifier;
    this.stopPrice = stopPrice;
  }
  // also equals(), hashCode(), toString()
}
```

Introducing the Item class is an example of *budding off* that we described in "Value Types" (page 59). It's a placeholder type that we use to identify a concept and that gives us somewhere to attach relevant new features as the code grows.

We push Item into the code and see what breaks, starting with UserRequestListener:

```
public interface UserRequestListener extends EventListener {
  void joinAuction(Item item);
}
```

First we fix MainWindowTest, the integration test we wrote for the Swing implementation in Chapter 16. The language is already beginning to shift. In the previous version of this test, the probe variable was called buttonProbe, which describes the structure of the user interface. That doesn't make sense any more, so we've renamed it itemProbe, which describes a collaboration between MainWindow and its neighbors.

```
@Test public void
makesUserRequestWhenJoinButtonClicked() {
  final ValueMatcherProbe<Item> itemProbe =
    new ValueMatcherProbe<Item>(equalTo(new Item("an item-id", 789)), "item request");
  mainWindow.addUserRequestListener(
      new UserRequestListener() {
        public void joinAuction(Item item) {
          itemProbe.setReceivedValue(item);
        }
      });
  driver.startBiddingFor("an item-id", 789);
  driver.check(itemProbe);
}
```

We make this test pass by extracting the stop price value within MainWindow.

```
joinAuctionButton.addActionListener(new ActionListener() {
  public void actionPerformed(ActionEvent e) {
    userRequests.announce().joinAuction(new Item(itemId(), stopPrice()));
  }
  private String itemId() {
    return itemIdField.getText();
  }
  private int stopPrice() {
    return ((Number)stopPriceField.getValue()).intValue();
  }
});
```

This pushes Item into SniperLauncher which, in turn, pushes it through to its dependent types such as AuctionHouse and AuctionSniper. We fix the compilation errors and make all the tests pass again—except for the outstanding end-to-end test which we have yet to implement.

We've now made explicit another concept in the domain. We realize that an item's identifier is only one part of how a user bids in an auction. Now the code can tell us exactly where decisions are made about bidding choices, so we don't have to follow a chain of method calls to see which strings are relevant.

Restraining the AuctionSniper

The last step to finish the task is to make the AuctionSniper observe the stop price we've just passed to it and stop bidding. In practice, we can ensure that we've covered everything by writing unit tests for each of the new state transitions drawn in Figure 18.1. Our first test triggers the Sniper to start bidding and then announces a bid outside its limit—the stop price is set to 1234. We've also extracted a common expectation into a helper method.[1]

```
@Test public void
doesNotBidAndReportsLosingIfSubsequentPriceIsAboveStopPrice() {
  allowingSniperBidding();
  context.checking(new Expectations() {{
    int bid = 123 + 45;
    allowing(auction).bid(bid);
    atLeast(1).of(sniperListener).sniperStateChanged(
                    new SniperSnapshot(ITEM_ID, 2345, bid, LOSING));
                                      when(sniperState.is("bidding"));
  }});
  sniper.currentPrice(123, 45, PriceSource.FromOtherBidder);
  sniper.currentPrice(2345, 25, PriceSource.FromOtherBidder);
}
private void allowingSniperBidding() {
  context.checking(new Expectations() {{
    allowing(sniperListener).sniperStateChanged(with(aSniperThatIs(BIDDING)));
                                      then(sniperState.is("bidding"));
  }});
}
```

---

1. jMock allows checking() to be called multiple times within a test.

Distinguishing between Test Setup and Assertions

Once again we're using the `allowing` clause to distinguish between the test setup (getting the `AuctionSniper` into the right state) and the significant test assertion (that the `AuctionSniper` is now losing). We're very picky about this kind of expressiveness because we've found it's the only way for the tests to remain meaningful, and therefore useful, over time. We return to this at length in Chapter 21 and Chapter 24.

The other tests are similar:

```
doesNotBidAndReportsLosingIfFirstPriceIsAboveStopPrice()
reportsLostIfAuctionClosesWhenLosing()
continuesToBeLosingOnceStopPriceHasBeenReached()
doesNotBidAndReportsLosingIfPriceAfterWinningIsAboveStopPrice()
```

We change `AuctionSniper`, with supporting features in `SniperSnapshot` and `Item`, to make the test pass:

```
public class AuctionSniper { […]
  public void currentPrice(int price, int increment, PriceSource priceSource) {
    switch(priceSource) {
    case FromSniper:
      snapshot = snapshot.winning(price);
      break;
    case FromOtherBidder:
      int bid = price + increment;
      if (item.allowsBid(bid)) {
        auction.bid(bid);
        snapshot = snapshot.bidding(price, bid);
      } else {
        snapshot = snapshot.losing(price);
      }
      break;
    }
    notifyChange();
  } […]

public class SniperSnapshot { […]
  public SniperSnapshot losing(int newLastPrice) {
    return new SniperSnapshot(itemId, newLastPrice, lastBid, LOSING);
  } […]

public class Item { […]
  public boolean allowsBid(int bid) {
    return bid <= stopPrice;
  } […]
```

The end-to-end tests pass and we can cross the feature off our list, Figure 18.3.

TO DO

~~single item-join, lose without bidding~~

~~single item-join, bid & lose~~

~~single item-join, bid & win~~

~~single item - show price details~~

~~multiple items~~

~~add new items through the GUI~~

~~stop bidding at stop price~~

translator — invalid message from Auction

translator - incorrect message version

auction — handle XMPPException on send

Figure 18.3 *The Sniper stops bidding at the stop price*

Observations

User Interfaces, Incrementally

It looks like we're making significant changes *again* to the user interface at a late stage in our development. Shouldn't we have seen this coming? This is an active topic for discussion in the Agile User Experience community and, as always, the answer is "it depends, but you have more flexibility than you might think."

In truth, for a simple application like this it would make sense to work out the user interface in more detail at the start, to make sure it's usable and coherent. That said, we also wanted to make a point that we *can* respond to changing needs, especially if we structure our tests and code so that they're flexible, not a dead weight. We all know that requirements will change, especially once we put our application into production, so we should be able to respond.

Other Modeling Techniques Still Work

Some presentations of TDD appear to suggest that it supersedes all previous software design techniques. We think TDD works best when it's based on skill and judgment acquired from as wide an experience as possible—which includes taking advantage of older techniques and formats (we hope we're not being too controversial here).

State transition diagrams are one example of taking another view. We regularly come across teams that have never quite figured out what the valid states and transitions are for key concepts in their domain, and applying this simple formalism often means we can clean up a lucky-dip of snippets of behavior scattered across the code. What's nice about state transitions diagrams is that they map directly onto tests, so we can show that we've covered all the possibilities.

The trick is to understand and use other modeling techniques for support and guidance, not as an end in themselves—which is how they got a bad name in the first place. When we're doing TDD and we're uncertain what to do, sometimes stepping back and opening a pack of index cards, or sketching out the interactions, can help us regain direction.

Domain Types Are Better Than Strings

> *The string is a stark data structure and everywhere it is passed there is much duplication of process. It is a perfect vehicle for hiding information.*
>
> —Alan Perlis

Looking back, we wish we'd created the `Item` type earlier, probably when we extracted `UserRequestListener`, instead of just using a `String` to represent the thing a Sniper bids for. Had we done so, we could have added the stop price to the existing `Item` class, and it would have been delivered, by definition, to where it was needed.

We might also have noticed sooner that we do not want to index our table on item identifier but on an `Item`, which would open up the possibility of trying multiple policies in a single auction. We're not saying that we should have designed more speculatively for a need that hasn't been proved. Rather, when we take the trouble to express the domain clearly, we often find that we have more options.

It's often better to define domain types to wrap not only `Strings` but other built-in types too, including collections. All we have to do is remember to apply our own advice. As you see, sometimes we forget.

Chapter 19

Handling Failure

In which we address the reality of programming in an imperfect world, and add failure reporting. We add a new auction event that reports failure. We attach a new event listener that will turn off the Sniper if it fails. We also write a message to a log and write a unit test that mocks a class, for which we're very sorry.

To avoid trying your patience any further, we close our example here.

So far, we've been prepared to assume that everything just works. This might be reasonable if the application is not supposed to last—perhaps it's acceptable if it just crashes and we restart it or, as in this case, we've been mainly concerned with demonstrating and exploring the domain. Now it's time to start being explicit about how we deal with failures.

What If It Doesn't Work?

Our product people are concerned that Southabee's On-Line has a reputation for occasionally failing and sending incorrectly structured messages, so they want us to show that we can cope. It turns out that the system we talk to is actually an aggregator for multiple auction feeds, so the failure of an individual auction does not imply that the whole system is unsafe. Our policy will be that when we receive a message that we cannot interpret, we will mark that auction as `Failed` and ignore any further updates, since it means we can no longer be sure what's happening. Once an auction has failed, we make no attempt to recover.[1]

In practice, reporting a message failure means that we flush the price and bid values, and show the status as `Failed` for the offending item. We also record the event somewhere so that we can deal with it later. We could make the display of the failure more obvious, for example by coloring the row, but we'll keep this version simple and leave any extras as an exercise for the reader.

The end-to-end test shows that a working Sniper receives a bad message, displays and records the failure, and then ignores further updates from this auction:

---

1. We admit that it's unlikely that an auction site that regularly garbles its messages will survive for long, but it's a simple example to work through. We also doubt that any serious bidder will be happy to let their bid lie hanging, not knowing whether they've bought something or lost to a rival. On the other hand, we've seen less plausible systems succeed in the world, propped up by an army of special handling, so perhaps you can let us get away with this one.

```
@Test public void
sniperReportsInvalidAuctionMessageAndStopsRespondingToEvents()
    throws Exception
{
  String brokenMessage = "a broken message";
  auction.startSellingItem();
  auction2.startSellingItem();

  application.startBiddingIn(auction, auction2);
  auction.hasReceivedJoinRequestFrom(ApplicationRunner.SNIPER_XMPP_ID);

  auction.reportPrice(500, 20, "other bidder");
  auction.hasReceivedBid(520, ApplicationRunner.SNIPER_XMPP_ID);

  auction.sendInvalidMessageContaining(brokenMessage);
  application.showsSniperHasFailed(auction);

  auction.reportPrice(520, 21, "other bidder");
  waitForAnotherAuctionEvent();

  application.reportsInvalidMessage(auction, brokenMessage);
  application.showsSniperHasFailed(auction);
}

private void waitForAnotherAuctionEvent() throws Exception {
  auction2.hasReceivedJoinRequestFrom(ApplicationRunner.SNIPER_XMPP_ID);
  auction2.reportPrice(600, 6, "other bidder");
  application.hasShownSniperIsBidding(auction2, 600, 606);
}
```

where sendInvalidMessageContaining() sends the given invalid string via a chat
to the Sniper, and showsSniperHasFailed() checks that the status for the item is
Failed and that the price values have been zeroed. We park the implementation
of reportsInvalidMessage() for the moment; we'll come back to it later in this
chapter.

 ## Testing That Something Doesn't Happen

You'll have noticed the waitForAnotherAuctionEvent() method which forces an
unrelated Sniper event and then waits for it to work through the system. Without
this call, it would be possible for the final showSniperHasFailed() check to pass
incorrectly because it would pick up the previous Sniper state—before the system
has had time to process the relevant price event. The additional event holds back
the test just long enough to make sure that the system has caught up. See
Chapter 27 for more on testing with asynchrony.

To get this test to fail appropriately, we add a FAILED value to the SniperState
enumeration, with an associated text mapping in SnipersTabelModel. The
test fails:

[...] but...
```
  it is not table with row with cells
    <label with text "item-54321">, <label with text "0">,
    <label with text "0">, <label with text "Failed">
  because
    in row 0: component 1 text was "500"
    in row 1: component 0 text was "item-65432"
```

It shows that there are two rows in the table: the second is for the other auction, and the first is showing that the current price is 500 when it should have been flushed to 0. This failure is our marker for what we need to build next.

Detecting the Failure

The failure will actually occur in the `AuctionMessageTranslator` (last shown in Chapter 14) which will throw a runtime exception when it tries to parse the message. The Smack library drops exceptions thrown by `MessageHandlers`, so we have to make sure that our handler catches everything. As we write a unit test for a failure in the translator, we realize that we need to report a new type of auction event, so we add an `auctionFailed()` method to the `AuctionEventListener` interface.

```
@Test public void
notifiesAuctionFailedWhenBadMessageReceived() {
  context.checking(new Expectations() {{
    exactly(1).of(listener).auctionFailed();
  }});

  Message message = new Message();
  message.setBody("a bad message");

  translator.processMessage(UNUSED_CHAT, message);
}
```

This fails with an `ArrayIndexOutOfBoundsException` when it tries to unpack a name/value pair from the string. We could be precise about which exceptions to catch but in practice it doesn't really matter here: we either parse the message or we don't, so to make the test pass we extract the bulk of `processMessage()` into a `translate()` method and wrap a try/catch block around it.

```
public class AuctionMessageTranslator implements MessageListener {
  public void processMessage(Chat chat, Message message) {
    try {
      translate(message.getBody());
    } catch (Exception parseException) {
      listener.auctionFailed();
    }
  }
}
```

While we're here, there's another failure mode we'd like to check. It's possible that a message is well-formed but incomplete: it might be missing one of its fields such as the event type or current price. We write a couple of tests to confirm that we can catch these, for example:

```
@Test public void
notifiesAuctionFailedWhenEventTypeMissing() {
  context.checking(new Expectations() {{
    exactly(1).of(listener).auctionFailed();
  }});
  Message message = new Message();
  message.setBody("SOLVersion: 1.1; CurrentPrice: 234; Increment: 5; Bidder: "
                  + SNIPER_ID + ";");
  translator.processMessage(UNUSED_CHAT, message);
}
```

Our fix is to throw an exception whenever we try to get a value that has not been set, and we define MissingValueException for this purpose.

```
public static class AuctionEvent { [...]
  private String get(String name) throws MissingValueException {
    String value = values.get(name);
    if (null == value) {
      throw new MissingValueException(name);
    }
    return value;
  }
}
```

Displaying the Failure

We added an auctionFailed() method to AuctionEventListener while unit-testing AuctionMessageTranslator. This triggers a compiler warning in AuctionSniper, so we added an empty implementation to keep going. Now it's time to make it work, which turns out to be easy. We write some tests in AuctionSniperTest for the new state transitions, for example:

```
@Test public void
reportsFailedIfAuctionFailsWhenBidding() {
  ignoringAuction();
  allowingSniperBidding();

  expectSniperToFailWhenItIs("bidding");

  sniper.currentPrice(123, 45, PriceSource.FromOtherBidder);
  sniper.auctionFailed();
}

private void expectSniperToFailWhenItIs(final String state) {
  context.checking(new Expectations() {{
    atLeast(1).of(sniperListener).sniperStateChanged(
        new SniperSnapshot(ITEM_ID, 00, 0, SniperState.FAILED));
                                  when(sniperState.is(state));
  }});
}
```

We've added a couple more helper methods: `ignoringAuction()` says that we don't care what happens to `auction`, allowing events to pass through so we can get to the failure; and, `expectSniperToFailWhenItIs()` describes what a failure should look like, including the previous state of the Sniper.

All we have to do is add a `failed()` transition to `SniperSnapshot` and use it in the new method.

```
public class AuctionSniper implements AuctionEventListener {
  public void auctionFailed() {
    snapshot = snapshot.failed();
    listeners.announce().sniperStateChanged(snapshot);
  } […]

public class SniperSnapshot {
  public SniperSnapshot failed() {
    return new SniperSnapshot(itemId, 0, 0, SniperState.FAILED);
  } […]
```

This displays the failure, as we can see in Figure 19.1.

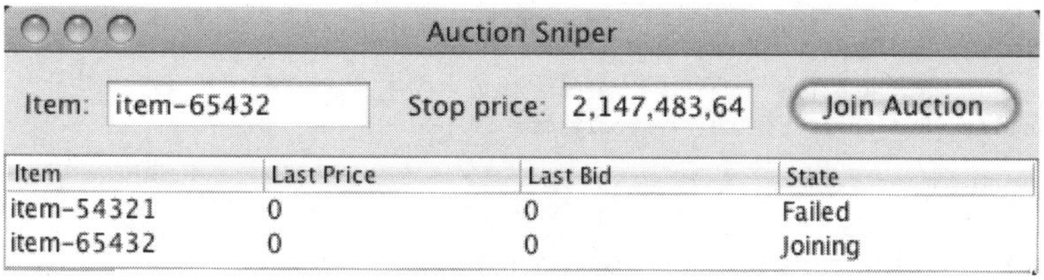

Auction Sniper
Item:
item-65432
Stop price:
2,147,483,64
Join Auction
Item
Last Price
Last Bid
State
item-54321
0
0
Failed
item-65432
0
0
Joining

Figure 19.1 *The Sniper shows a failed auction*

The end-to-end test, however, still fails. The synchronization hook we added reveals that we haven't disconnected the Sniper from receiving further events from the auction.

Disconnecting the Sniper

We turn off a Sniper by removing its `AuctionMessageTranslator` from its `Chat`'s set of `MessageListeners`. We can do this safely while processing a message because `Chat` stores its listeners in a thread-safe "copy on write" collection. One obvious place to do this is within `processMessage()` in `AuctionMessageTranslator`, which receives the `Chat` as an argument, but we have two doubts about this. First, as we pointed out in Chapter 12, constructing a real `Chat` is painful. Most of the mocking frameworks support creating a mock class, but it makes us uncomfortable because then we're defining a relationship with an implementation, not a role—we're being too precise about our dependencies. Second, we might be assigning too many responsibilities to `AuctionMessageTranslator`; it would have to translate the message *and* decide what to do when it fails.

Our alternative approach is to attach another object to the translator that implements this disconnection policy, using the infrastructure we already have for notifying `AuctionEventListeners`.

```
public final class XMPPAuction implements Auction {
  public XMPPAuction(XMPPConnection connection, String auctionJID) {
    AuctionMessageTranslator translator = translatorFor(connection);
    this.chat = connection.getChatManager().createChat(auctionJID, translator);
    addAuctionEventListener(chatDisconnectorFor(translator));
  }

  private AuctionMessageTranslator translatorFor(XMPPConnection connection) {
    return new AuctionMessageTranslator(connection.getUser(),
                                   auctionEventListeners.announce());
  }

z

  private AuctionEventListener
  chatDisconnectorFor(final AuctionMessageTranslator translator) {
    return new AuctionEventListener() {
      public void auctionFailed() {
        chat.removeMessageListener(translator);
      }
      public void auctionClosed(// empty method
      public void currentPrice( // empty method
    };
  } [...]
```

The end-to-end test, as far as it goes, passes.

 ## The Composition Shell Game

The issue in this design episode is not the fundamental complexity of the feature, which is constant, but how we divide it up. The design we chose (attaching a disconnection listener) could be argued to be more complicated than its alternative (detaching the chat within the translator). It certainly takes more lines of code, but that's not the only metric. Instead, we're emphasizing the "single responsibility" principle, which means each object does just one thing well and the system behavior comes from how we assemble those objects.

Sometimes this feels as if the behavior we're looking for is always somewhere else (as Gertrude Stein said, "There is no there there"), which can be frustrating for developers not used to the style. Our experience, on the other hand, is that focused responsibilities make the code more maintainable because we don't have to cut through unrelated functionality to get to the piece we need. See Chapter 6 for a longer discussion.

Recording the Failure

Now we want to return to the end-to-end test and the `reportsInvalidMessage()` method that we parked. Our requirement is that the Sniper application must log a message about these failures so that the user's organization can recover the situation. This means that our test should look for a log file and check its contents.

Filling In the Test

We implement the missing check and flush the log before each test, delegating the management of the log file to an `AuctionLogDriver` class which uses the Apache Commons IO library. It also cheats slightly by resetting the log manager (we're not really supposed to be in the same address space), since deleting the log file can confuse a cached logger.

```java
public class ApplicationRunner { [...]
  private AuctionLogDriver logDriver = new AuctionLogDriver();

  public void reportsInvalidMessage(FakeAuctionServer auction, String message)
    throws IOException
  {
    logDriver.hasEntry(containsString(message));
  }

  public void startBiddingWithStopPrice(FakeAuctionServer auction, int stopPrice) {
    startSniper();
    openBiddingFor(auction, stopPrice);
  }
  private startSniper() {
    logDriver.clearLog()
    Thread thread = new Thread("Test Application") {
      @Override public void run() { // Start the application [...]
  }
}

public class AuctionLogDriver {
  public static final String LOG_FILE_NAME = "auction-sniper.log";
  private final File logFile = new File(LOG_FILE_NAME);

  public void hasEntry(Matcher<String> matcher) throws IOException  {
    assertThat(FileUtils.readFileToString(logFile), matcher);
  }
  public void clearLog() {
    logFile.delete();
    LogManager.getLogManager().reset();
  }
}
```

This new check only reassures us that we've fed a message through the system and into some kind of log record—it tells us that the pieces fit together. We'll write a more thorough test of the contents of a log record later. The end-to-end test now fails because, of course, there's no log file to read.

Failure Reporting in the Translator

Once again, the first change is in the `AuctionMessageTranslator`. We'd like the record to include the auction identifier, the received message, and the thrown exception. The "single responsibility" principle suggests that the `AuctionMessageTranslator` should not be responsible for deciding *how* to report the event, so we invent a new collaborator to handle this task. We call it `XMPPFailureReporter`:

```
public interface XMPPFailureReporter {
  void cannotTranslateMessage(String auctionId, String failedMessage,
                              Exception exception);
}
```

We amend our existing failure tests, wrapping up message creation and common expectations in helper methods, for example:

```
@Test public void
notifiesAuctionFailedWhenBadMessageReceived() {
  String badMessage = "a bad message";
  expectFailureWithMessage(badMessage);
  translator.processMessage(UNUSED_CHAT, message(badMessage));
}
private Message message(String body) {
  Message message = new Message();
  message.setBody(body);
  return message;
}
private void expectFailureWithMessage(final String badMessage) {
  context.checking(new Expectations() {{
    oneOf(listener).auctionFailed();
    oneOf(failureReporter).cannotTranslateMessage(
                         with(SNIPER_ID), with(badMessage),
                         with(any(Exception.class)));
  }});
}
```

The new reporter is a dependency for the translator, so we feed it in through the constructor and call it just before notifying any listeners. We know that `message.getBody()` will not throw an exception, it's just a simple bean, so we can leave it outside the catch block.

```
public class AuctionMessageTranslator implements MessageListener {
  public void processMessage(Chat chat, Message message) {
    String messageBody = message.getBody();
    try {
      translate(messageBody);
    } catch (RuntimeException exception) {
      failureReporter.cannotTranslateMessage(sniperId, messageBody, exception);
      listener.auctionFailed();
    }
  } [...]
```

The unit test passes.

Generating the Log Message

The next stage is to implement the XMPPFailureReporter with something that generates a log file. This is where we actually check the format and contents of a log entry. We start a class LoggingXMPPFailureReporter and decide to use Java's built-in logging framework. We could make the tests for this new class write and read from a real file. Instead, we decide that file access is sufficiently covered by the end-to-end test we've just set up, so we'll run everything in memory to reduce the test's dependencies. We're confident we can take this shortcut, because the example is so simple; for more complex behavior we would write some integration tests.

The Java logging framework has no interfaces, so we have to be more concrete than we'd like. Exceptionally, we decide to use a class-based mock to override the relevant method in Logger; in jMock we turn on class-based mocking with the setImposteriser() call. The AfterClass annotation tells JUnit to call resetLogging() after all the tests have run to flush any changes we might have made to the logging environment.

```
@RunWith(JMock.class)
public class LoggingXMPPFailureReporterTest {
  private final Mockery context = new Mockery() {{
    setImposteriser(ClassImposteriser.INSTANCE);
  }};
  final Logger logger = context.mock(Logger.class);
  final LoggingXMPPFailureReporter reporter = new LoggingXMPPFailureReporter(logger);

  @AfterClass
  public static void resetLogging() {
    LogManager.getLogManager().reset();
  }

  @Test public void
  writesMessageTranslationFailureToLog() {
    context.checking(new Expectations() {{
      oneOf(logger).severe("<auction id> "
                  + "Could not translate message \"bad message\" "
                  + "because \"java.lang.Exception: bad\"");
    }});
    reporter.cannotTranslateMessage("auction id", "bad message", new Exception("bad"));
  }
}
```

We pass this test with an implementation that just calls the logger with a string formatted from the inputs to cannotTranslateMessage().

 Breaking Our Own Rules?

We already wrote that we don't like to mock classes, and we go on about it further in Chapter 20. So, how come we're doing it here?

What we care about in this test is the rendering of the values into a failure message with a severity level. The class is very limited, just a shim above the logging layer, so we don't think it's worth introducing another level of indirection to define the logging role. As we wrote before, we also don't think it worth running against a real file since that introduces dependencies (and, even worse, asynchrony) not really relevant to the functionality we're developing. We also believe that, as part of the Java runtime, the logging API is unlikely to change.

So, just this once, as a special favor, setting no precedents, making no promises, we mock the Logger class. There are a couple more points worth making before we move on. First, we would not do this for a class that is internal to our code, because then we would be able write an interface to describe the role it's playing. Second, if the LoggingXMPPFailureReporter were to grow in complexity, we would probably find ourselves discovering a supporting message formatter class that could be tested directly.

Closing the Loop

Now we have the pieces in place to make the whole end-to-end test pass. We plug an instance of the LoggingXMPPFailureReporter into the XMPPAuctionHouse so that, via its XMPPAuctions, every AuctionMessageTranslator is constructed with the reporter. We also move the constant that defines the log file name there from AuctionLogDriver, and define a new XMPPAuctionException to gather up any failures within the package.

```
public class XMPPAuctionHouse implements AuctionHouse {
  public XMPPAuctionHouse(XMPPConnection connection)
    throws XMPPAuctionException
  {
    this.connection = connection;
    this.failureReporter = new LoggingXMPPFailureReporter(makeLogger());
  }
  public Auction auctionFor(String itemId) {
    return new XMPPAuction(connection, auctionId(itemId, connection), failureReporter);
  }
  private Logger makeLogger() throws XMPPAuctionException {
    Logger logger = Logger.getLogger(LOGGER_NAME);
    logger.setUseParentHandlers(false);
    logger.addHandler(simpleFileHandler());
    return logger;
  }
  private FileHandler simpleFileHandler() throws XMPPAuctionException {
    try {
      FileHandler handler = new FileHandler(LOG_FILE_NAME);
      handler.setFormatter(new SimpleFormatter());
      return handler;
    } catch (Exception e) {
      throw new XMPPAuctionException("Could not create logger FileHandler "
                              + getFullPath(LOG_FILE_NAME), e);
    }
  }
} [...]
```

The end-to-end test passes completely and we can cross another item off our list: Figure 19.2.

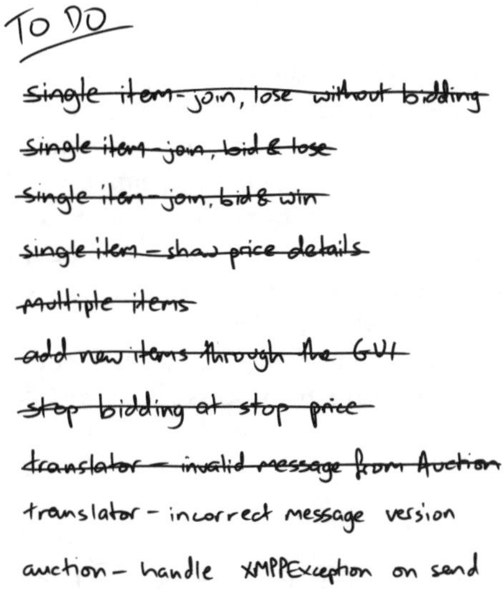

TO DO

~~single item—join, lose without bidding~~
~~single item—join, bid & lose~~
~~single item—join, bid & win~~
~~single item—show price details~~
~~multiple items~~
~~add new items through the GUI~~
~~stop bidding at stop price~~
~~translator — invalid message from Auction~~
translator — incorrect message version
auction — handle XMPPException on send

Figure 19.2 *The Sniper reports failed messages from an auction*

Observations

"Inverse Salami" Development

We hope that by now you're getting a sense of the rhythm of incrementally growing software, adding functionality in thin but coherent slices. For each new feature, write some tests that show what it should do, work through each of those tests changing just enough code to make it pass, restructure the code as needed either to open up space for new functionality or to reveal new concepts—then ship it. We discuss how this fits into the larger development picture in Chapter 5. In static languages, such as Java and C#, we can often use the compiler to help us navigate the chain of implementation dependencies: change the code to accept the new triggering event, see what breaks, fix that breakage, see what that change breaks in turn, and repeat the process until the functionality works.

The skill is in learning how to divide requirements up into incremental slices, always having something working, always adding just one more feature. The process should feel relentless—it just keeps moving. To make this work, we have to understand how to change the code incrementally and, critically, keep the code well structured so that we can take it wherever we need to go (and we don't know where that is yet). This is why the refactoring part of a test-driven development cycle is so critical—we always get into trouble when we don't keep up that side of the bargain.

Small Methods to Express Intent

We have a habit of writing helper methods to wrap up small amounts of code—for two reasons. First, this reduces the amount of syntactic noise in the calling code that languages like Java force upon us. For example, when we disconnect the Sniper, the translatorFor() method means we don't have to type "AuctionMessageTranslator" twice in the same line. Second, this gives a meaningful name to a structure that would not otherwise be obvious. For example, chatDisconnectorFor() describes what its anonymous class does and is less intrusive than defining a named inner class.

Our aim is to do what we can to make each level of code as readable and self-explanatory as possible, repeating the process all the way down until we actually have to use a Java construct.

Logging Is Also a Feature

We defined XMPPFailureReporter to package up failure reporting for the AuctionMessageTranslator. Many teams would regard this as overdesign and just write the log message in place. We think this would weaken the design by mixing levels (message translation and logging) in the same code.

We've seen many systems where logging has been added ad hoc by developers wherever they find a need. However, production logging is an external interface that should be driven by the requirements of those who will depend on it, not by the structure of the current implementation. We find that when we take the trouble to describe runtime reporting *in the caller's terms*, as we did with the XMPPFailureReporter, we end up with more useful logs. We also find that we end up with the logging infrastructure clearly isolated, rather than scattered throughout the code, which makes it easier to work with.

This topic is such a bugbear (for Steve at least) that we devote a whole section to it in Chapter 20.

Part IV

Sustainable Test-Driven Development

This part discusses the qualities we look for in test code that keep the development "habitable." We want to make sure the tests pull their weight by making them expressive, so that we can tell what's important when we read them and when they fail, and by making sure they don't become a maintenance drag themselves. We need to apply as much care and attention to the tests as we do to the production code, although the coding styles may differ. Difficulty in testing might imply that we need to change our test code, but often it's a hint that our design ideas are wrong and that we ought to change the production code.

We've written up these guidelines as separate chapters, but that has more to do with our need for a linear structure that will fit into a book. In practice, these qualities are all related to and support each other. Test-driven development combines testing, specification, and design into one holistic activity.[1]

---

1. For us, a sign of this interrelatedness was the difficulty we had in breaking up the material into coherent chapters.

Chapter 20

Listening to the Tests

You can see a lot just by observing.

—Yogi Berra

Introduction

Sometimes we find it difficult to write a test for some functionality we want to add to our code. In our experience, this usually means that our design can be improved—perhaps the class is too tightly coupled to its environment or does not have clear responsibilities. When this happens, we first check whether it's an opportunity to improve our code, before working around the design by making the test more complicated or using more sophisticated tools. We've found that the qualities that make an object easy to test also make our code responsive to change.

The trick is to let our tests *drive* our design (that's why it's called test-*driven* development). TDD is about testing code, verifying its externally visible qualities such as functionality and performance. TDD is *also* about feedback on the code's internal qualities: the coupling and cohesion of its classes, dependencies that are explicit or hidden, and effective information hiding—the qualities that keep the code maintainable.

With practice, we've become more sensitive to the rough edges in our tests, so we can use them for rapid feedback about the design. Now when we find a feature that's difficult to test, we don't just ask ourselves *how* to test it, but also *why* is it difficult to test.

In this chapter, we look at some common "test smells" that we've encountered and discuss what they might imply about the design of the code. There are two categories of test smell to consider. One is where the test itself is not well written—it may be unclear or brittle. Meszaros [Meszaros07] covers several such patterns in his "Test Smells" chapter. This chapter is concerned with the other category, where a test is highlighting that the target code is the problem. Meszaros has one pattern for this, called "Hard-to-Test Code." We've picked out some common cases that we've seen that are relevant to our approach to TDD.

I Need to Mock an Object I Can't Replace (without Magic)

Singletons Are Dependencies

One interpretation of reducing complexity in code is making commonly useful objects accessible through a global structure, usually implemented as a *singleton*. Any code that needs access to a feature can just refer to it by its global name instead of receiving it as an argument. Here's a common example:

```
Date now = new Date();
```

Under the covers, the constructor calls the singleton System and sets the new instance to the current time using System.currentTimeMillis(). This is a convenient technique, but it comes at a cost. Let's say we want to write a test like this:

```
@Test public void rejectsRequestsNotWithinTheSameDay() {
  receiver.acceptRequest(FIRST_REQUEST);
  // the next day
  assertFalse("too late now", receiver.acceptRequest(SECOND_REQUEST));
}
```

The implementation looks like this:

```
public boolean acceptRequest(Request request) {
  final Date now = new Date();
  if (dateOfFirstRequest == null) {
    dateOfFirstRequest = now;
  } else if (firstDateIsDifferentFrom(now)) {
    return false;
  }
  // process the request
  return true;
}
```

where dateOfFirstRequest is a field and firstDateIsDifferentFrom() is a helper method that hides the unpleasantness of working with the Java date library.

To test this timeout, we must either make the test wait overnight or do something clever (perhaps with aspects or byte-code manipulation) to intercept the constructor and return suitable Date values for the test. This difficulty in testing is a hint that we should change the code. To make the test easier, we need to control how Date objects are created, so we introduce a Clock and pass it into the Receiver. If we stub Clock, the test might look like this:

```
@Test public void rejectsRequestsNotWithinTheSameDay() {
  Receiver receiver = new Receiver(stubClock);
  stubClock.setNextDate(TODAY);
  receiver.acceptRequest(FIRST_REQUEST);

  stubClock.setNextDate(TOMORROW);
  assertFalse("too late now", receiver.acceptRequest(SECOND_REQUEST));
}
```

and the implementation like this:

```
public boolean acceptRequest(Request request) {
  final Date now = clock.now();
  if (dateOfFirstRequest == null) {
   dateOfFirstRequest = now;
  } else if (firstDateIsDifferentFrom(now)) {
   return false;
  }
  // process the request
  return true;
}
```

Now we can test the Receiver without any special tricks. More importantly, however, we've made it obvious that Receiver is dependent on time—we can't even create one without a Clock. Some argue that this is breaking encapsulation by exposing the internals of a Receiver—we should be able to just create an instance and not worry—but we've seen so many systems that are impossible to test because the developers did not isolate the concept of time. We *want* to know about this dependency, especially when the service is rolled out across the world, and New York and London start complaining about different results.

From Procedures to Objects

Having taken the trouble to introduce a Clock object, we start wondering if our code is missing a concept: date checking *in terms of our domain*. A Receiver doesn't need to know all the details of a calendar system, such as time zones and locales; it just need to know if the date has changed *for this application*. There's a clue in the fragment:

```
firstDateIsDifferentFrom(now)
```

which means that we've had to wrap up some date manipulation code in Receiver. It's the wrong object; that kind of work should be done in Clock. We write the test again:

```
@Test public void rejectsRequestsNotWithinTheSameDay() {
  Receiver receiver = new Receiver(clock);
  context.checking(new Expectations() {{
   allowing(clock).now(); will(returnValue(NOW));
   one(clock).dayHasChangedFrom(NOW); will(returnValue(false));
  }});

  receiver.acceptRequest(FIRST_REQUEST);
  assertFalse("too late now", receiver.acceptRequest(SECOND_REQUEST));
}
```

The implementation looks like this:

```
public boolean acceptRequest(Request request) {
  if (dateOfFirstRequest == null) {
    dateOfFirstRequest = clock.now();
  } else if (clock.dayHasChangedFrom(dateOfFirstRequest)) {
    return false;
  }
  // process the request
  return true;
}
```

This version of Receiver is more focused: it doesn't need to know how to distinguish one date from another and it only needs to get a date to set the first value. The Clock interface defines exactly those date services Receiver needs from its environment.

But we think we can push this further. Receiver only retains a date so that it can detect a change of day; perhaps we should delegate all the date functionality to another object which, for want of a better name, we'll call a SameDayChecker.

```
@Test public void rejectsRequestsOutsideAllowedPeriod() {
  Receiver receiver = new Receiver(sameDayChecker);
  context.checking(new Expectations() {{
    allowing(sameDayChecker).hasExpired(); will(returnValue(false));
  }});

  assertFalse("too late now", receiver.acceptRequest(REQUEST));
}
```

with an implementation like this:

```
public boolean acceptRequest(Request request) {
  if (sameDayChecker.hasExpired()) {
    return false;
  }
  // process the request
  return true;
}
```

All the logic about dates has been separated out from Receiver, which can concentrate on processing the request. With two objects, we can make sure that each behavior (date checking and request processing) is unit-tested cleanly.

Implicit Dependencies Are Still Dependencies

We can hide a dependency from the caller of a component by using a global value to bypass encapsulation, but that doesn't make the dependency go away—it just makes it inaccessible. For example, Steve once had to work with a Microsoft .Net library that couldn't be loaded without installing ActiveDirectory—which wasn't actually required for the features he wanted to use and which he couldn't install on his machine anyway. The library developer was trying to be helpful and to make it "just work," but the result was that Steve couldn't get it to work at all.

One goal of object orientation as a technique for structuring code is to make the boundaries of an object clearly visible. An object should only deal with values and instances that are either local—created and managed within its scope—or passed in explicitly, as we emphasized in "Context Independence" (page 54).

In the example above, the act of making date checking testable forced us to make the Receiver's requirements more explicit and to think more clearly about the domain.

Use the Same Techniques to Break Dependencies in Unit Tests as in Production Code

There are several frameworks available that use techniques such as manipulating class loaders or bytecodes to allow unit tests to break dependencies without changing the target code. As a rule, these are advanced techniques that most developers would not use when writing production code. Sometimes these tools really are necessary, but developers should be aware that they come with a hidden cost.

Unit-testing tools that let the programmer sidestep poor dependency management in the design waste a valuable source of feedback. When the developers eventually do need to address these design weaknesses to add some urgent feature, they will find it harder to do. The poor structure will have influenced other parts of the system that rely on it, and any understanding of the original intent will have evaporated. As with dirty pots and pans, it's easier to get the grease off before it's been baked in.

Logging Is a Feature

We have a more contentious example of working with objects that are hard to replace: *logging*. Take a look at these two lines of code:

```
log.error("Lost touch with Reality after " + timeout + "seconds");
log.trace("Distance traveled in the wilderness: " + distance);
```

These are two separate features that happen to share an implementation. Let us explain.

- *Support* logging (errors and info) is part of the user interface of the application. These messages are intended to be tracked by support staff, as well as perhaps system administrators and operators, to diagnose a failure or monitor the progress of the running system.

- *Diagnostic* logging (debug and trace) is infrastructure for programmers. These messages should not be turned on in production because they're intended to help the programmers understand what's going on inside the system they're developing.

Given this distinction, we should consider using different techniques for these two type of logging. Support logging should be test-driven from somebody's requirements, such as auditing or failure recovery. The tests will make sure we've thought about what each message is for and made sure it works. The tests will also protect us from breaking any tools and scripts that other people write to analyze these log messages. Diagnostic logging, on the other hand, is driven by the programmers' need for fine-grained tracking of what's happening in the system. It's scaffolding—so it probably doesn't need to be test-driven and the messages might not need to be as consistent as those for support logs. After all, didn't we just agree that these messages are not to be used in production?

Notification Rather Than Logging

To get back to the point of the chapter, writing unit tests against static global objects, including loggers, is clumsy. We have to either read from the file system or manage an extra appender object for testing; we have to remember to clean up afterwards so that tests don't interfere with each other *and* set the right level on the right logger. The noise in the test reminds us that our code is working at two levels: our domain and the logging infrastructure. Here's a common example of code with logging:

```
Location location = tracker.getCurrentLocation();
for (Filter filter : filters) {
  filter.selectFor(location);
  if (logger.isInfoEnabled()) {
    logger.info("Filter " + filter.getName() + ", " + filter.getDate()
                + " selected for " + location.getName()
                + ", is current: " + tracker.isCurrent(location));
  }
}
```

Notice the shift in vocabulary and style between the functional part of the loop and the (emphasized) logging part. The code is doing two things at once—something to do with locations and rendering support information—which breaks the single responsibility principle. Maybe we could do this instead:

```
Location location = tracker.getCurrentLocation();
for (Filter filter : filters) {
  filter.selectFor(location);
  support.notifyFiltering(tracker, location, filter);}
```

where the support object might be implemented by a logger, a message bus, pop-up windows, or whatever's appropriate; this detail is not relevant to the code at this level.

This code is also easier to test, as you saw in Chapter 19. We, not the logging framework, own the support object, so we can pass in a mock implementation at our convenience and keep it local to the test case. The other simplification is that now we're testing for objects, rather than formatted contents of a string. Of course, we will still need to write an implementation of support and some focused integration tests to go with it.

But That's Crazy Talk...

The idea of encapsulating support reporting sounds like over-design, but it's worth thinking about for a moment. It means we're writing code in terms of our *intent* (helping the support people) rather than *implementation* (logging), so it's more expressive. All the support reporting is handled in a few known places, so it's easier to be consistent about how things are reported and to encourage reuse. It can also help us structure and control our reporting in terms of the application domain, rather than in terms of Java packages. Finally, the act of writing a test for each report helps us avoid the "I don't know what to do with this exception, so I'll log it and carry on" syndrome, which leads to log bloat and production failures because we haven't handled obscure error conditions.

One objection we've heard is, "I can't pass in a logger for testing because I've got logging all over my domain objects. I'd have to pass one around everywhere." We think this is a test smell that is telling us that we haven't clarified our design enough. Perhaps some of our support logging should really be diagnostic logging, or we're logging more than we need because of something that we wrote when we hadn't yet understood the behavior. Most likely, there's still too much duplication in our domain code and we haven't yet found the "choke points" where most of the production logging should go.

So what about diagnostic logging? Is it disposable scaffolding that should be taken down once the job is done, or essential infrastructure that should be tested and maintained? That depends on the system, but once we've made the distinction we have more freedom to think about using different techniques for support and diagnostic logging. We might even decide that in-line code is the wrong technique for diagnostic logging because it interferes with the readability of the production code that matters. Perhaps we could weave in some aspects instead (since that's the canonical example of their use); perhaps not—but at least we've now clarified the choice.

One final data point. One of us once worked on a system where so much content was written to the logs that they had to be deleted after a week to fit on the disks. This made maintenance very difficult as the relevant logs were usually gone by the time a bug was assigned to be fixed. If they'd logged nothing at all, the system would have run faster with no loss of useful information.

Mocking Concrete Classes

One approach to interaction testing is to mock concrete classes rather than interfaces. The technique is to inherit from the class you want to mock and override the methods that will be called within the test, either manually or with any of the mocking frameworks. We think this is a technique that should be used only when you really have no other options.

Here's an example of mocking by hand. The test verifies that the music centre starts the CD player at the requested time. Assume that setting the schedule on a CdPlayer object involves triggering some behavior we don't want in the test, so we override scheduleToStartAt() and verify afterwards that we've called it with the right argument.

```
public class MusicCentreTest {
  @Test public void
  startsCdPlayerAtTimeRequested() {
    final MutableTime scheduledTime = new MutableTime();
    CdPlayer player = new CdPlayer() {
      @Override public void scheduleToStartAt(Time startTime) {
        scheduledTime.set(startTime);
      }
    }

    MusicCentre centre = new MusicCentre(player);
    centre.startMediaAt(LATER);

    assertEquals(LATER, scheduledTime.get());
  }
}
```

The problem with this approach is that it leaves the relationship between the CdPlayer and MusicCentre implicit. We hope we've made clear by now that our intention in test-*driven* development is to use mock objects to bring out relationships between objects. If we subclass, there's nothing in the domain code to make such a relationship visible—just methods on an object. This makes it harder to see if the service that supports this relationship might be relevant elsewhere, and we'll have to do the analysis again next time we work with the class. To make the point, here's a possible implementation of CdPlayer:

```
public class CdPlayer {
  public void scheduleToStartAt(Time startTime) { [...]
  public void stop() { [...]
  public void gotoTrack(int trackNumber) { [...]
  public void spinUpDisk() { [...]
  public void eject() { [...]
}
```

It turns out that our MusicCentre only uses the starting and stopping methods on the CdPlayer; the rest are used by some other part of the system. We would be overspecifying the MusicCentre by requiring it to talk to a CdPlayer; what it actually needs is a ScheduledDevice. Robert Martin made the point (back in 1996) in his *Interface Segregation Principle* that "Clients should not be forced to depend upon interfaces that they do not use," but that's exactly what we do when we mock a concrete class.

There's a more subtle but powerful reason for not mocking concrete classes. When we extract an interface as part of our test-driven development process, we have to think up a name to describe the relationship we've just discovered—in this example, the ScheduledDevice. We find that this makes us think harder about the domain and teases out concepts that we might otherwise miss. Once something has a name, we can talk about it.

"Break Glass in Case of Emergency"

There are a few occasions when we have to put up with this smell. The least un-acceptable situation is where we're working with legacy code that we control but can't change all at once. Alternatively, we might be working with third-party code that we can't change at all (see Chapter 8). We find that it's almost always better to write a veneer over an external library rather than mock it directly—but occasionally, it's just not worth it. We broke the rule with Logger in Chapter 19 but apologized a lot and felt bad about it. In any case, these are unfortunate but necessary compromises that we would try to work our way out of when possible. The longer we leave them in the code, the more likely it is that some brittleness in the design will cause us grief.

Above all, do not override a class' internal features—this just locks down your test to the quirks of the current implementation. Only override visible methods. This rule also prohibits exposing internal methods just to override them in a test. If you can't get to the structure you need, then the tests are telling you that it's time to break up the class into smaller, composable features.

Don't Mock Values

There's no point in writing mocks for values (which should be immutable any-way). Just create an instance and use it. For example, in this test Video holds details of a part of a show:

```
@Test public void sumsTotalRunningTime() {
  Show show = new Show();
  Video video1 = context.mock(Video.class); // Don't do this
  Video video2 = context.mock(Video.class);

  context.checking(new Expectations(){{
    one(video1).time(); will(returnValue(40));
    one(video2).time(); will(returnValue(23));
  }});

  show.add(video1);
  show.add(video2);
  assertEqual(63, show.runningTime())
}
```

Here, it's not worth creating an interface/implementation pair to control which time values are returned; just create instances with the appropriate times and use them.

There are a couple of heuristics for when a class is likely to be a value and so not worth mocking. First, its values are immutable—although that might also mean that it's an *adjustment* object, as described in "Object Peer Stereotypes" (page 52). Second, we can't think of a meaningful name for a class that would implement an interface for the type. If Video were an interface, what would we call its class other than VideoImpl or something equally vague? We discuss class naming in "Impl Classes Are Meaningless" on page 63.

If you're tempted to mock a value because it's too complicated to set up an instance, consider writing a builder; see Chapter 22.

Bloated Constructor

Sometimes during the TDD process, we end up with a constructor that has a long, unwieldy list of arguments. We most likely got there by adding the object's dependencies one at a time, and it got out of hand. This is not dreadful, since the process helped us sort out the design of the class and its neighbors, but now it's time to clean up. We will still need the functionality that depends on all the current constructor arguments, so we should see if there's any implicit structure there that we can tease out.

One possibility is that some of the arguments together define a concept that should be packaged up and replaced with a new object to represent it. Here's a small example:

```
public class MessageProcessor {
  public MessageProcessor(MessageUnpacker unpacker,
                          AuditTrail auditor,
                          CounterPartyFinder counterpartyFinder,
                          LocationFinder locationFinder,
                          DomesticNotifier domesticNotifier,
                          ImportedNotifier importedNotifier)
  {
    // set the fields here
  }

  public void onMessage(Message rawMessage) {
    UnpackedMessage unpacked = unpacker.unpack(rawMessage, counterpartyFinder);
    auditor.recordReceiptOf(unpacked);
    // some other activity here
    if (locationFinder.isDomestic(unpacked)) {
      domesticNotifier.notify(unpacked.asDomesticMessage());
    } else {
      importedNotifier.notify(unpacked.asImportedMessage())
    }
  }
}
```

Just the thought of writing expectations for all these objects makes us wilt, which suggests that things are too complicated. A first step is to notice that the unpacker and counterpartyFinder are always used together—they're fixed at construction and one calls the other. We can remove one argument by pushing the counterpartyFinder into the unpacker.

```
public class MessageProcessor {
  public MessageProcessor(MessageUnpacker unpacker,
                          AuditTrail auditor,
                          LocationFinder locationFinder,
                          DomesticNotifier domesticNotifier,
                          ImportedNotifier importedNotifier) { […]

  public void onMessage(Message rawMessage) {
    UnpackedMessage unpacked = unpacker.unpack(rawMessage);
    // etc.
  }
```

Then there's the triple of locationFinder and the two notifiers, which seem to go together. It might make sense to package them into a MessageDispatcher.

```
public class MessageProcessor {
  public MessageProcessor(MessageUnpacker unpacker,
                          AuditTrail auditor,
                          MessageDispatcher dispatcher) { […]

  public void onMessage(Message rawMessage) {
    UnpackedMessage unpacked = unpacker.unpack(rawMessage);
    auditor.recordReceiptOf(unpacked);
    // some other activity here
    dispatcher.dispatch(unpacked);
  }
}
```

Although we've forced this example to fit within a section, it shows that being sensitive to complexity in the tests can help us clarify our designs. Now we have a message handling object that clearly performs the usual three stages: receive, process, and forward. We've pulled out the message routing code (the MessageDispatcher), so the MessageProcessor has fewer responsibilities and we know where to put routing decisions when things get more complicated. You might also notice that this code is easier to unit-test.

When extracting implicit components, we start by looking for two conditions: arguments that are always used together in the class, and those that have the same lifetime. Once we've found a coincidence, we have the harder task of finding a good name that explains the concept.

As an aside, one sign that a design is developing nicely is that this kind of change is easy to integrate. All we have to do is find where the MessageProcessor is created and change this:

```
messageProcessor =
  new MessageProcessor(new XmlMessageUnpacker(),
                       auditor, counterpartyFinder,
                       locationFinder, domesticNotifier,
                       importedNotifier);
```

to this:

```
messageProcessor =
  new MessageProcessor(new XmlMessageUnpacker(counterpartyFinder),
                       auditor,
                       new MessageDispatcher(
                         locationFinder,
                         domesticNotifier, importedNotifier));
```

Later we can reduce the syntax noise by extracting out the creation of the `MessageDispatcher`.

Confused Object

Another diagnosis for a "bloated constructor" might be that the object itself is too large because it has too many responsibilities. For example,

```
public class Handset {
  public Handset(Network network, Camera camera, Display display,
              DataNetwork dataNetwork, AddressBook addressBook,
              Storage storage, Tuner tuner, …)
  {
    // set the fields here
  }
  public void placeCallTo(DirectoryNumber number) {
    network.openVoiceCallTo(number);
  }
  public void takePicture() {
    Frame frame = storage.allocateNewFrame();
    camera.takePictureInto(frame);
    display.showPicture(frame);
  }
  public void showWebPage(URL url) {
    display.renderHtml(dataNetwork.retrievePage(url));
  }
  public void showAddress(SearchTerm searchTerm) {
    display.showAddress(addressBook.findAddress(searchTerm));
  }
  public void playRadio(Frequency frequency) {
    tuner.tuneTo(frequency);
    tuner.play();
  }
  // and so on
}
```

Like our mobile phones, this class has several unrelated responsibilities which force it to pull in many dependencies. And, like our phones, the class is confusing to use because unrelated features interfere with each other. We're prepared to put up with these compromises in a handset because we don't have enough pockets for all the devices it includes, but that doesn't apply to code. This class should be broken up; Michael Feathers describes some techniques for doing so in Chapter 20 of [Feathers04].

An associated smell for this kind of class is that its test suite will look confused too. The tests for its various features will have no relationship with each other, so we'll be able to make major changes in one area without touching others. If we can break up the test class into slices that don't share anything, it might be best to go ahead and slice up the object too.

Too Many Dependencies

A third diagnosis for a bloated constructor might be that not all of the arguments are *dependencies*, one of the peer stereotypes we defined in "Object Peer Stereotypes" (page 52). As discussed in that section, we insist on dependencies being passed in to the constructor, but notifications and adjustments can be set to defaults and reconfigured later. When a constructor is too large, and we don't believe there's an implicit new type amongst the arguments, we can use more default values and only overwrite them for particular test cases.

Here's an example—it's not quite bad enough to need fixing, but it'll do to make the point. The application is a racing game; players can try out different configurations of car and driving style to see which one wins.[1] A RacingCar represents a competitor within a race:

```java
public class RacingCar {
  private final Track track;
  private Tyres tyres;
  private Suspension suspension;
  private Wing frontWing;
  private Wing backWing;
  private double fuelLoad;
  private CarListener listener;
  private DrivingStrategy driver;
  public RacingCar(Track track, DrivingStrategy driver, Tyres tyres,
                   Suspension suspension, Wing frontWing, Wing backWing,
                   double fuelLoad, CarListener listener)
  {
    this.track = track;
    this.driver = driver;
    this.tyres = tyres;
    this.suspension = suspension;
    this.frontWing = frontWing;
    this.backWing = backWing;
    this.fuelLoad = fuelLoad;
    this.listener = listener;
  }
}
```

---

1. Nat once worked in a job that involved following the Formula One circuit.

242

It turns out that track is the only dependency of a RacingCar; the hint is that it's the only field that's final. The listener is a notification, and everything else is an adjustment; all of these can be modified by the user before or during the race. Here's a reworked constructor:

```
public class RacingCar {
  private final Track track;

  private DrivingStrategy driver = DriverTypes.borderlineAggressiveDriving();
  private Tyres tyres = TyreTypes.mediumSlicks();
  private Suspension suspension = SuspensionTypes.mediumStiffness();
  private Wing frontWing = WingTypes.mediumDownforce();
  private Wing backWing = WingTypes.mediumDownforce();
  private double fuelLoad = 0.5;

  private CarListener listener = CarListener.NONE;

  public RacingCar(Track track) {
    this.track = track;
  }

  public void setSuspension(Suspension suspension) { [...]
  public void setTyres(Tyres tyres) { [...]
  public void setEngine(Engine engine) { [...]

  public void setListener(CarListener listener) { [...]
}
```

Now we've initialized these peers to common defaults; the user can configure them later through the user interface, and we can configure them in our unit tests. We've initialized the listener to a null object, again this can be changed later by the object's environment.

Too Many Expectations

When a test has too many expectations, it's hard to see what's important and what's really under test. For example, here's a test:

```
@Test public void
decidesCasesWhenFirstPartyIsReady() {
  context.checking(new Expectations(){{
    one(firstPart).isReady(); will(returnValue(true));
    one(organizer).getAdjudicator(); will(returnValue(adjudicator));
    one(adjudicator).findCase(firstParty, issue); will(returnValue(case));
    one(thirdParty).proceedWith(case);
  }});

  claimsProcessor.adjudicateIfReady(thirdParty, issue);
}
```

that might be implemented like this:

```
public void adjudicateIfReady(ThirdParty thirdParty, Issue issue) {
  if (firstParty.isReady()) {
    Adjudicator adjudicator = organization.getAdjudicator();
    Case case = adjudicator.findCase(firstParty, issue);
    thirdParty.proceedWith(case);
  } else{
    thirdParty.adjourn();
  }
}
```

What makes the test hard to read is that everything is an expectation, so everything looks equally important. We can't tell what's significant and what's just there to get through the test.

In fact, if we look at all the methods we call, there are only two that have any side effects outside this class: `thirdParty.proceedWith()` and `thirdParty.adjourn()`; it would be an error to call these more than once. All the other methods are queries; we can call `organization.getAdjudicator()` repeatedly without breaking any behavior. `adjudicator.findCase()` might go either way, but it happens to be a lookup so it has no side effects.

We can make our intentions clearer by distinguishing between *stubs*, simulations of real behavior that help us get the test to pass, and *expectations*, assertions we want to make about how an object interacts with its neighbors. There's a longer discussion of this distinction in "Allowances and Expectations" (page 277). Reworking the test, we get:

```
@Test public void decidesCasesWhenFirstPartyIsReady() {
  context.checking(new Expectations(){{
    allowing(firstPart).isReady(); will(returnValue(true));
    allowing(organizer).getAdjudicator(); will(returnValue(adjudicator));
    allowing(adjudicator).findCase(firstParty, issue); will(returnValue(case));

    one(thirdParty).proceedWith(case);
  }});

  claimsProcessor.adjudicateIfReady(thirdParty, issue);
}
```

which is more explicit about how we expect the object to change the world around it.

 ## Write Few Expectations

A colleague, Romilly Cocking, when he first started working with us, was surprised by how few expectations we usually write in a unit test. Just like "everyone" has now learned to avoid too many assertions in a test, we try to avoid too many expectations. If we have more than a few, then either we're trying to test too large a unit, or we're locking down too many of the object's interactions.

Special Bonus Prize

We always have problems coming up with good examples. There's actually a better improvement to this code, which is to notice that we've pulled out a chain of objects to get to the case object, exposing dependencies that aren't relevant here. Instead, we should have told the nearest object to do the work for us, like this:

```java
public void adjudicateIfReady(ThirdParty thirdParty, Issue issue) {
  if (firstParty.isReady()) {
    organization.adjudicateBetween(firstParty, thirdParty, issue);
  } else {
    thirdParty.adjourn();
  }
}
```

or, possibly,

```java
public void adjudicateIfReady(ThirdParty thirdParty, Issue issue) {
  if (firstParty.isReady()) {
    thirdParty.startAdjudication(organization, firstParty, issue);
  } else{
    thirdParty.adjourn();
  }
}
```

which looks more balanced. If you spotted this, we award you a Moment of Smugness™ to be exercised at your convenience.

What the Tests Will Tell Us (If We're Listening)

We've found these benefits from learning to listen to test smells:

Keep knowledge local

Some of the test smells we've identified, such as needing "magic" to create mocks, are to do with knowledge leaking between components. If we can keep knowledge local to an object (either internal or passed in), then its implementation is independent of its context; we can safely move it wherever we like. Do this consistently and your application, built out of pluggable components, will be easy to change.

If it's explicit, we can name it

One reason why we don't like mocking concrete classes is that we like to have names for the relationships *between* objects as well the objects themselves. As the legends say, if we have something's true name, we can control it. If we can see it, we have a better chance of finding its other uses and so reducing duplication.

More names mean more domain information

We find that when we emphasize how objects communicate, rather than what they are, we end up with types and roles defined more in terms of the domain than of the implementation. This might be because we have a greater number of smaller abstractions, which gets us further away from the underlying language. Somehow we seem to get more domain vocabulary into the code.

Pass behavior rather than data

We find that by applying "Tell, Don't Ask" consistently, we end up with a coding style where we tend to pass behavior (in the form of callbacks) into the system instead of pulling values up through the stack. For example, in Chapter 17, we introduced a `SniperCollector` that responds when told about a new `Sniper`. Passing this listener into the Sniper creation code gives us better information hiding than if we'd exposed a collection to be added to. More precise interfaces give us better information-hiding and clearer abstractions.

We care about keeping the tests and code clean as we go, because it helps to ensure that we understand our domain and reduces the risk of being unable to cope when a new requirement triggers changes to the design. It's much easier to keep a codebase clean than to recover from a mess. Once a codebase starts to "rot," the developers will be under pressure to botch the code to get the next job done. It doesn't take many such episodes to dissipate a team's good intentions.

We once had a posting to the jMock user list that included this comment:

I was involved in a project recently where jMock was used quite heavily. Looking back, here's what I found:

1. The unit tests were at times unreadable (no idea what they were doing).

2. Some tests classes would reach 500 lines in addition to inheriting an abstract class which also would have up to 500 lines.

3. Refactoring would lead to massive changes in test code.

A unit test shouldn't be 1000 lines long! It should focus on at most a few classes and should not need to create a large fixture or perform lots of preparation just to get the objects into a state where the target feature can be exercised. Such tests are hard to understand—there's just so much to remember when reading them. And, of course, they're brittle, all the objects in play are too tightly coupled and too difficult to set to the state the test requires.

Test-driven development can be unforgiving. Poor quality tests can slow development to a crawl, and poor internal quality of the system being tested will result in poor quality tests. By being alert to the internal quality feedback we get from writing tests, we can nip this problem in the bud, long before our unit tests approach 1000 lines of code, and end up with tests we can live with. Conversely, making an effort to write tests that are readable and flexible gives us more feedback about the internal quality of the code we are testing. We end up with tests that help, rather than hinder, continued development.

Chapter 21

Test Readability

> *To design is to communicate clearly by whatever means you can control or master.*
>
> —Milton Glaser

Introduction

Teams that adopt TDD usually see an early boost in productivity because the tests let them add features with confidence and catch errors immediately. For some teams, the pace then slows down as the tests themselves become a maintenance burden. For TDD to be sustainable, the tests must do more than verify the behavior of the code; they must also express that behavior clearly—they must be *readable*. This matters for the same reason that code readability matters: every time the developers have to stop and puzzle through a test to figure out what it means, they have less time left to spend on creating new features, and the team velocity drops.

We take as much care about writing our test code as about production code, but with differences in style since the two types of code serve different purposes. Test code should describe *what* the production code does. That means that it tends to be concrete about the values it uses as examples of what results to expect, but abstract about how the code works. Production code, on the other hand, tends to be abstract about the values it operates on but concrete about how it gets the job done. Similarly, when writing production code, we have to consider how we will compose our objects to make up a working system, and manage their dependencies carefully. Test code, on the other hand, is at the end of the dependency chain, so it's more important for it to express the intention of its target code than to plug into a web of other objects. We want our test code to read like a declarative description of what is being tested.

In this chapter, we'll describe some practices that we've found helpful to keep our tests readable and expressive.

247

Could Do Better[1]

We've seen many unit test suites that could be much more effective given a little extra attention. They have too many "test smells" of the kind cataloged in [Meszaros07], as well as in our own Chapters 20 and 24. When cleaning up tests, or just trying to write new ones, the readability problems we watch out for are:

- Test names that do not clearly describe the point of each test case and its differences from the other test cases;

- Single test cases that seem to be exercising multiple features;

- Tests with different structure, so the reader cannot skim-read them to understand their intention;

- Tests with lots of code for setting up and handling exceptions, which buries their essential logic; and,

- Tests that use literal values ("magic numbers") but are not clear about what, if anything, is significant about those values.

Test Names Describe Features

The name of the test should be the first clue for a developer to understand what is being tested and how the target object is supposed to behave.

Not every team we've worked with follows this principle. Some naive developers use names that don't mean anything at all:

```
public class TargetObjectTest {
  @Test public void test1() { […]
  @Test public void test2() { […]
  @Test public void test3() { […]
```

We don't see many of these nowadays; the world has moved on. A common approach is to name a test after the method it's exercising:

```
public class TargetObjectTest {
  @Test public void isReady() { […]
  @Test public void choose() { […]
  @Test public void choose1() { […]

public class TargetObject  {
  public void isReady() { […]
  public void choose(Picker picker) { […]
```

perhaps with multiple tests for different paths through the same method.

---

1. This is (or was) a common phrase in UK school reports for children whose schoolwork isn't as good as it could be.

At best, such names duplicate the information a developer could get just by looking at the target class; they break the "Don't Repeat Yourself" principle [Hunt99]. We don't need to know that `TargetObject` has a `choose()` method—we need to know what the object does in different situations, what the method is *for*.

A better alternative is to name tests in terms of the features that the target object provides. We use a *TestDox* convention (invented by Chris Stevenson) where each test name reads like a sentence, with the target class as the implicit subject. For example,

- A `List` holds items in the order they were added.

- A `List` can hold multiple references to the same item.

- A `List` throws an exception when removing an item it doesn't hold.

We can translate these directly to method names:

```
public class ListTests {
  @Test public void holdsItemsInTheOrderTheyWereAdded() { […] }
  @Test public void canHoldMultipleReferencesToTheSameItem() { […] }
  @Test public void throwsAnExceptionWhenRemovingAnItemItDoesntHold() { […] }
```

These names can be as long as we like because they're only called through reflection—we never have to type them in to call them.

The point of the convention is to encourage the developer to think in terms of what the target object *does*, not what it *is*. It's also very compatible with our incremental approach of adding a feature at a time to an existing codebase. It gives us a consistent style of naming all the way from user stories, through tasks and acceptance tests, to unit tests—as you saw in Part III.

As a matter of style, the test name should say something about the expected result, the action on the object, and the motivation for the scenario. For example, if we were testing a `ConnectionMonitor` class, then

```
pollsTheServersMonitoringPort()
```

doesn't tell us enough: why does it poll, what happens when it gets a result? On the other hand,

```
notifiesListenersThatServerIsUnavailableWhenCannotConnectToItsMonitoringPort()
```

explains both the scenario and the expected behavior. We'll show later how this style of naming maps onto our standard test structures.

Test Name First or Last?

We've noticed that some developers start with a placeholder name, fill out the body of the test, and then decide what to call it. Others (such as Steve) like to decide the test name first, to clarify their intentions, before writing any test code. Both approaches work as long as the developer follows through and makes sure that the test is, in the end, consistent and expressive.

The TestDox format fulfills the early promise of TDD—that the tests should act as documentation for the code. There are tools and IDE plug-ins that unpack the "camel case" method names and link them to the class under test, such as the TestDox plug-in for the IntelliJ IDE; Figure 21.1 shows the automatic documentation for a KeyboardLayout class.

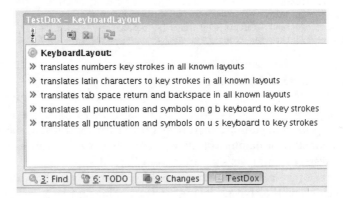

Figure 21.1   *The TestDox IntelliJ plug-in*

Regularly Read Documentation Generated from Tests

We find that such generated documentation gives us a fresh perspective on the test names, highlighting the problems we're too close to the code to see. For example, when generating the screenshot for Figure 21.1, Nat noticed that the name of the first test is unclear—it should be "translates numbers *to* key strokes in all known layouts."

We make an effort to at least skim-read the documentation regularly during development.

Canonical Test Structure

We find that if we write our tests in a standard form, they're easier to understand. We can skim-read to find expectations and assertions quickly and see how they relate to the code under test. If we're finding it difficult to write a test in a standard form, that's often a hint that the code is too complicated or that we haven't quite clarified our ideas.

The most common form for a test is:

1. *Setup:* prepare the context of the test, the environment in which the target code will run;

2. *Execute:* call the target code, triggering the tested behavior;

3. *Verify:* check for a visible effect that we expect from the behavior; and,

4. *Teardown:* clean up any leftover state that might corrupt other tests.

There are other versions of this form, such as "Arrange, Act, Assert," which collapse some of the stages.

For example:

```java
public class StringTemplateTest {
  @Test public void expandsMacrosSurroundedWithBraces() {
    StringTemplate template = new StringTemplate("{a}{b}"); // Setup
    HashMap<String,Object> macros = new HashMap<String,Object>();
    macros.put("a", "A");
    macros.put("b", "B");

    String expanded = template.expand(macros);             // Execute
    assertThat(expanded, equalTo("AB"));                   // Assert
  }                                                        // No Teardown
}
```

Tests that set expectations on mock objects use a variant of this structure where some of the assertions are declared before the execute stage and are implicitly checked afterwards—for example, in `LoggingXMPPFailureReporterTest` from Chapter 19:

```java
@RunWith(JMock.class)
public class LoggingXMPPFailureReporterTest {
  private final Mockery context = new Mockery() {{  // Setup
   setImposteriser(ClassImposteriser.INSTANCE);
  }};

  final Logger logger = context.mock(Logger.class);
  final LoggingXMPPFailureReporter reporter = new LoggingXMPPFailureReporter(logger);
```

```
@Test public void writesMessageTranslationFailureToLog() {
  Exception exception = new Exception("an exception");
  context.checking(new Expectations() {{           // Expect
    oneOf(logger).severe( expected log message here);
  }});

  reporter.cannotTranslateMessage("auction id",   // Execute
                           "failed message", exception);
  // implicitly check expectations are satisfied  // Assert
}

@AfterClass public static void resetLogging() {  // Teardown
  LogManager.getLogManager().reset();
}
}
```

Write Tests Backwards

Although we stick to a canonical format for test code, we don't necessarily write tests from top to bottom. What we often do is: write the test name, which helps us decide what we want to achieve; write the call to the target code, which is the entry point for the feature; write the expectations and assertions, so we know what effects the feature should have; and, write the setup and teardown to define the context for the test. Of course, there may be some blurring of these steps to help the compiler, but this sequence reflects how we tend to think through a new unit test. Then we run it and watch it fail.

How Many Assertions in a Test Method?

Some TDD practitioners suggest that each test should only contain one expectation or assertion. This is useful as a training rule when learning TDD, to avoid asserting everything the developer can think of, but we don't find it practical. A better rule is to think of one coherent feature per test, which might be represented by up to a handful of assertions. If a single test seems to be making assertions about different features of a target object, it might be worth splitting up. Once again, expressiveness is the key: as a reader of this test, can I figure out what's significant?

Streamline the Test Code

All code should emphasize "what" it does over "how," including test code; the more implementation detail is included in a test method, the harder it is for the reader to understand what's important. We try to move everything out of the test method that doesn't contribute to the description, in domain terms, of the feature being exercised. Sometimes that involves restructuring the code, sometimes just ignoring the syntax noise.

Use Structure to Explain

As you'll have seen throughout Part III, we make a point of following "Small Methods to Express Intent" (page 226), even to the extent of writing a tiny method like `translatorFor()` just to reduce the Java syntax noise. This fits nicely into the Hamcrest approach, where the `assertThat()` and jMock expectation syntaxes are designed to allow developers to compose small features into a (more or less) readable description of an assertion. For example,

```
assertThat(instruments, hasItem(instrumentWithPrice(greaterThan(81))));
```

checks whether the collection `instruments` has at least one `Instrument` with a `strikePrice` property greater than 81. The assertion line expresses our intent, the helper method creates a matcher that checks the value:

```
private Matcher<? super Instrument>
instrumentWithPrice(Matcher<? super Integer> priceMatcher) {
  return new FeatureMatcher<Instrument, Integer>(
              priceMatcher, "instrument at price", "price") {
    @Override protected Integer featureValueOf(Instrument actual) {
      return actual.getStrikePrice();
    }
  };
}
```

This may create more program text in the end, but we're prioritizing expressiveness over minimizing the source lines.

Use Structure to Share

We also extract common features into methods that can be shared between tests for setting up values, tearing down state, making assertions, and occasionally triggering the event. For example, in Chapter 19, we exploited jMock's facility for setting multiple expectation blocks to write a `expectSniperToFailWhenItIs()` method that wraps up repeated behavior behind a descriptive name.

The only caution with factoring out test structure is that, as we said in the introduction to this chapter, we have to be careful not to make a test so abstract that we cannot see what it does any more. Our highest concern is making the test describe what the target code does, so we refactor enough to be able to see its flow, but we don't always refactor as hard as we would for production code.

Accentuate the Positive

We only catch exceptions in a test if we want to assert something about them. We sometimes see tests like this:

```java
@Test public void expandsMacrosSurroundedWithBraces() {
  StringTemplate template = new StringTemplate("{a}{b}");

  try {
    String expanded = template.expand(macros);
    assertThat(expanded, equalTo("AB"));
  } catch (TemplateFormatException e) {
    fail("Template failed: " + e);
  }
}
```

If this test is intended to pass, then converting the exception actually drops information from the stack trace. The simplest thing to do is to let the exception propagate for the test runtime to catch. We can add arbitrary exceptions to the test method signature because it's only called by reflection. This removes at least half the lines of the test, and we can compact it further to be:

```java
@Test public void expandsMacrosSurroundedWithBraces() throws Exception {
  assertThat(new StringTemplate("{a}{b}").expand(macros),
             equalTo("AB"));
}
```

which tells us just what is supposed to happen and ignores everything else.

Delegate to Subordinate Objects

Sometimes helper methods aren't enough and we need helper *objects* to support the tests. We saw this in the test rig we built in Chapter 11. We developed the `ApplicationRunner`, `AuctionSniperDriver`, and `FakeAuctionServer` classes so we could write tests in terms of auctions and Snipers, not in terms of Swing and messaging.

A more common technique is to write *test data builders* to build up complex data structures with just the appropriate values for a test; see Chapter 22 for more detail. Again, the point is to include in the test just the values that are relevant, so that the reader can understand the intent; everything else can be defaulted.

There are two approaches to writing subordinate objects. In Chapter 11 we started by writing the test we wanted to see and then filling in the supporting objects: start from a statement of the problem and see where it goes. The alternative is to write the code directly in the tests, and then refactor out any clusters of behavior. This is the origin of the WindowLicker framework, which started out as helper code in JUnit tests for interacting with the Swing event dispatcher and eventually grew into a separate project.

Assertions and Expectations

The assertions and expectations of a test should communicate *precisely* what matters in the behavior of the target code. We regularly see code where tests assert too much detail, which makes them difficult to read and brittle when things change; we discuss what this might mean in "Too Many Expectations" (page 242).

For the expectations and assertions we write, we try to keep them as narrowly defined as possible. For example, in the "instrument with price" assertion above, we check only the strike price and ignore the rest of the values as irrelevant in that test. In other cases, we're not interested in all of the arguments to a method, so we ignore them in the expectation. In Chapter 19, we define an expectation that says that we care about the Sniper identifier and message, but that any RuntimeException object will do for the third argument:

```
oneOf(failureReporter).cannotTranslateMessage(
                        with(SNIPER_ID), with(badMessage),
                        with(any(RuntimeException.class)));
```

If you learned about pre- and postconditions in college, this is when that training will come in useful.

Finally, a word of caution on assertFalse(). The combination of the failure message and negation makes it easy to read this as meaning that the two dates should *not* be different:

```
assertFalse("end date", first.endDate().equals(second.endDate()));
```

We could use assertTrue() and add a "!" to the result but, again, the single character is easy to miss. That's why we prefer to use matchers to make the code more explicit:

```
assertThat("end date", first.endDate(), not(equalTo(second.endDate())));
```

which also has the advantage of showing the actual date received in the failure report:

```
java.lang.AssertionError: end date
Expected: not <Thu Jan 01 02:34:38 GMT 1970>
     but: was <Thu Jan 01 02:34:38 GMT 1970>
```

Literals and Variables

One last point. As we wrote in the introduction to this chapter, test code tends to be more concrete than production code, which means it has more literal values. Literal values without explanation can be difficult to understand because the programmer has to interpret whether a particular value is significant (e.g. just outside the allowed range) or just an arbitrary placeholder to trace behavior (e.g. should be doubled and passed on to a peer). A literal value does not describe its role, although there are some techniques for doing so that we will show in Chapter 23

One solution is to allocate literal values to variables and constants with names that describe their function. For example, in Chapter 12 we declared

```
public static final Chat UNUSED_CHAT = null;
```

to show that we were using `null` to represent an argument that was unused in the target code. We weren't expecting the code to receive `null` in production, but it turns out that we don't care and it makes testing easier. Similarly, a team might develop conventions for naming common values, such as:

```
public final static INVALID_ID = 666;
```

We name variables to show the roles these values or objects play in the test and their relationships to the target object.

Chapter 22

Constructing Complex Test Data

Many attempts to communicate are nullified by saying too much.

—Robert Greenleaf

Introduction

If we are strict about our use of constructors and immutable value objects, constructing objects in tests can be a chore. In production code, we construct such objects in relatively few places and all the required values are available to hand from, for example, user input, a database query, or a received message. In tests, however, we have to provide all the constructor arguments every time we want to create an object:

```
@Test public void chargesCustomerForTotalCostOfAllOrderedItems() {
  Order order = new Order(
      new Customer("Sherlock Holmes",
          new Address("221b Baker Street",
                      "London",
                      new PostCode("NW1", "3RX"))));
  order.addLine(new OrderLine("Deerstalker Hat", 1));
  order.addLine(new OrderLine("Tweed Cape", 1));
  [...]
}
```

The code to create all these objects makes the tests hard to read, filling them with information that doesn't contribute to the behavior being tested. It also makes tests brittle, as changes to the constructor arguments or the structure of the objects will break many tests. The *object mother* pattern [Schuh01] is one attempt to avoid this problem. An object mother is a class that contains a number of factory methods [Gamma94] that create objects for use in tests. For example, we could write an object mother for orders:

```
Order order = ExampleOrders.newDeerstalkerAndCapeOrder();
```

An object mother makes tests more readable by packaging up the code that creates new object structures and giving it a name. It also helps with maintenance since its features can be reused between tests. On the other hand, the object mother pattern does not cope well with variation in the test data—every minor difference requires a new factory method:

```
Order order1 = ExampleOrders.newDeerstalkerAndCapeAndSwordstickOrder();
Order order2 = ExampleOrders.newDeerstalkerAndBootsOrder();
[...]
```

Over time, an object mother may itself become too messy to support, either full of duplicated code or refactored into an infinity of fine-grained methods.

Test Data Builders

Another solution is to use the *builder pattern* to build instances in tests, most often for values. For a class that requires complex setup, we create a *test data builder* that has a field for each constructor parameter, initialized to a safe value. The builder has "chainable" public methods for overwriting the values in its fields and, by convention, a build() method that is called last to create a new instance of the target object from the field values.[1] An optional refinement is to add a static factory method for the builder itself so that it's clearer in the test what is being built. For example, a builder for Order objects might look like:

```java
public class OrderBuilder {
  private Customer customer = new CustomerBuilder().build();
  private List<OrderLine> lines = new ArrayList<OrderLine>();
  private BigDecimal discountRate = BigDecimal.ZERO;

  public static OrderBuilder anOrder() {
    return new OrderBuilder();
  }
  public OrderBuilder withCustomer(Customer customer) {
    this.customer = customer;
    return this;
  }
  public OrderBuilder withOrderLines(OrderLines lines) {
    this.lines = lines;
    return this;
  }
  public OrderBuilder withDiscount(BigDecimal discountRate) {
    this.discountRate = discountRate;
    return this;
  }
  public Order build() {
    Order order = new Order(customer);
    for (OrderLine line : lines) order.addLine(line);
      order.setDiscountRate(discountRate);
    }
  }
}
```

---

1. This pattern is essentially the same as a Smalltalk cascade.

Tests that just need an `Order` object and are not concerned with its contents can create one in a single line:

```
Order order = new OrderBuilder().build();
```

Tests that need particular values within an object can specify just those values that are relevant and use defaults for the rest. This makes the test more expressive because it includes only the values that are relevant to the expected results. For example, if a test needed an `Order` for a `Customer` with no postcode, we would write:

```
new OrderBuilder()
  .fromCustomer(
    new CustomerBuilder()
      .withAddress(new AddressBuilder().withNoPostcode().build())
      .build())
  .build();
```

We find that test data builders help keep tests expressive and resilient to change. First, they wrap up most of the syntax noise when creating new objects. Second, they make the default case simple, and special cases not much more complicated. Third, they protect the test against changes in the structure of its objects. If we add an argument to a constructor, then all we have to change is the relevant builder and those tests that drove the need for the new argument.

A final benefit is that we can write test code that's easier to read and spot errors in, because each builder method identifies the purpose of its parameter. For example, in this code it's not obvious that "London" has been passed in as the second street line rather than the city name:

```
TestAddresses.newAddress("221b Baker Street", "London", "NW1 6XE");
```

A test data builder makes the mistake more obvious:

```
new AddressBuilder()
  .withStreet("221b Baker Street")
  .withStreet2("London")
  .withPostCode("NW1 6XE")
  .build();
```

Creating Similar Objects

We can use builders when we need to create multiple similar objects. The most obvious approach is to create a new builder for each new object, but this leads to duplication and makes the test code harder to work with. For example, these two orders are identical apart from the discount. If we didn't highlight the difference, it would be difficult to find:

```
Order orderWithSmallDiscount = new OrderBuilder()
  .withLine("Deerstalker Hat", 1)
  .withLine("Tweed Cape", 1)
  .withDiscount(0.10)
  .build();

Order orderWithLargeDiscount = new OrderBuilder()
  .withLine("Deerstalker Hat", 1)
  .withLine("Tweed Cape", 1)
  .withDiscount(0.25)
  .build();
```

Instead, we can initialize a single builder with the common state and then, for each object to be built, define the differing values and call its build() method:

```
OrderBuilder hatAndCape = new OrderBuilder()
  .withLine("Deerstalker Hat", 1)
  .withLine("Tweed Cape", 1);

Order orderWithSmallDiscount = hatAndCape.withDiscount(0.10).build();
Order orderWithLargeDiscount = hatAndCape.withDiscount(0.25).build();
```

This produces a more focused test with less code. We can name the builder after the features that are common, and the domain objects after their differences.

This technique works best if the objects differ by the same fields. If the objects vary by different fields, each build() will pick up the changes from the previous uses. For example, it's not obvious in this code that orderWithGiftVoucher will carry the 10% discount as well as a gift voucher:

```
Order orderWithDiscount = hatAndCape.withDiscount(0.10).build();
Order orderWithGiftVoucher = hatAndCape.withGiftVoucher("abc").build();
```

To avoid this problem, we could add a copy constructor or a method that duplicates the state from another builder:

```
Order orderWithDiscount = new OrderBuilder(hatAndCape)
  .withDiscount(0.10)
  .build();

Order orderWithGiftVoucher = new OrderBuilder(hatAndCape)
  .withGiftVoucher("abc")
  .build();
```

Alternatively, we could add a factory method that returns a copy of the builder with its current state:

```
Order orderWithDiscount = hatAndCape.but().withDiscount(0.10).build();
Order orderWithGiftVoucher = hatAndCape.but().withGiftVoucher("abc").build();
```

For complex setups, the safest option is to make the "with" methods functional and have each one return a new copy of the builder instead of itself.

Combining Builders

Where a test data builder for an object uses other "built" objects, we can pass in those builders as arguments rather than their objects. This will simplify the test code by removing the build() methods. The result is easier to read because it emphasizes the important information—*what* is being built—rather than the mechanics of building it. For example, this code builds an order with no postcode, but it's dominated by the builder infrastructure:

```
Order orderWithNoPostcode = new OrderBuilder()
  .fromCustomer(
    new CustomerBuilder()
        .withAddress(new AddressBuilder().withNoPostcode().build())
        .build())
    .build();
```

We can remove much of the noise by passing around builders:

```
Order order = new OrderBuilder()
  .fromCustomer(
    new CustomerBuilder()
      .withAddress(new AddressBuilder().withNoPostcode())))
  .build();
```

Emphasizing the Domain Model with Factory Methods

We can further reduce the noise in the test code by wrapping up the construction of the builders in factory methods:

```
Order order =
  anOrder().fromCustomer(
            aCustomer().withAddress(anAddress().withNoPostcode())).build();
```

As we compress the test code, the duplication in the builders becomes more obtrusive; we have the name of the constructed type in both the "with" and "builder" methods. We can take advantage of Java's method overloading by collapsing this to a single with() method, letting the Java type system figure out which field to update:

```
Order order =
  anOrder().from(aCustomer().with(anAddress().withNoPostcode())).build();
```

Obviously, this will only work with one argument of each type. For example, if we introduce a Postcode, we can use overloading, whereas the rest of the builder methods must have explicit names because they use String:

```
Address aLongerAddress = anAddress()
    .withStreet("221b Baker Street")
    .withCity("London")
    .with(postCode("NW1", "3RX"))
    .build();
```

This should encourage us to introduce domain types, which, as we wrote in "Domain Types Are Better Than Strings" (page 213), leads to more expressive and maintainable code.

Removing Duplication at the Point of Use

We've made the process of assembling complex objects for tests simpler and more expressive by using test data builders. Now, let's look at how we can structure our tests to make the best use of these builders in context. We often find ourselves writing tests with similar code to create supporting objects and pass them to the code under test, so we want to clean up this duplication. We've found that some refactorings are better than others; here's an example.

First, Remove Duplication

We have a system that processes orders asynchronously. The test feeds orders into the system, tracks their progress on a monitor, and then looks for them in a user interface. We've packaged up all the infrastructure so the test looks like this:

```
@Test public void reportsTotalSalesOfOrderedProducts() {
  Order order1 = anOrder()
    .withLine("Deerstalker Hat", 1)
    .withLine("Tweed Cape", 1)
    .withCustomersReference(1234)
    .build();
  requestSender.send(order1);
  progressMonitor.waitForCompletion(order1);

  Order order2 = anOrder()
    .withLine("Deerstalker Hat", 1)
    .withCustomersReference(5678)
    .build();
  requestSender.send(order2);
  progressMonitor.waitForCompletion(order2);

  TotalSalesReport report = gui.openSalesReport();
  report.checkDisplayedTotalSalesFor("Deerstalker Hat", is(equalTo(2)));
  report.checkDisplayedTotalSalesFor("Tweed Cape", is(equalTo(1)));
}
```

There's an obvious duplication in the way the orders are created, sent, and tracked. Our first thought might be to pull that into a helper method:

```
@Test public void reportsTotalSalesOfOrderedProducts() {
  submitOrderFor("Deerstalker Hat", "Tweed Cape");
  submitOrderFor("Deerstalker Hat");

  TotalSalesReport report = gui.openSalesReport();
  report.checkDisplayedTotalSalesFor("Deerstalker Hat", is(equalTo(2)));
  report.checkDisplayedTotalSalesFor("Tweed Cape", is(equalTo(1)));
}
```

```
void submitOrderFor(String ... products) {
  OrderBuilder orderBuilder = anOrder()
    .withCustomersReference(nextCustomerReference());

  for (String product : products) {
    orderBuilder = orderBuilder.withLine(product, 1);
  }

  Order order = orderBuilder.build();
  requestSender.send(order);
  progressMonitor.waitForCompletion(order);
}
```

This refactoring works fine when there's a single case but, like the object mother pattern, does not scale well when we have variation. As we deal with orders with different contents, amendments, cancellations, and so on, we end up with this sort of mess:

```
void submitOrderFor(String ... products) { [...]
void submitOrderFor(String product, int count,
                    String otherProduct, int otherCount) { [...]
void submitOrderFor(String product, double discount) { [...]
void submitOrderFor(String product, String giftVoucherCode) { [...]
```

We think a bit harder about what varies between tests and what is common, and realize that a better alternative is to pass the *builder* through, not its arguments; it's similar to when we started combining builders. The helper method can use the builder to add any supporting detail to the order before feeding it into the system:

```
@Test public void reportsTotalSalesOfOrderedProducts() {
  sendAndProcess(anOrder()
    .withLine("Deerstalker Hat", 1)
    .withLine("Tweed Cape", 1));
  sendAndProcess(anOrder()
    .withLine("Deerstalker Hat", 1));

  TotalSalesReport report = gui.openSalesReport();
  report.checkDisplayedTotalSalesFor("Deerstalker Hat", is(equalTo(2)));
  report.checkDisplayedTotalSalesFor("Tweed Cape", is(equalTo(1)));
}

void sendAndProcess(OrderBuilder orderDetails) {
  Order order = orderDetails
    .withDefaultCustomersReference(nextCustomerReference())
    .build();
  requestSender.send(order);
  progressMonitor.waitForCompletion(order);
}
```

Then, Raise the Game

The test code is looking better, but it still reads like a script. We can change its emphasis to *what* behavior is expected, rather than *how* the test is implemented, by rewording some of the names:

```java
@Test public void reportsTotalSalesOfOrderedProducts() {
  havingReceived(anOrder()
      .withLine("Deerstalker Hat", 1)
      .withLine("Tweed Cape", 1));
  havingReceived(anOrder()
      .withLine("Deerstalker Hat", 1));

  TotalSalesReport report = gui.openSalesReport();
  report.displaysTotalSalesFor("Deerstalker Hat", equalTo(2));
  report.displaysTotalSalesFor("Tweed Cape", equalTo(1));
}

@Test public void takesAmendmentsIntoAccountWhenCalculatingTotalSales() {
  Customer theCustomer = aCustomer().build();

  havingReceived(anOrder().from(theCustomer)
    .withLine("Deerstalker Hat", 1)
    .withLine("Tweed Cape", 1));

  havingReceived(anOrderAmendment().from(theCustomer)
    .withLine("Deerstalker Hat", 2));

  TotalSalesReport report = user.openSalesReport();
  report.containsTotalSalesFor("Deerstalker Hat", equalTo(2));
  report.containsTotalSalesFor("Tweed Cape", equalTo(1));
}
```

We started with a test that looked procedural, extracted some of its behavior into builder objects, and ended up with a declarative description of what the feature does. We're nudging the test code towards the sort of language we could use when discussing the feature with someone else, even someone non-technical; we push everything else into supporting code.

Communication First

We use test data builders to reduce duplication *and* make the test code more expressive. It's another technique that reflects our obsession with the language of code, driven by the principle that code is there to be read. Combined with factory methods and test scaffolding, test data builders help us write more literate, declarative tests that describe the *intention* of a feature, not just a sequence of steps to drive it.

Using these techniques, we can even use higher-level tests to communicate directly with non-technical stakeholders, such as business analysts. If they're willing to ignore the obscure punctuation, we can use the tests to help us narrow down exactly what a feature should do, and why.

There are other tools that are designed to foster collaboration across the technical and non-technical members in a team, such as FIT [Mugridge05]. We've found, as have others such as the LiFT team [LIFT], that we can achieve much of this while staying within our development toolset—and, of course, we can write better tests for ourselves.

Chapter 23

Test Diagnostics

Mistakes are the portals of discovery.

—James Joyce

Design to Fail

The point of a test is not to pass but to *fail*. We want the production code to pass its tests, but we also want the tests to detect and report any errors that do exist. A "failing" test has actually succeeded at the job it was designed to do. Even unexpected test failures, in an area unrelated to where we are working, can be valuable because they reveal implicit relationships in the code that we hadn't noticed.

One situation we want to avoid, however, is when we can't diagnose a test failure that has happened. The last thing we should have to do is crack open the debugger and step through the tested code to find the point of disagreement. At a minimum, it suggests that our tests don't yet express our requirements clearly enough. In the worst case, we can find ourselves in "debug hell," with deadlines to meet but no idea of how long a fix will take. At this point, the temptation will be high to just delete the test—and lose our safety net.

 Stay Close to Home

Synchronize frequently with the source code repository—up to every few minutes—so that if a test fails unexpectedly it won't cost much to revert your recent changes and try another approach.

The other implication of this tip is not to be too inhibited about dropping code and trying again. Sometimes it's quicker to roll back and restart with a clear head than to keep digging.

We've learned the hard way to make tests fail *informatively*. If a failing test clearly explains what has failed and why, we can quickly diagnose and correct the code. Then, we can get on with the next task.

Chapter 21 addressed the static readability of tests. This chapter describes some practices that we find helpful to make sure the tests give us the information we need at runtime.

267

Small, Focused, Well-Named Tests

The easiest way to improve diagnostics is to keep each test small and focused and give tests readable names, as described in Chapter 21. If a test is small, its name should tell us most of what we need to know about what has gone wrong.

Explanatory Assertion Messages

JUnit's assertion methods all have a version in which the first parameter is a message to display when the assertion fails. From what we've seen, this feature is not used as often as it should be to make assertion failures more helpful.

For example, when this test fails:

```
Customer customer  = order.getCustomer();
assertEquals("573242", customer.getAccountId());
assertEquals(16301, customer.getOutstandingBalance());
```

the report does not make it obvious which of the assertions has failed:

```
ComparisonFailure: expected:<[16301]> but was:<[16103]>
```

The message is describing the symptom (the balance is 16103) rather than the cause (the outstanding balance calculation is wrong).

If we add a message to identify the value being asserted:

```
assertEquals("account id", "573242", customer.getAccountId());
assertEquals("outstanding balance", 16301, customer.getOustandingBalance());
```

we can immediately see what the point is:

```
ComparisonFailure: outstanding balance expected:<[16301]> but was:<[16103]>
```

Highlight Detail with Matchers

Developers can provide another level of diagnostic detail by using assertThat() with Hamcrest matchers. The Matcher API includes support for describing the value that mismatched, to help with understanding exactly what is different. For example, the instrument strike price assertion on page 252 generates this failure report:

```
Expected: a collection containing instrument at price a value greater than <81>
     but: price was <50>, price was <72>, price was <31>
```

which shows exactly which values are relevant.

Self-Describing Value

An alternative to adding detail to the assertion is to build the detail into values in the assertion. We can take this in the same spirit as the idea that comments are a hint that the code needs to be improved: if we have to add detail to an assertion, maybe that's a hint that we could make the failure more obvious.

In the customer example above, we could improve the failure message by setting the account identifier in the test `Customer` to the self-describing value `"a customer account id"`:

```
ComparisonFailure: expected:<[a customer account id]> but was:<[id not set]>
```

Now we don't need to add an explanatory message, because the value itself explains its role.

We might be able to do more when we're working with reference types. For example, in a test that has this setup:

```
Date startDate = new Date(1000);
Date endDate = new Date(2000);
```

the failure message reports that a payment date is wrong but doesn't describe where the wrong value might have come from:

```
java.lang.AssertionError: payment date
Expected: <Thu Jan 01 01:00:01 GMT 1970>
    got: <Thu Jan 01 01:00:02 GMT 1970>
```

What we really want to know is the *meaning* of these dates. If we force the display string:

```
Date startDate = namedDate(1000, "startDate");
Date endDate = namedDate(2000, "endDate");

Date namedDate(long timeValue, final String name) {
    return new Date(timeValue) { public String toString() { return name; } };
}
```

we get a message that describes the role that each date plays:

```
java.lang.AssertionError: payment date
Expected: <startDate>
    got: <endDate>
```

which makes it clear that we've assigned the wrong field to the payment date.[1]

---

1. This is yet another motivation for defining more domain types to hide the basic types in the language. As we discussed in "Domain Types Are Better Than Strings" (page 213), it gives us somewhere to hang useful behavior like this.

Obviously Canned Value

Sometimes, the values being checked can't easily explain themselves. There's not enough information in a char or int, for example. One option is to use improbable values that will be obviously different from the values we would expect in production. For an int, for example, we might use a negative value (if that doesn't break the code) or Integer.MAX_VALUE (if it's wildly out of range). Similarly, the original version of startDate in the previous example was an obviously canned value because nothing in the system dated back to 1970.

When a team develops conventions for common values, it can ensure that they stand out. The INVALID_ID at the end of the last chapter was three digits long; that would be very obviously wrong if real system identifiers were five digits and up.

Tracer Object

Sometimes we just want to check that an object is passed around by the code under test and routed to the appropriate collaborator. We can create a *tracer object*, a type of Obviously Canned Value, to represent this value. A tracer object is a dummy object that has no supported behavior of its own, except to describe its role when something fails. For example, this test:

```
@RunWith(JMock.class)
public class CustomerTest {
  final LineItem item1 = context.mock(LineItem.class, "item1");
  final LineItem item2 = context.mock(LineItem.class, "item2");
  final Billing billing = context.mock(Billing.class);

  @Test public void
  requestsInvoiceForPurchasedItems() {
    context.checking(new Expectations() {{
      oneOf(billing).add(item1);
      oneOf(billing).add(item2);
    }});

    customer.purchase(item1, item2);
    customer.requestInvoice(billing);
  }
}
```

might generate a failure report like this:

```
not all expectations were satisfied
expectations:
  expected once, already invoked 1 time: billing.add(<item1>)
  ! expected once, never invoked: billing.add(<item2>>)
what happened before this:
  billing.add(<item1>)
```

Notice that jMock can accept a name when creating a mock object that will be used in failure reporting. In fact, where there's more than one mock object of the same type, jMock insists that they are named to avoid confusion (the default is to use the class name).

Tracer objects can be a useful design tool when TDD'ing a class. We sometimes use an empty interface to mark (and name) a domain concept and show how it's used in a collaboration. Later, as we grow the code, we fill in the interface with methods to describe its behavior.

Explicitly Assert That Expectations Were Satisfied

A test that has both expectations and assertions can produce a confusing failure. In jMock and other mock object frameworks, the expectations are checked after the body of the test. If, for example, a collaboration doesn't work properly and returns a wrong value, an assertion might fail before any expectations are checked. This would produce a failure report that shows, say, an incorrect calculation result rather than the missing collaboration that actually caused it.

In a few cases, then, it's worth calling the `assertIsSatisfied()` method on the `Mockery` before any of the test assertions to get the right failure report:

```
context.assertIsSatisfied();
assertThat(result, equalTo(expectedResult));
```

This demonstrates why it is important to "Watch the Test Fail" (page 42). If you expect the test to fail because an expectation is not satisfied but a postcondition assertion fails instead, you will see that you should add an explicit call to assert that all expectations have been satisfied.

Diagnostics Are a First-Class Feature

Like everyone else, we find it easy to get carried away with the simple three-step TDD cycle: fail, pass, refactor. We're making good progress and *we* know what the failures mean because we've just written the test. But nowadays, we try to follow the four-step TDD cycle (fail, *report,* pass, refactor) we described in Chapter 5, because that's how we know we've understood the feature—and whoever has to change it in a month's time will also understand it. Figure 23.1 shows again that we need to maintain the quality of the tests, as well as the production code.

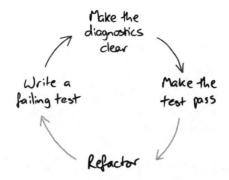

Figure 23.1 *Improve the diagnostics as part of the TDD cycle*

Chapter 24

Test Flexibility

Living plants are flexible and tender;
the dead are brittle and dry.
[...]
The rigid and stiff will be broken.
The soft and yielding will overcome.

—Lao Tzu (c.604—531 B.C.)

Introduction

As the system and its associated test suite grows, maintaining the tests can become a burden if they have not been written carefully. We've described how we can reduce the ongoing cost of tests by making them easy to read and generating helpful diagnostics on failure. We also want to make sure that each test fails only when its relevant code is broken. Otherwise, we end up with *brittle* tests that slow down development and inhibit refactoring. Common causes of test brittleness include:

- The tests are too tightly coupled to unrelated parts of the system or unrelated behavior of the object(s) they're testing;

- The tests overspecify the expected behavior of the target code, constraining it more than necessary; and,

- There is duplication when multiple tests exercise the same production code behavior.

Test brittleness is not just an attribute of how the tests are written; it's also related to the design of the system. If an object is difficult to decouple from its environment because it has many dependencies or its dependencies are hidden, its tests will fail when distant parts of the system change. It will be hard to judge the knock-on effects of altering the code. So, we can use test brittleness as a valuable source of feedback about design quality.

There's a virtuous relationship with test readability and resilience. A test that is focused, has clean set-up, and has minimal duplication is easier to name and is more obvious about its purpose. This chapter expands on some of the techniques we discussed in Chapter 21. Actually, the whole chapter can be collapsed into a single rule:

273

Specify Precisely What Should Happen and No More

JUnit, Hamcrest, and jMock allow us to specify just what we want from the target code (there are equivalents in other languages). The more precise we are, the more the code can flex in other unrelated dimensions without breaking tests misleadingly. Our experience is that the other benefit of keeping tests flexible is that they're easier for us to understand because they are clearer about what they're testing—about what is and is not important in the tested code.

Test for Information, Not Representation

A test might need to pass a value to trigger the behavior it's supposed to exercise in its target object. The value could either be passed in as a parameter to a method on the object, or returned as a result from a query the object makes on one of its neighbors stubbed by the test. If the test is structured in terms of how the value is represented by other parts of the system, then it has a dependency on those parts and will break when they change.

For example, imagine we have a system that uses a `CustomerBase` to store and find information about our customers. One of its features is to look up a `Customer` given an email address; it returns `null` if there's no customer with the given address.

```
public interface CustomerBase {
  // Returns null if no customer found
  Customer findCustomerWithEmailAddress(String emailAddress);
  [...]
}
```

When we test the parts of the code that search for customers by email address, we stub `CustomerBase` as a collaborating object. In some of those tests, no customer will be found so we return `null`:

```
allowing(customerBase).findCustomerWithEmailAddress(theAddress);
                            will(returnValue(null));
```

There are two problems with this use of `null` in a test. First, we have to remember what `null` means here, and when it's appropriate; the test is not self-explanatory. The second concern is the cost of maintenance.

Some time later, we experience a `NullPointerException` in production and track the source of the null reference down to the `CustomerBase`. We realize we've broken one of our design rules: "Never Pass Null between Objects." Ashamed, we change the `CustomerBase`'s search methods to return a `Maybe` type, which implements an iterable collection of at most one result.

```
public interface CustomerBase {
  Maybe<Customer> findCustomerWithEmailAddress(String emailAddress);
}

public abstract class Maybe<T> implements Iterable<T> {
  abstract boolean hasResult();

  public static Maybe<T> just(T oneValue) { …
  public static Maybe<T> nothing() { …
}
```

We still, however, have the tests that stub CustomerBase to return null, to represent missing customers. The compiler cannot warn us of the mismatch because null is a valid value of type Maybe<Customer> too, so the best we can do is to watch all these tests fail and change each one to the new design.

If, instead, we'd given the tests their own representation of "no customer found" as a single well-named constant instead of the literal null, we could have avoided this drudgery. We would have changed one line:

```
public static final Customer NO_CUSTOMER_FOUND = null;
```

to

```
public static final Maybe<Customer> NO_CUSTOMER_FOUND = Maybe.nothing();
```

without changing the tests themselves.

Tests should be written in terms of the information passed between objects, not of how that information is represented. Doing so will both make the tests more self-explanatory and shield them from changes in implementation controlled elsewhere in the system. Significant values, like NO_CUSTOMER_FOUND, should be defined in one place as a constant. There's another example in Chapter 12 when we introduce UNUSED_CHAT. For more complex structures, we can hide the details of the representation in test data builders (Chapter 22).

Precise Assertions

In a test, focus the assertions on just what's relevant to the scenario being tested. Avoid asserting values that aren't driven by the test inputs, and avoid reasserting behavior that is covered in other tests.

We find that these heuristics guide us towards writing tests where each method exercises a unique aspect of the target code's behavior. This makes the tests more robust because they're not dependent on unrelated results, and there's less duplication.

Most test assertions are simple checks for equality; for example, we assert the number of rows in a table model in "Extending the Table Model" (page 180). Testing for equality doesn't scale well as the value being returned becomes more complex. Different test scenarios may make the tested code return results that differ only in specific attributes, so comparing the entire result each time is misleading and introduces an implicit dependency on the behavior of the whole tested object.

There are a couple of ways in which a result can be more complex. First, it can be defined as a structured value type. This is straightforward since we can just reference directly any attributes we want to assert. For example, if we take the financial instrument from "Use Structure to Explain" (page 253), we might need to assert only its strike price:

```
assertEquals("strike price", 92, instrument.getStrikePrice());
```

without comparing the whole instrument.

We can use Hamcrest matchers to make the assertions more expressive and more finely tuned. For example, if we want to assert that a transaction identifier is larger than its predecessor, we can write:

```
assertThat(instrument.getTransactionId(), largerThan(PREVIOUS_TRANSACTION_ID));
```

This tells the programmer that the only thing we really care about is that the new identifier is larger than the previous one—its actual value is not important in this test. The assertion also generates a helpful message when it fails.

The second source of complexity is implicit, but very common. We often have to make assertions about a text string. Sometimes we know exactly what the text should be, for example when we have the FakeAuctionServer look for specific messages in "Extending the Fake Auction" (page 107). Sometimes, however, all we need to check is that certain values are included in the text.

A frequent example is when generating a failure message. We don't want all our unit tests to be locked to its current formatting, so that they fail when we add whitespace, and we don't want to have to do anything clever to cope with timestamps. We just want to know that the critical information is included, so we write:

```
assertThat(failureMessage,
        allOf(containsString("strikePrice=92"),
            containsString("id=FGD.430"),
            containsString("is expired")));
```

which asserts that all these strings occur somewhere in failureMessage. That's enough reassurance for us, and we can write other tests to check that a message is formatted correctly if we think it's significant.

One interesting effect of trying to write precise assertions against text strings is that the effort often suggests that we're missing an intermediate structure object—in this case perhaps an InstrumentFailure. Most of the code would be written in terms of an InstrumentFailure, a structured value that carries all the relevant fields. The failure would be converted to a string only at the last possible moment, and that string conversion can be tested in isolation.

Precise Expectations

We can extend the concept of being precise about assertions to being precise about expectations. Each mock object test should specify just the relevant details of the interactions between the object under test and its neighbors. The combined unit tests for an object describe its protocol for communicating with the rest of the system.

We've built a lot of support into jMock for specifying this communication between objects as precisely as it should be. The API is designed to produce tests that clearly express how objects relate to each other and that are flexible because they're not too restrictive. This may require a little more test code than some of the alternatives, but we find that the extra rigor keeps the tests clear.

Precise Parameter Matching

We want to be as precise about the values passed in to a method as we are about the value it returns. For example, in "Assertions and Expectations" (page 254) we showed an expectation where one of the accepted arguments was any type of RuntimeException; the specific class doesn't matter. Similarly, in "Extracting the SnipersTableModel" (page 197), we have this expectation:

```
oneOf(auction).addAuctionEventListener(with(sniperForItem(itemId)));
```

The method sniperForItem() returns a Matcher that checks only the item identifier when given an AuctionSniper. This test doesn't care about anything else in the sniper's state, such as its current bid or last price, so we don't make it more brittle by checking those values.

The same precision can be applied to expecting input strings. If, for example, we have an auditTrail object to accept the failure message we described above, we can write a precise expectation for that auditing:

```
oneOf(auditTrail).recordFailure(with(allOf(containsString("strikePrice=92"),
                                           containsString("id=FGD.430"),
                                           containsString("is expired"))));
```

Allowances and Expectations

We introduced the concept of *allowances* in "The Sniper Acquires Some State" (page 144). jMock insists that all *expectations* are met during a test, but allowances may be matched or not. The point of the distinction is to highlight what matters in a particular test. Expectations describe the interactions that are essential to the protocol we're testing: if we send *this* message to the object, we expect to see it send *this* other message to *this* neighbor.

Allowances *support* the interaction we're testing. We often use them as stubs to feed values into the object, to get the object into the right state for the behavior we want to test. We also use them to ignore other interactions that aren't relevant to the current test. For example, in "Repurposing sniperBidding()" we have a test that includes:

```
ignoring(auction);
allowing(sniperListener).sniperStateChanged(with(aSniperThatIs(BIDDING)));
                                then(sniperState.is("bidding"));
```

The `ignoring()` clause says that, in this test, we don't care about messages sent to the `auction`; they will be covered in other tests. The `allowing()` clause matches any call to `sniperStateChanged()` with a Sniper that is currently bidding, but doesn't insist that such a call happens. In this test, we use the allowance to record what the Sniper has told us about its state. The method `aSniperThatIs()` returns a `Matcher` that checks only the `SniperState` when given a `SniperSnapshot`.

In other tests we attach "action" clauses to allowances, so that the call will return a value or throw an exception. For example, we might have an allowance that stubs the `catalog` to return a `price` that will be returned for use later in the test:

```
allowing(catalog).getPriceForItem(item); will(returnValue(74));
```

The distinction between allowances and expectations isn't rigid, but we've found that this simple rule helps:

 ### Allow Queries; Expect Commands

Commands are calls that are likely to have side effects, to change the world outside the target object. When we tell the `auditTrail` above to record a failure, we expect that to change the contents of some kind of log. The state of the system will be different if we call the method a different number of times.

Queries don't change the world, so they can be called any number of times, including none. In our example above, it doesn't make any difference to the system how many times we ask the `catalog` for a price.

The rule helps to decouple the test from the tested object. If the implementation changes, for example to introduce caching or use a different algorithm, the test is still valid. On the other hand, if we were writing a test for a cache, we would want to know exactly how often the query was made.

jMock supports more varied checking of how often a call is made than just `allowing()` and `oneOf()`. The number of times a call is expected is defined by the "cardinality" clause that starts the expectation. In "The AuctionSniper Bids," we saw the example:

```
atLeast(1).of(sniperListener).sniperBidding();
```

which says that we care that this call is made, but not how many times. There are other clauses which allow fine-tuning of the number of times a call is expected, listed in Appendix A.

Ignoring Irrelevant Objects

As you've seen, we can simplify a test by "ignoring" collaborators that are not relevant to the functionality being exercised. jMock will not check *any* calls to ignored objects. This keeps the test simple and focused, so we can immediately see what's important and changes to one aspect of the code do not break unrelated tests.

As a convenience, jMock will provide "zero" results for ignored methods that return a value, depending on the return type:

Type	"Zero" value
Boolean	`false`
Numeric type	`0`
String	`""` (an empty string)
Array	Empty array
A type that can be mocked by the Mockery	An ignored mock
Any other type	`null`

The ability to dynamically mock returned types can be a powerful tool for narrowing the scope of a test. For example, for code that uses the Java Persistence API (JPA), a test can ignore the `EntityManagerFactory`. The factory will return an ignored `EntityManager`, which will return an ignored `EntityTransaction` on which we can ignore `commit()` or `rollback()`. With one ignore clause, the test can focus on the code's domain behavior by disabling everything to do with transactions.

Like all "power tools," `ignoring()` should be used with care. A chain of ignored objects might suggest that the functionality ought to be pulled out into a new collaborator. As programmers, we must also make sure that ignored features are tested somewhere, and that there are higher-level tests to make sure everything works together. In practice, we usually introduce `ignoring()` only when writing specialized tests after the basics are in place, as for example in "The Sniper Acquires Some State" (page 144).

Invocation Order

jMock allows invocations on a mock object to be called in any order; the expectations don't have to be declared in the same sequence.[1] The less we say in the tests about the order of interactions, the more flexibility we have with the implementation of the code. We also gain flexibility in how we structure the tests; for example, we can make test methods more readable by packaging up expectations in helper methods.

 Only Enforce Invocation Order When It Matters

Sometimes the order in which calls are made is significant, in which case we add explicit constraints to the test. Keeping such constraints to a minimum avoids locking down the production code. It also helps us see whether each case is necessary—ordered constraints are so uncommon that each use stands out.

---

jMock has two mechanisms for constraining invocation order: *sequences*, which define an ordered list of invocations, and *state machines*, which can describe more sophisticated ordering constraints. Sequences are simpler to understand than state machines, but their restrictiveness can make tests brittle if used inappropriately.

Sequences are most useful for confirming that an object sends notifications to its neighbors in the right order. For example, we need an `AuctionSearcher` object that will search its collection of `Auctions` to find which ones match anything from a given set of keywords. Whenever it finds a match, the searcher will notify its `AuctionSearchListener` by calling `searchMatched()` with the matching auction. The searcher will tell the listener that it's tried all of its available auctions by calling `searchFinished()`.

Our first attempt at a test looks like this:

```
public class AuctionSearcherTest { […]
  @Test public void
  announcesMatchForOneAuction() {
    final AuctionSearcher auctionSearch =
                new AuctionSearcher(searchListener, asList(STUB_AUCTION1));
    context.checking(new Expectations() {{
      oneOf(searchListener).searchMatched(STUB_AUCTION1);
      oneOf(searchListener).searchFinished();
    }});
    auctionSearch.searchFor(KEYWORDS);
  }
}
```

---

1. Some early mock frameworks were strictly "record/playback": the actual calls had to match the sequence of the expected calls. No frameworks enforce this any more, but the misconception is still common.

where searchListener is a mock AuctionSearchListener, KEYWORDS is a set of keyword strings, and STUB_AUCTION1 is a stub implementation of Auction that will match one of the strings in KEYWORDS.

The problem with this test is that there's nothing to stop searchFinished() being called before searchMatched(), which doesn't make sense. We have an interface for AuctionSearchListener, but we haven't described its *protocol*. We can fix this by adding a Sequence to describe the relationship between the calls to the listener. The test will fail if searchFinished() is called first.

```
@Test public void
announcesMatchForOneAuction() {
    final AuctionSearcher auctionSearch =
                    new AuctionSearcher(searchListener, asList(STUB_AUCTION1));

  context.checking(new Expectations() {{
    Sequence events = context.sequence("events");

    oneOf(searchListener).searchMatched(STUB_AUCTION1); inSequence(events);
    oneOf(searchListener).searchFinished();             inSequence(events);
  }});

  auctionSearch.searchFor(KEYWORDS);
}
```

We continue using this sequence as we add more auctions to match:

```
@Test public void
announcesMatchForTwoAuctions() {
  final AuctionSearcher auctionSearch = new AuctionSearcher(searchListener,
                  new AuctionSearcher(searchListener,
                                  asList(STUB_AUCTION1, STUB_AUCTION2));

  context.checking(new Expectations() {{
    Sequence events = context.sequence("events");

    oneOf(searchListener).searchMatched(STUB_AUCTION1); inSequence(events);
    oneOf(searchListener).searchMatched(STUB_AUCTION2); inSequence(events);
    oneOf(searchListener).searchFinished();             inSequence(events);
  }});

  auctionSearch.searchFor(KEYWORDS);
}
```

But is this overconstraining the protocol? Do we have to match auctions in the same order that they're initialized? Perhaps all we care about is that the right matches are made before the search is closed. We can relax the ordering constraint with a States object (which we first saw in "The Sniper Acquires Some State" on page 144).

A States implements an abstract state machine with named states. We can trigger state transitions by attaching a then() clause to an expectation. We can enforce that an invocation only happens when object is (or is not) in a particular state with a when() clause. We rewrite our test:

```
@Test public void
announcesMatchForTwoAuctions() {
  final AuctionSearcher auctionSearch = new AuctionSearcher(searchListener,
                   new AuctionSearcher(searchListener,
                                     asList(STUB_AUCTION1, STUB_AUCTION2)));

  context.checking(new Expectations() {{
    States searching = context.states("searching");

    oneOf(searchListener).searchMatched(STUB_AUCTION1);
                                    when(searching.isNot("finished"));
    oneOf(searchListener).searchMatched(STUB_AUCTION2);
                                    when(searching.isNot("finished"));
    oneOf(searchListener).searchFinished(); then(searching.is("finished"));
  }});

  auctionSearch.searchFor(KEYWORDS);
}
```

When the test opens, searching is in an undefined (default) state. The searcher can report matches as long as searching is not finished. When the searcher reports that it has finished, the then() clause switches searching to finished, which blocks any further matches.

States and sequences can be used in combination. For example, if our requirements change so that auctions have to be matched in order, we can add a sequence for just the matches, in addition to the existing searching states. The new sequence would confirm the order of search results and the existing states would confirm that the results arrived before the search is finished. An expectation can belong to multiple states and sequences, if that's what the protocol requires. We rarely need such complexity—it's most common when responding to external feeds of events where we don't own the protocol—and we always take it as a hint that something should be broken up into smaller, simpler pieces.

When Expectation Order Matters

Actually, the order in which jMock expectations are declared is sometimes significant, but not because they have to shadow the order of invocation. Expectations are appended to a list, and invocations are matched by searching this list in order. If there are two expectations that can match an invocation, the one declared first will win. If that first expectation is actually an allowance, the second expectation will never see a match and the test will fail.

The Power of jMock States

jMock States has turned out to be a useful construct. We can use it to model each of the three types of participants in a test: the object being tested, its peers, and the test itself.

We can represent our understanding of the state of the object being tested, as in the example above. The test listens for the events the object sends out to its peers and uses them to trigger state transitions and to reject events that would break the object's protocol.

As we wrote in "Representing Object State" (page 146), this is a *logical* representation of the state of the tested object. A States describes what the test finds relevant about the object, not its internal structure. We don't want to constrain the object's implementation.

We can represent how a peer changes state as it's called by the tested object. For instance, in the example above, we might want to insist that the listener must be ready before it can receive any results, so the searcher must query its state. We could add a new States, listenerState:

```
allowing(searchListener).isReady(); will(returnValue(true));
                                    then(listenerState.is("ready"));
oneOf(searchListener).searchMatched(STUB_AUCTION1);
                                    when(listenerState.is("ready"));
```

Finally, we can represent the state of the test itself. For example, we could enforce that some interactions are ignored while the test is being set up:

```
ignoring(auction); when(testState.isNot("running"));
testState.become("running");
oneOf(auction).bidMore(); when(testState.is("running"));
```

Even More Liberal Expectations

Finally, jMock has plug-in points to support the definition of arbitrary expectations. For example, we could write an expectation to accept any getter method:

```
allowing(aPeerObject).method(startsWith("get")).withNoArguments();
```

or to accept a call to one of a set of objects:

```
oneOf (anyOf(same(o1),same(o2),same(o3))).method("doSomething");
```

Such expectations move us from a statically typed to a dynamically typed world, which brings both power and risk. These are our strongest "power tool" features—sometimes just what we need but always to be used with care. There's more detail in the jMock documentation.

"Guinea Pig" Objects

In the "ports and adapters" architecture we described in "Designing for Maintainability" (page 47), the adapters map application domain objects onto the system's technical infrastructure. Most of the adapter implementations we see are generic; for example, they often use reflection to move values between domains. We can apply such mappings to any type of object, which means we can change our domain model without touching the mapping code.

The easiest approach when writing tests for the adapter code is to use types from the application domain model, but this makes the test brittle because it binds together the application and adapter domains. It introduces a risk of mis- leadingly breaking tests when we change the application model, because we haven't separated the concerns.

Here's an example. A system uses an XmlMarshaller to marshal objects to and from XML so they can be sent across a network. This test exercises XmlMarshaller by round-tripping an AuctionClosedEvent object: a type that the production system really does send across the network.

```
public class XmlMarshallerTest {
  @Test public void
  marshallsAndUnmarshallsSerialisableFields() {
    XMLMarshaller marshaller = new XmlMarshaller();

    AuctionClosedEvent original = new AuctionClosedEventBuilder().build();

    String xml = marshaller.marshall(original);
    AuctionClosedEvent unmarshalled = marshaller.unmarshall(xml);

    assertThat(unmarshalled, hasSameSerialisableFieldsAs(original));
  }
}
```

Later we decide that our system won't send an AuctionClosedEvent after all, so we should be able to delete the class. Our refactoring attempt will fail because AuctionClosedEvent is still being used by the XmlMarshallerTest. The irrelevant coupling will force us to rework the test unnecessarily.

There's a more significant (and subtle) problem when we couple tests to domain types: it's harder to see when test assumptions have been broken. For example, our XmlMarshallerTest also checks how the marshaller handles transient and non-transient fields. When we wrote the tests, AuctionClosedEvent included both kind of fields, so we were exercising all the paths through the marshaller. Later, we removed the transient fields from AuctionClosedEvent, which means that we have tests that are no longer meaningful but *do not fail*. Nothing is alerting us that we have tests that have stopped working and that important features are not being covered.

We should test the XmlMarshaller with specific types that are clear about the features that they represent, unrelated to the real system. For example, we can introduce helper classes in the test:

```java
public class XmlMarshallerTest {
  public static class MarshalledObject {
    private String privateField = "private";
    public final String publicFinalField = "public final";
    public int primitiveField;
    // constructors, accessors for private field, etc.
  }
  public static class WithTransient extends MarshalledObject {
    public transient String transientField = "transient";
  }

  @Test public void
  marshallsAndUnmarshallsSerialisableFields() {
    XMLMarshaller marshaller = new XmlMarshaller();

    WithTransient original = new WithTransient();

    String xml = marshaller.marshall(original);
    AuctionClosedEvent unmarshalled = marshaller.unmarshall(xml);

    assertThat(unmarshalled, hasSameSerialisableFieldsAs(original));
  }
}
```

The WithTransient class acts as a "guinea pig," allowing us to exhaustively exercise the behavior of our XmlMarshaller before we let it loose on our production domain model. WithTransient also makes our test more readable because the class and its fields are examples of "Self-Describing Value" (page 269), with names that reflect their roles in the test.

Part V

Advanced Topics

In this part, we cover some topics that regularly cause teams to struggle with test-driven development. What's common to these topics is that they cross the boundary between feature-level and system-level design. For example, when we look at multi-threaded code, we need to test both the behavior that runs within a thread and the way different threads interact.

Our experience is that such code is difficult to test when we're not clear about which aspect we're addressing. Lumping everything together produces tests that are confusing, brittle, and sometimes misleading. When we take the time to listen to these "test smells," they often lead us to a better design with a clearer separation of responsibilities.

Chapter 25

Testing Persistence

It is always during a passing state of mind that we make lasting resolutions.

—Marcel Proust

Introduction

As we saw in Chapter 8, when we define an abstraction in terms of a third-party API, we have to test that our abstraction behaves as we expect when integrated with that API, but cannot use our tests to get feedback about its design.

A common example is an abstraction implemented using a persistence mechanism, such as Object/Relational Mapping (ORM). ORM hides a lot of sophisticated functionality behind a simple API. When we build an abstraction upon an ORM, we need to test that our implementation sends correct queries, has correctly configured the mappings between our objects and the relational schema, uses a dialect of SQL that is compatible with the database, performs updates and deletes that are compatible with the integrity constraints of the database, interacts correctly with the transaction manager, releases external resources in a timely manner, does not trip over any bugs in the database driver, and much more.

When testing persistence code, we also have more to worry about with respect to the quality of our tests. There are components running in the background that the test must set up correctly. Those components have persistent state that could make tests interfere with each other. Our test code has to deal with all this extra complexity. We need to spend additional effort to ensure that our tests remain readable and to generate reasonable diagnostics that pinpoint why tests fail—to tell us in which component the failure occurred and why.

This chapter describes some techniques for dealing with this complexity. The example code uses the standard Java Persistence API (JPA), but the techniques will work just as well with other persistence mechanisms, such as Java Data Objects (JDO), open source ORM technologies like Hibernate, or even when dumping objects to files using a data-mapping mechanism such as XStream[1] or the standard Java API for XML Binding (JAXB).[2]

---

1. http://xstream.codehaus.org
2. Apologies for all the acronyms. The Java standardization process does not require standards to have memorable names.

An Example Scenario

The examples in this chapter will all use the same scenario. We now have a web service that performs auction sniping on behalf of our customers.

A customer can log in to different auction sites and has one or more payment methods by which they pay for our service and the lots they bid for. The system supports two payment methods: credit cards and an online payment service called PayMate. A customer has a contact address and, if they have a credit card, the card has a billing address.

This domain model is represented in our system by the persistent entities shown in Figure 25.1 (which only includes the fields that show what the purpose of the entity is.)

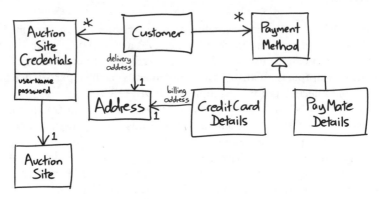

Figure 25.1   *Persistent entities*

Isolate Tests That Affect Persistent State

Since persistent data hangs around from one test to the next, we have to take extra care to ensure that persistence tests are isolated from one another. JUnit cannot do this for us, so the test fixture must ensure that the test starts with its persistent resources in a known state.

For database code, this means deleting rows from the database tables before the test starts. The process of cleaning the database depends on the database's integrity constraints. It might only be possible to clear tables in a strict order. Furthermore, if some tables have foreign key constraints between them that cascade deletes, cleaning one table will automatically clean others.

Clean Up Persistent Data at the Start of a Test, Not at the End

Each test should initialize the persistent store to a known state when it starts. When a test is run individually, it will leave data in the persistent store that can help you diagnose test failures. When it is run as part of a suite, the next test will clean up the persistent state first, so tests will be isolated from each other. We used this technique in "Recording the Failure" (page 221) when we cleared the log before starting the application at the start of the test.

The order in which tables must be cleaned up should be captured in one place because it must be kept up-to-date as the database schema evolves. It's an ideal candidate to be extracted into a *subordinate object* to be used by any test that uses the database:

```java
public class DatabaseCleaner {
  private static final Class<?>[] ENTITY_TYPES = {
    Customer.class,
    PaymentMethod.class,
    AuctionSiteCredentials.class,
    AuctionSite.class,
    Address.class
  };
  private final EntityManager entityManager;

  public DatabaseCleaner(EntityManager entityManager) {
    this.entityManager = entityManager;
  }

  public void clean() throws SQLException {
    EntityTransaction transaction = entityManager.getTransaction();
    transaction.begin();

    for (Class<?> entityType : ENTITY_TYPES) {
      deleteEntities(entityType);
    }

    transaction.commit();
  }

  private void deleteEntities(Class<?> entityType) {
    entityManager
      .createQuery("delete from " + entityNameOf(entityType))
      .executeUpdate();
  }
}
```

We use an array, ENTITY_TYPES, to ensure that the entity types (and, therefore, database tables) are cleaned in an order that does not violate referential integrity when rows are deleted from the database.[3] We add DatabaseCleaner to a setup method, to initialize the database before each test. For example:

```
public class ExamplePersistenceTest {
  final EntityManagerFactory factory =
                          Persistence.createEntityManagerFactory("example");
  final EntityManager entityManager = factory.createEntityManager();

  @Before
  public void cleanDatabase() throws Exception {
    new DatabaseCleaner(entityManager).clean();
  }
  […]
}
```

For brevity, we won't show this cleanup in the test examples. You should assume that every persistence test starts with the database in a known, clean state.

Make Tests Transaction Boundaries Explicit

A common technique to isolate tests that use a transactional resource (such as a database) is to run each test in a transaction which is then rolled back at the end of the test. The idea is to leave the persistent state the same after the test as before.

The problem with this technique is that it doesn't test what happens on commit, which is a significant event. The ORM flushes the state of the objects it is managing in memory to the database. The database, in turn, checks its integrity constraints. A test that never commits does not fully exercise how the code under test interacts with the database. Neither can it test interactions between distinct transactions. Another disadvantage of rolling back is that the test discards data that might be useful for diagnosing failures.

Tests should explicitly delineate transactions. We also prefer to make transaction boundaries stand out, so they're easy to see when reading the test. We usually extract transaction management into a subordinate object, called a *transactor*, that runs a unit of work within a transaction. In this case, the transactor will coordinate JPA transactions, so we call it a JPATransactor.[4]

---

3. We've left entityNameOf() out of this code excerpt. The JPA says the the name of an entity is derived from its related Java class but doesn't provide a standard API to do so. We implemented just enough of this mapping to allow DatabaseCleaner to work.

4. In other systems, tests might also use a JMSTransactor for coordinating transactions in a Java Messaging Service (JMS) broker, or a JTATransactor for coordinating distributed transactions via the standard Java Transaction API (JTA).

```
public interface UnitOfWork {
  void work() throws Exception;
}

public class JPATransactor {
  private final EntityManager entityManager;

  public JPATransactor(EntityManager entityManager) {
    this.entityManager = entityManager;
  }

  public void perform(UnitOfWork unitOfWork) throws Exception {
    EntityTransaction transaction = entityManager.getTransaction();

    transaction.begin();
    try {
      unitOfWork.work();
      transaction.commit();
    }
    catch (PersistenceException e) {
      throw e;
    }
    catch (Exception e) {
      transaction.rollback();
      throw e;
    }
  }
}
```

The transactor is called by passing in a `UnitOfWork`, usually created as an anonymous class:

```
transactor.perform(new UnitOfWork() {
  public void work() throws Exception {
    customers.addCustomer(aNewCustomer());
  }
});
```

This pattern is so useful that we regularly use it in our production code as well. We'll show more of how the transactor is used in the next section.

"Container-Managed" Transactions

Many Java applications use declarative *container-managed transactions*, where the application framework manages the application's transaction boundaries. The framework starts each transaction when it receives a request to an application component, includes the application's transactional resources in transaction, and commits or rolls back the transaction when the request succeeds or fails. Java EE is the canonical example of such frameworks in the Java world.

The techniques we describe in this chapter are compatible with this kind of framework. We have used them to test applications built within Java EE and Spring, and with "plain old" Java programs that use JPA, Hibernate, or JDBC directly.

The frameworks wrap transaction management around the objects that make use of transactional resources, so there's nothing in their code to mark the application's transaction boundaries. The tests for those objects, however, need to manage transactions explicitly—which is what a transactor is for.

In the tests, the transactor uses the same transaction manager as the application, configured in the same way. This ensures that the tests and the full application run the same transactional code. It should make no difference whether a transaction is controlled by a block wrapped around our code by the framework, or by a transactor in our tests. But if we've made a mistake and it does make a difference, our end-to-end tests should catch such failures by exercising the application code in the container.

Testing an Object That Performs Persistence Operations

Now that we've got some test scaffolding we can write tests for an object that performs persistence.

In our domain model, a *customer base* represents all the customers we know about. We can add customers to our customer base and find customers that match certain criteria. For example, we need to find customers with credit cards that are about to expire so that we can send them a reminder to update their payment details.

```
public interface CustomerBase {  […]
  void addCustomer(Customer customer);
  List<Customer> customersWithExpiredCreditCardsAt(Date deadline);
}
```

When unit-testing code that calls a `CustomerBase` to find and notify the relevant customers, we can mock the interface. In a deployed system, however, this code will call a real implementation of `CustomerBase` that is backed by JPA to save and load customer information from a database. We must also test that this persistent implementation works correctly—that the queries it makes and the object/relational mappings are correct. For example, below is a test of the `customersWithExpiredCreditCardsAt()` query. There are two helper methods that interact with `customerBase` within a transaction: `addCustomer()` adds a set of example customers, and `assertCustomersExpiringOn()` queries for customers with expired cards.

```
public class PersistentCustomerBaseTest { […]
  final PersistentCustomerBase customerBase =
                            new PersistentCustomerBase(entityManager);
  @Test
  @SuppressWarnings("unchecked")
  public void findsCustomersWithCreditCardsThatAreAboutToExpire() throws Exception {
    final String deadline = "6 Jun 2009";

    addCustomers(
      aCustomer().withName("Alice (Expired)")
        .withPaymentMethods(aCreditCard().withExpiryDate(date("1 Jan 2009"))),
      aCustomer().withName("Bob (Expired)")
        .withPaymentMethods(aCreditCard().withExpiryDate(date("5 Jun 2009"))),
      aCustomer().withName("Carol (Valid)")
        .withPaymentMethods(aCreditCard().withExpiryDate(date(deadline))),
      aCustomer().withName("Dave (Valid)")
        .withPaymentMethods(aCreditCard().withExpiryDate(date("7 Jun 2009")))
    );
    assertCustomersExpiringOn(date(deadline),
                        containsInAnyOrder(customerNamed("Alice (Expired)"),
                                           customerNamed("Bob (Expired)")));
  }

  private void addCustomers(final CustomerBuilder... customers) throws Exception {
    transactor.perform(new UnitOfWork() {
      public void work() throws Exception {
        for (CustomerBuilder customer : customers) {
          customerBase.addCustomer(customer.build());
        }
      }
    });
  }

  private void assertCustomersExpiringOn(final Date date,
                                     final Matcher<Iterable<Customer>> matcher)
    throws Exception
  {
    transactor.perform(new UnitOfWork() {
      public void work() throws Exception {
        assertThat(customerBase.customersWithExpiredCreditCardsAsOf(date), matcher);
      }
    });
  }
}
```

We call addCustomers() with CustomerBuilders set up to include a name and an expiry date for the credit card. The expiry date is the significant field for this test, so we create customers with expiry dates before, on, and after the deadline to demonstrate the boundary condition. We also set the name of each customer to identify the instances in a failure (notice that the names self-describe the relevant status of each customer). An alternative to matching on name would have been to use each object's persistence identifier, which is assigned by JPA. That would have been more complex to work with (it's not exposed as a property on Customer), and would not be self-describing.

The `assertCustomersExpiringOn()` method runs the query we're testing for the given deadline and checks that the result conforms to the Hamcrest matcher we pass in. The `containsInAnyOrder()` method returns a matcher that checks that there's a sub-matcher for each of the elements in a collection. We've written a `customerNamed()` method to return a custom matcher that tests whether an object is a `Customer` with a given name (there's more on custom matchers in Appendix B). So, this test says that we expect to receive back exactly two `Customer` objects, named `"Alice (Expired)"` and `"Bob (Expired)"`.

The test implicitly exercises `CustomerBase.addCustomer()` by calling it to set up the database for the query. Thinking further, what we actually care about is the relationship between the result of calling `addCustomer()` and subsequent queries, so we probably won't test `addCustomer()` independently. If there's an effect of `addCustomer()` that is not visible through *some* feature of the system, then we'd have to ask some hard questions about its purpose before writing a special test query to cover it.

 ## Better Test Structure with Matchers

This test includes a nice example of using Hamcrest to create a clean test structure. The test method constructs a matcher, which gives a concise description of a valid result for the query. It passes the matcher to `assertCustomersExpiringOn()`, which just runs the query and passes the result to the matcher. We have a clean separation between the test method, which knows what is expected to be retrieved, and the query/assert method, which knows how to make a query and can be used in other tests.

Here is an implementation of `PersistentCustomerBase` that passes the test:

```
public class PersistentCustomerBase implements CustomerBase {
  private final EntityManager entityManager;

  public PersistentCustomerBase(EntityManager entityManager) {
    this.entityManager = entityManager;
  }

  public void addCustomer(Customer customer) {
    entityManager.persist(customer);
  }

  public List<Customer> customersWithExpiredCreditCardsAt(Date deadline) {
    Query query = entityManager.createQuery(
        "select c from Customer c, CreditCardDetails d " +
        "where d member of c.paymentMethods " +
        "  and d.expiryDate < :deadline");
    query.setParameter("deadline", deadline);
    return query.getResultList();
  }
}
```

This implementation looks trivial—it's so much shorter than its test—but it relies on a lot of XML configuration that we haven't included and on a third-party framework that implements the `EntityManager`'s simple API.

On Patterns and Type Names

The `CustomerBase` interface and `PersistentCustomerBase` class implement the *repository* or *data access object* pattern (often abbreviated to DAO). We have not used the terms "Repository," "DataAccessObject," or "DAO" in the name of the interface or class that implements it because:

- Using such terms leaks knowledge about the underlying technology layers (persistence) into the application domain, and so breaks the "ports and adapters" architecture. The objects that use a `CustomerBase` are persistence-agnostic: they do not care whether the `Customer` objects they interact with are written to disk or not. The `Customer` objects are also persistence-agnostic: a program does not need to have a database to create and use `Customer` objects. Only `PersistentCustomerBase` knows how it maps `Customer` objects in and out of persistent storage.

- We prefer not to name classes or interfaces after patterns; what matters to us is their relationship to other classes in the system. The clients of `CustomerBase` do not care what patterns it uses. As the system evolves, we might make the `CustomerBase` class work in some other way and the name would then be misleading.

- We avoid generic words like "data," "object," or "access" in type names. We try to give each class a name that identifies a concept within its domain or expresses how it bridges between the application and technical domains.

Testing That Objects Can Be Persisted

The `PersistentCustomerBase` relies on so much configuration and underlying third-party code that the error messages from its test can be difficult to diagnose. A test failure could be caused by a defect in a query, the mapping of the `Customer` class, the mapping of any of the classes that it uses, the configuration of the ORM, invalid database connection parameters, or a misconfiguration of the database itself.

We can write more tests to help us pinpoint the cause of a persistence failure when it occurs. A useful test is to "round-trip" instances of all persistent entity types through the database to check that the mappings are configured correctly for each class.

Round-trip tests are useful whenever we reflectively translate objects to and from other forms. Many serialization and mapping technologies have the same advantages and difficulties as ORM. The mapping can be defined by compact, declarative code or configuration, but misconfiguration creates defects that are difficult to diagnose. We use round-trip tests so we can quickly identify the cause of such defects.

Round-Tripping Persistent Objects

We can use a list of "test data builders" (page 257) to represent the persistent entity types. This makes it easy for the test to instantiate each instance. We can also use builder types more than once, with differing set-ups, to create entities for round-tripping in different states or with different relationships to other entities.

This test loops through a list of builders (we'll show how we create the list in a moment). For each builder, it creates and persists an entity in one transaction, and retrieves and compares the result in another. As in the last test, we have two transactor methods that perform transactions. The setup method is persistedObjectFrom() and the query method is assertReloadsWithSameStateAs().

```
public class PersistabilityTest { [...]
  final List<? extends Builder<?>> persistentObjectBuilders = [...]

  @Test public void roundTripsPersistentObjects() throws Exception {
    for (Builder<?> builder : persistentObjectBuilders) {
      assertCanBePersisted(builder);
    }
  }
  private void assertCanBePersisted(Builder<?> builder) throws Exception {
    try {
      assertReloadsWithSameStateAs(persistedObjectFrom(builder));
    } catch (PersistenceException e) {
      throw new PersistenceException("could not round-trip " + typeNameFor(builder), e);
    }
  }
  private Object persistedObjectFrom(final Builder<?> builder) throws Exception {
    return transactor.performQuery(new QueryUnitOfWork() {
      public Object query() throws Exception {
        Object original = builder.build();
        entityManager.persist(original);
        return original;
      }
    });
  }
  private void assertReloadsWithSameStateAs(final Object original) throws Exception {
    transactor.perform(new UnitOfWork() {
      public void work() throws Exception {
        assertThat(entityManager.find(original.getClass(), idOf(original)),
                 hasSamePersistentFieldsAs(original));
      }
    });
  }
```

```
  private String typeNameFor(Builder<?> builder) {
    return builder.getClass().getSimpleName().replace("Builder", "");
  }
}
```

The persistedObjectFrom() method asks its given builder to create an entity instance which it persists within a transaction. Then it returns the new instance to the test, for later comparison; QueryUnitOfWork is a variant of UnitOfWork that allows us to return a value from a transaction.

The assertReloadsWithSameStateAs() method extracts the persistence identifier that the EntityManager assigned to the expected object (using reflection), and uses that identifier to ask the EntityManager to retrieve another copy of the entity from the database. Then it calls a custom matcher that uses reflection to check that the two copies of the entity have the same values in their persistent fields.

On the Use of Reflection

We have repeatedly stated that we should test through an object's public API, so that our tests give us useful feedback about the design of that API. So, why are we using reflection here to bypass our objects' encapsulation boundaries and reach into their private state? Why are we using the persistence API in a way we wouldn't do in production code?

We're using these round-trip tests to test-drive the *configuration* of the ORM, as it maps our objects into the database. We're not test-driving the design of the objects themselves. The state of our objects is encapsulated and hidden from other objects in the system. The ORM uses reflection to save that state to, and retrieve it from, the database—so here, we use the same technique as the ORM does to verify its behavior.

Round-Tripping Related Entities

Creating a list of builders is complicated when there are relationships between entities, and saving of one entity is not cascaded to its related entities. This is the case when an entity refers to reference data that is never created during a transaction.

For example, our system knows about a limited number of auction sites. Customers have AuctionSiteCredentials that refer to those sites. When the system creates a Customer entity, it associates it with existing AuctionSites that it loads from the database. Saving the Customer will save its AuctionSiteCredentials, but won't save the referenced AuctionSites because they should already exist in the database. At the same time, we must associate a new AuctionSiteCredentials with an AuctionSite that is already in the database, or we will violate referential integrity constraints when we save.

The fix is to make sure that there's a persisted `AuctionSite` before we save a new `AuctionSiteCredentials`. The `AuctionSiteCredentialsBuilder` delegates to another builder to create the `AuctionSite` for the `AuctionSiteCredentials` under construction (see "Combining Builders" on page 261). We ensure referential integrity by wrapping the `AuctionSite` builder in a *Decorator* [Gamma94] that persists the `AuctionSite` before it is associated with the `AuctionSiteCredentials`. This is why we call the entity builder within a transaction—some of the related builders will perform database operations that require an active transaction.

```
public class PersistabilityTest { [...]
  final List<? extends Builder<?>> persistentObjectBuilders = Arrays.asList(
  new AddressBuilder(),
  new PayMateDetailsBuilder(),
  new CreditCardDetailsBuilder(),
  new AuctionSiteBuilder(),
  new AuctionSiteCredentialsBuilder().forSite(persisted(new AuctionSiteBuilder())),
  new CustomerBuilder()
    .usingAuctionSites(
      new AuctionSiteCredentialsBuilder().forSite(persisted(new AuctionSiteBuilder())))
    .withPaymentMethods(
      new CreditCardDetailsBuilder(),
      new PayMateDetailsBuilder()));
  private <T> Builder<T> persisted(final Builder<T> builder) {
    return new Builder<T>() {
      public T build() {
        T entity = builder.build();
        entityManager.persist(entity);
        return entity;
      }
    };
  }
}
```

But Database Tests Are S-l-o-w!

Tests that run against realistic infrastructure are much slower than unit tests that run everything in memory. We can unit-test our code by defining a clean interface to the persistence infrastructure (defined in terms of our code's domain) and using a mock persistence implementation—as we described in "Only Mock Types That You Own" (page 69). We then test the implementation of this interface with fine-grained integration tests so we don't have to bring up the entire system to test the technical layers.

This lets us organize our tests into a chain of phases: *unit* tests that run very quickly in memory; slower *integration* tests that reach outside the process, usually through third-party APIs, and that depend on the configuration of external services such as databases and messaging brokers; and, finally, *end-to-end* tests that run against a system packaged and deployed into a production-like environment. This gives us rapid feedback if we break the application's core logic, and incremental feedback about integration at increasingly coarse levels of granularity.

Chapter 26

Unit Testing and Threads

It is decreed by a merciful Nature that the human brain cannot think of two things simultaneously.

—Sir Arthur Conan Doyle

Introduction

There's no getting away from it: concurrency complicates matters. It is a challenge when doing test-driven development. Unit tests cannot give you as much confidence in system quality because concurrency and synchronization are system-wide concerns. When writing tests, you have to worry about getting the synchronization right within the system *and* between the test and the system. Test failures are harder to diagnose because exceptions may be swallowed by background threads or tests may just time out with no clear explanation.

It's hard to diagnose and correct synchronization problems in existing code, so it's worth thinking about the system's concurrency architecture ahead of time. You don't need to design it in great detail, just decide on a broad-brush architecture and principles by which the system will cope with concurrency.

This design is often prescribed by the frameworks or libraries that an application uses. For example:

- Swing dispatches user events on its own thread. If an event handler runs for a long time, the user interface becomes unresponsive because Swing does not process user input while the event handler is running. Event callbacks must spawn "worker" threads to perform long-running tasks, and those worker threads must synchronize with the event dispatch thread to update the user interface.

- A servlet container has a pool of threads that receive HTTP requests and pass them to servlets for processing. Many threads can be active in the same servlet instance at once.

- Java EE containers manage all the threading in the application. The container guarantees that only one thread will call into a component at a time. Components cannot start their own threads.

- The Smack library used by the Auction Sniper application starts a daemon thread to receive XMPP messages. It will deliver messages on a single thread, but the application must synchronize the Smack thread and the Swing thread to avoid the GUI components being corrupted.

When you must design a system's concurrency architecture from scratch, you can use modeling tools to prove your design free of certain classes of synchronization errors, such as deadlock, livelock, or starvation. Design tools that help you model concurrency are becoming increasingly easy to use. The book *Concurrency: State Models & Java Programs* [Magee06] is an introduction to concurrent programming that stresses a combination of formal modeling and implementation and describes how to do the formal modeling with the LTSA analysis tool.

Even with a proven design, however, we have to cross the chasm between design and implementation. We need to ensure that our components conform to the architectural constraints of the system. Testing can help at this point. Once we've designed how the system will manage concurrency, we can test-drive the objects that will fit into that architecture. Unit tests give us confidence that an object performs its synchronization responsibilities, such as locking its state or blocking and waking threads. Coarser-grained tests, such as system tests, give us confidence that the entire system manages concurrency correctly.

Separating Functionality and Concurrency Policy

Objects that cope with multiple threads mix functional concerns with synchronization concerns, either of which can be the cause of test failures. Tests must also synchronize with the background threads, so that they don't make assertions before the threads have finished working or leave threads running that might interfere with later tests. Worse, in the presence of threads, unit tests do not usually report failures well. Exceptions get thrown on the hidden threads, killing them unexpectedly and breaking the behavior of the tested object. If a test times out waiting for background threads to finish, there's often no diagnostic other than a basic timeout message. All this makes unit testing difficult.

Searching for Auctions Concurrently

Let's look at an example. We will extend our Auction Sniper application to let the user search for auctions of interest. When the user enters search keywords, the application will run the search concurrently on all auction houses that the application can connect to. Each AuctionHouse will return a list of AuctionDescriptions that contain information about its auctions matching the search keywords. The application will combine the results it receives from all AuctionHouses and display a single list of auctions to the user. The user can then decide which of them to bid for.

The concurrent search is performed by an AuctionSearch object which passes the search keywords to each AuctionHouse and announces the results they return to an `AuctionSearchConsumer`. Our tests for the Auction Search are complicated because an `AuctionSearch` will spawn multiple threads per search, one for each `AuctionHouse`. If it hides those threads behind its API, we will have to implement the searching and notification functionality *and* the synchronization at the same time. When a test fails, we will have to work out which of those concerns is at fault. That's why we prefer our usual practice of incrementally adding functionality test by test.

It would be easier to test and implement the `AuctionSearch` if we could tackle the functional behavior and the synchronization separately. This would allow us to test the functional behavior within the test thread. We want to separate the logic that splits a request into multiple tasks from the technical details of how those tasks are executed concurrently. So we pass a "task runner" in to the `AuctionSearch`, which can then delegate managing tasks to the runner instead of starting threads itself. In our unit tests we'll give the `AuctionSearch` a fake task runner that calls tasks directly. In the real system, we'll give it a task runner that creates threads for tasks.

Introducing an Executor

We need an interface between the `AuctionHouse` and the task runner. We can use this one from Java's standard `java.util.concurrent` package:

```
public interface Executor {
  void execute(Runnable command);
}
```

How should we implement `Executor` in our unit tests? For testing, we need to run the tasks in the same thread as the test runner instead of creating new task threads. We could use jMock to mock `Executor` and write a custom action to capture all calls so we can run them later, but that sounds too complicated. The easiest option is to write a class to implement `Executor`. We can use it explicitly to run the tasks on the test thread after the call to the tested object has returned. jMock includes such a class, called `DeterministicExecutor`. We use this executor to write our first unit test. It checks that `AuctionSearch` notifies its `AuctionSearchConsumer` whenever an `AuctionHouse` returns search results and when the entire search has finished.

In the test setup, we mock the consumer because we want to show how it's notified by `AuctionSearch`. We represent auction houses with a simple `StubAuctionHouse` that just returns a list of descriptions if it matches keywords, or an empty list if not (real ones would communicate to auction services over the Internet). We wrote a custom stub, instead of using a jMock allowance, to reduce the "noise" in the failure reports; you'll see how this matters when we start stress-testing in the next section. We also pass an instance of `DeterministicExecutor` to `AuctionSearch` so that we can run the tasks within the test thread.

```
@RunWith(JMock.class)
public class AuctionSearchTests {
  Mockery context = new JUnit4Mockery();
  final DeterministicExecutor executor = new DeterministicExecutor();
  final StubAuctionHouse houseA = new StubAuctionHouse("houseA");
  final StubAuctionHouse houseB = new StubAuctionHouse("houseB");

  List<AuctionDescription> resultsFromA = asList(auction(houseA, "1"));
  List<AuctionDescription> resultsFromB = asList(auction(houseB, "2"));;

  final AuctionSearchConsumer consumer = context.mock(AuctionSearchConsumer.class);
  final AuctionSearch search =
                      new AuctionSearch(executor, houses(houseA, houseB), consumer);

  @Test public void
  searchesAllAuctionHouses() throws Exception {
    final Set<String> keywords = set("sheep", "cheese");
    houseA.willReturnSearchResults(keywords, resultsFromA);
    houseB.willReturnSearchResults(keywords, resultsFromB);

    context.checking(new Expectations() {{
      final States searching = context.states("searching");

      oneOf(consumer).auctionSearchFound(resultsFromA);   when(searching.isNot("done"));
      oneOf(consumer).auctionSearchFound(resultsFromB);   when(searching.isNot("done"));
      oneOf(consumer).auctionSearchFinished();            then(searching.is("done"));
    }});

    search.search(keywords);
    executor.runUntilIdle();
  }
}
```

In the test, we configure the StubAuctionHouses to return example results when they're queried with the given keywords. We specify our expectations that the consumer will be notified of the two search results (in any order), and then that the search has finished.

When we call search.search(keywords), the AuctionSearch hands a task for each of its auction houses to the executor. By the time search() returns, the tasks to run are queued in the executor. Finally, we call executor.runUntilIdle() to tell the executor to run queued tasks until its queue is empty. The tasks run on the test thread, so any assertion failures will be caught and reported by JUnit, and we don't have to worry about synchronizing the test thread with background threads.

Implementing AuctionSearch

This implementation of AuctionSearch calls its executor to start a search for each of its auction houses. It tracks how many searches are unfinished in its runningSearchCount field, so that it can notify the consumer when it's finished.

```java
public class AuctionSearch {
  private final Executor executor;
  private final List<AuctionHouse> auctionHouses;
  private final AuctionSearchConsumer consumer;

  private int runningSearchCount = 0;

  public AuctionSearch(Executor executor,
                       List<AuctionHouse> auctionHouses,
                       AuctionSearchConsumer consumer)
  {
    this.executor = executor;
    this.auctionHouses = auctionHouses;
    this.consumer = consumer;
  }

  public void search(Set<String> keywords) {
    for (AuctionHouse auctionHouse : auctionHouses) {
      startSearching(auctionHouse, keywords);
    }
  }

  private void startSearching(final AuctionHouse auctionHouse,
                              final Set<String> keywords)
  {
    runningSearchCount++;

    executor.execute(new Runnable() {
      public void run() {
        search(auctionHouse, keywords);
      }
    });
  }

  private void search(AuctionHouse auctionHouse, Set<String> keywords) {
    consumer.auctionSearchFound(auctionHouse.findAuctions(keywords));

    runningSearchCount--;
    if (runningSearchCount == 0) {
      consumer.auctionSearchFinished();
    }
  }
}
```

Unfortunately, this version is unsafe because it doesn't synchronize access to runningSearchCount. Different threads may overwrite each other when they decrement the field. So far, we've clarified the core behavior. We'll drive out this synchronization issue in the next test. Pulling out the Executor has given us two advantages. First, it makes development easier as we can unit-test the basic functionality without getting confused by threading issues. Second, the object's API no longer hides its concurrency policy.

Concurrency is a system-wide concern that should be controlled outside the objects that need to run concurrent tasks. By passing an appropriate Executor to the constructor, we're following the "context independence" design principle.

The application can now easily adapt the object to the application's threading policy without changing its implementation. For example, we could introduce a thread pool should we need to limit the number of active threads.

Unit-Testing Synchronization

Separating the functional and synchronization concerns has let us test-drive the functional behavior of our `AuctionSearch` in isolation. Now it's time to test-drive the synchronization. We will do this by writing stress-tests that run multiple threads through the `AuctionSearch` implementation to cause synchronization errors. Without precise control over the thread scheduler, we can't *guarantee* that our tests will find synchronization errors. The best we can do is run the same code enough times on enough threads to give our tests a reasonable likelihood of detecting the errors.

One approach to designing stress tests is to think about the aspects of an object's observable behavior that are independent of the number of threads calling into the object. These are the object's *observable invariants with respect to concurrency*.[1] By focusing on these invariants, we can tune the number of threads in a test without having to change its assertions. This gives us a process for writing stress tests:

- Specify one of the object's observable invariants with respect to concurrency;

- Write a stress test for the invariant that exercises the object multiple times from multiple threads;

- Watch the test fail, and tune the stress test until it reliably fails on every test run; and,

- Make the test pass by adding synchronization.

We'll demonstrate this with an example.

 Safety First

In this chapter we have made the unit tests of functional behavior pass before we covered stress testing at the unit level because that allowed us to explain each technique on its own. In practice, however, we often write both a unit test for functionality and a stress test of the synchronization before writing any code, make sure they *both* fail, then make them both pass. This helps us avoid checking in code that passes its tests but contains concurrency errors.

---

1. This differs from the use of invariants in "design by contract" and formal methods of modeling concurrency. These define invariants over the object's *state*.

A Stress Test for AuctionSearch

One invariant of our AuctionSearch is that it notifies the consumer just once when the search has finished, no matter how many AuctionHouses it searches—that is, no matter how many threads it starts.

We can use jMock to write a stress test for this invariant. We don't *always* use jMock for stress tests because expectation failures interfere with the threads of the object under test. On the other hand, jMock reports the actual sequence of calls to its mock objects when there is a failure, which helps diagnose defects. It also provides convenient facilities for synchronizing between the test thread and the threads being tested.

In AuctionSearchStressTests, we set up AuctionSearch with a thread-pool executor that will run tasks in background threads, and a list of auction houses stubbed to match on the given keywords. jMock is not thread-safe by default, so we set up the Mockery with a Synchroniser, an implementation of its threading policy that allows us to call mocked objects from different threads. To make tuning the test easier, we define constants at the top for the "degree of stress" we'll apply during the run.

```
@RunWith(JMock.class)
public class AuctionSearchStressTests {
  private static final int NUMBER_OF_AUCTION_HOUSES = 4;
  private static final int NUMBER_OF_SEARCHES = 8;
  private static final Set<String> KEYWORDS = setOf("sheep", "cheese");

  final Synchroniser synchroniser = new Synchroniser();
  final Mockery context = new JUnit4Mockery() {{
    setThreadingPolicy(synchroniser);
  }};
  final AuctionSearchConsumer consumer = context.mock(AuctionSearchConsumer.class);
  final States searching = context.states("searching");

  final ExecutorService executor = Executors.newCachedThreadPool();
  final AuctionSearch search = new AuctionSearch(executor, auctionHouses(), consumer);
  [...]
  private List<AuctionHouse> auctionHouses() {
    ArrayList<AuctionHouse> auctionHouses = new ArrayList<AuctionHouse>();
    for (int i = 0; i < NUMBER_OF_AUCTION_HOUSES; i++) {
      auctionHouses.add(stubbedAuctionHouse(i));
    }
    return auctionHouses;
  }

  private AuctionHouse stubbedAuctionHouse(final int id) {
    StubAuctionHouse house = new StubAuctionHouse("house" + id);
    house.willReturnSearchResults(
        KEYWORDS, asList(new AuctionDescription(house, "id" + id, "description")));
    return house;
  }
```

```
@Test(timeout=500) public void
onlyOneAuctionSearchFinishedNotificationPerSearch() throws Exception {
  context.checking(new Expectations() {{
    ignoring (consumer).auctionSearchFound(with(anyResults()));
  }});

  for (int i = 0; i < NUMBER_OF_SEARCHES; i++) {
    completeASearch();
  }
}

private void completeASearch() throws InterruptedException {
  searching.startsAs("in progress");
  context.checking(new Expectations() {{
    exactly(1).of(consumer).auctionSearchFinished(); then(searching.is("done"));
  }});

  search.search(KEYWORDS);
  synchroniser.waitUntil(searching.is("done"));
}

@After
public void cleanUp() throws InterruptedException {
  executor.shutdown();
  executor.awaitTermination(1, SECONDS);
}
}
```

In the test method onlyOneAuctionSearchFinishedNotificationPerSearch(), we run a complete search NUMBER_OF_SEARCHES times, to increase the likelihood of finding any race conditions. It finishes each search by asking synchroniser to wait until it's collected all the background threads the executor has launched, or until it's timed out. Synchroniser provides a method that will safely wait until a state machine is (or is not) in a given state. The test ignores auctionSearchFound() notifications, since here we're only interested in making sure that the searches finish cleanly. Finally, we shut down executor in the test teardown.

It's important to watch a stress test fail. It's too easy to write a test that passes even though the tested object has a synchronization hole. So, we "test the test" by making it fail before we've synchronized the code, and checking that we get the failure report we expected. If we don't, then we might need to raise the numbers of threads or iterations per thread until we can trust the test to reveal the error.[2] *Then* we add the synchronization to make the test pass. Here's our test failure:

---

2. Of course, the stress parameters may differ between environments, such as development vs. build. We can't follow that through here, except to note that it needs addressing.

```
java.lang.AssertionError: unexpected invocation: consumer.auctionSearchFinished()
expectations:
  allowed, already invoked 5 times: consumer.auctionSearchFound(ANYTHING)
  expected once, already invoked 1 time: consumer.auctionSearchFinished();
                                          then searching is done
  expected once, already invoked 1 time: consumer.auctionSearchFinished();
                                          then searching is done
states:
  searching is done
what happened before this:
  consumer.auctionSearchFound(<[AuctionDescription[auctionHouse=houseA,[…]
  consumer.auctionSearchFound(<[AuctionDescription[auctionHouse=houseB,[…]
  consumer.auctionSearchFound(<[AuctionDescription[auctionHouse=houseB,[…]
  consumer.auctionSearchFinished()
  consumer.auctionSearchFound(<[AuctionDescription[auctionHouse=houseA,[…]
  consumer.auctionSearchFinished()
  consumer.auctionSearchFound(<[AuctionDescription[auctionHouse=houseB,[…]
```

This says that AuctionSearch has called auctionFinished() once too often.

Fixing the Race Condition (Twice)

We haven't synchronized access to runningSearchCount. If we use an AtomicInteger from the Java concurrency libraries instead of a plain int, the threads should be able to decrement it without interfering with each other.

```
public class AuctionSearch { […]
  private final AtomicInteger runningSearchCount = new AtomicInteger();

  public void search(Set<String> keywords) {
    for (AuctionHouse auctionHouse : auctionHouses) {
      startSearching(auctionHouse, keywords);
    }
  }

  private void startSearching(final AuctionHouse auctionHouse,
                              final Set<String> keywords)
  {
    runningSearchCount.incrementAndGet();

    executor.execute(new Runnable() {
      public void run() { search(auctionHouse, keywords); }
    });
  }

  private void search(AuctionHouse auctionHouse, Set<String> keywords) {
    consumer.auctionSearchFound(auctionHouse.findAuctions(keywords));

    if (runningSearchCount.decrementAndGet() == 0) {
      consumer.auctionSearchFinished();
    }
  }
}
```

We try this and, in spite of our use of an `AtomicInteger`, our test still fails! We haven't got our synchronization right after all.

We look again at the failure and see that now the `AuctionSearch` is reporting that the search has finished more than once per search. Previously, the unsafe concurrent access to `runningSearchCount` resulted in *fewer* `auctionSearchFinished()` notifications than expected, because `AuctionSearch` was losing updates to the field. Something else must be wrong.

As an eagle-eyed reader, you'll have noticed a race condition in the way `AuctionSearch` increments and decrements `runningSearchCount`. It increments the count *before* starting a task thread. Once the main thread has started creating task threads, the thread scheduler can preëmpt it and start running whatever task threads are ready—while the main thread still has search tasks left to create. If all these started task threads complete before the scheduler resumes the main thread, they will decrement the count to 0 and the last one will send an `auctionSearchFinshed()` notification. When the main thread finally resumes, it will continue by starting its remaining searches, which will eventually trigger another notification.

This sort of error shows why we need to write stress tests, to make sure that we see them fail, and to understand the failure messages—it's also a good motivation for us to write comprehensible failure reports. This example also highlights the benefits of splitting tests of "raw" functionality from threaded tests. With the single-threaded version stable, we know we can concentrate on looking for race conditions in the stress tests.

We fix the code by setting `runningSearchCount` to the expected number of searches before starting any threads:

```
public class AuctionSearch { [...]
  public void search(Set<String> keywords) {
    runningSearchCount.set(auctionHouses.size());

    for (AuctionHouse auctionHouse : auctionHouses) {
      startSearching(auctionHouse, keywords);
    }
  }

  private void startSearching(final AuctionHouse auctionHouse,
                              final Set<String> keywords)
  {
    // no longer increments the count here
    executor.execute(new Runnable() {
      public void run() { search(auctionHouse, keywords); }
    });
  }
}
```

Stress-Testing Passive Objects

AuctionSearch actively starts multiple threads by calling out to its executor. Most objects that are concerned with threading, however, don't start threads themselves but have multiple threads "pass through" them and alter their state. Servlets, for example, are required to support multiple threads touching the same instance. In such cases, an object must synchronize access to any state that might cause a race condition.

To stress-test the synchronization of a passive object, the test must start its own threads to call the object. When all the threads have finished, the state of the object should be the same as if those calls had happened in sequence. For example, AtomicBigCounter below does not synchronize access to its count variable. It works when called from a single thread but can lose updates when called from multiple threads:

```
public class AtomicBigCounter {
  private BigInteger count = BigInteger.ZERO;

  public BigInteger count() { return count; }
  public void inc() { count = count.add(BigInteger.ONE); }
}
```

We can show this failure by calling inc() from multiple threads enough times to give us a good chance of causing the race condition and losing an update. When this happens, the final result of count() will be less than the number of times we've called inc().

We could spin up multiple threads directly in our test, but the mess of detail for launching and synchronizing threads would get in the way of understanding the intent. The threading concerns are a good candidate for extracting into a *subordinate object*, MultiThreadedStressTester, which we use to call the counter's inc() method:

```
public class AtomicBigCounterTests { [...]
  final AtomicBigCounter counter = new AtomicBigCounter();

  @Test public void
  canIncrementCounterFromMultipleThreadsSimultaneously() throws InterruptedException {
    MultithreadedStressTester stressTester = new MultithreadedStressTester(50000);

    stressTester.stress(new Runnable() {
      public void run() {
        counter.inc();
      }
    });
    stressTester.shutdown();

    assertThat("final count", counter.count(),
            equalTo(BigInteger.valueOf(stressTester.totalActionCount())));
  }
}
```

The test fails, showing the race condition in `AtomicBigCounter`:

```
java.lang.AssertionError: final count
Expected: <50000>
     got: <36933>
```

We pass the test by making the `inc()` and `count()` methods synchronized.

Synchronizing the Test Thread with Background Threads

When writing a test for code that starts threads, the test cannot confirm the code's behavior until it has synchronized its thread with any threads the code has started. For example, in `AuctionSearchStressTests` we make the test thread wait until all the task threads launched by `AuctionSearch` have been completed. Synchronizing with background threads can be challenging, especially if the tested object does not delegate to an executor to run concurrent tasks.

The easiest way to ensure that threads have finished is for the test to sleep long enough for them all to run to completion. For example:

```
private void waitForSearchToFinish() throws InterruptedException {
  Thread.sleep(250);
}
```

This works for occasional use—a sub-second delay in a few tests won't be noticeable—but it doesn't scale. As the number of tests with delays grows, the total delay adds up and the test suite slows down so much that running it becomes a distraction. We must be able to run all the unit tests so quickly as to not even think about whether we should. The other problem with fixed sleeps is that our choice of delay has to apply across all the environments where the tests run. A delay suitable for an underpowered machine will slow the tests everywhere else, and introducing a new environment may force another round of tuning.

An alternative, as we saw in `AuctionSearchStressTests`, is to use jMock's `Synchroniser`. It provides support for synchronizing between test and background threads, based on whether a state machine has entered or left a given state:

```
synchroniser.waitUntil(searching.is("finished"));
synchroniser.waitUntil(searching.isNot("in progress"));
```

These methods will block forever for a failing test, where the state machine never meets the specified criteria, so they should be used with a timeout added to the test declaration:

```
@Test(timeout=500)
```

This tells the test runnner to force a failure if the test overruns the timeout period.

A test will run as fast as possible if successful (Synchroniser's implementation is based on Java monitors), and only wait the entire 500 ms for failures. So, most of the time, the synchronization will not slow down the test suite.

If not using jMock, you can write a utility similar to Synchroniser to synchronize between test and background threads. Alternatively, we describe other synchronization techniques in Chapter 27.

The Limitations of Unit Stress Tests

Having a separate set of tests for our object's synchronization behavior helps us pinpoint where to look for defects if tests fail. It is very difficult to diagnose race conditions with a debugger, as stepping through code (or even adding print statements) will alter the thread scheduling that's causing the clash.[3] If a change causes a stress test to fail but the functional unit tests still pass, at least we know that the object's functional logic is correct and we've introduced a defect into its synchronization, or vice versa.

Obviously, stress tests offer only a degree of reassurance that code is thread-safe, not a guarantee. There may be scheduling differences between different operating systems (or versions of an operating system) and between different processor combinations. Further, there may be other processes on a host that affect scheduling while the tests are running. The best we can do is to run the tests frequently in a range of environments—locally before committing new code, and on multiple build servers after commit. This should already be part of the development process. We can tune the amount of work and number of threads in the tests until they are reliable enough at detecting errors—where the meaning of "enough" is an engineering decision for the team.

To cover our backs, we take a "belt and braces" approach.[4] We run unit tests to check that our objects correctly synchronize concurrent threads and to pinpoint synchronization failures. We run end-to-end tests to check that unit-level synchronization policies integrate across the entire system. If the concurrency architecture is not imposed on us by the frameworks we are using, we sometimes use formal modeling tools, such as the LTSA tool described in [Magee06], to prove that our concurrency model avoids certain classes of errors. Finally, we run static analysis tools as part of our automated build process to catch further errors. There are now some excellent practical examples, such as Findbugs,[5] that can detect synchronization errors in everyday Java code.

---

3. These are known as "Heisenbugs," because trying to detect the bug alters it.
4. For American readers, this means "belt and suspenders," but suspenders are a significantly different garment in British English.
5. http://findbugs.sf.net

In this chapter, we've considered unit-level testing of concurrent code. Larger-scale testing of concurrent behavior is much more complex—the tested code might be running in multiple, distributed processes; the test setup might not be able to control the creation of threads with an executor; some of the synchronization events might not be easily detectable; and, the system might detect and swallow errors before they can be reported to a test. We address this level of testing in the next chapter.

Chapter 27

Testing Asynchronous Code

I can spell banana but I never know when to stop.

—Johnny Mercer (songwriter)

Introduction

Some tests must cope with asynchronous behavior—whether they're end-to-end tests probing a system from the outside or, as we've just seen, unit tests exercising multithreaded code. These tests trigger some activity within the system to run concurrently with the test's thread. The critical difference from "normal" tests, where there is no concurrency, is that control returns to the test before the tested activity is complete—returning from the call to the target code does not mean that it's ready to be checked.

For example, this test assumes that a `Set` has finished adding an element when the `add()` method returns. Asserting that `set` has a size of one verifies that it did not store duplicate elements.

```
@Test public void storesUniqueElements() {
  Set set = new HashSet<String>();

  set.add("bananana");
  set.add("bananana");

  assertThat(set.size(), equalTo(1));
}
```

By contrast, this system test is asynchronous. The `holdingOfStock()` method synchronously downloads a stock report by HTTP, but the `send()` method sends an asynchronous message to a server that updates its records of stocks held.

```
@Test public void buyAndSellOfSameStockOnSameDayCancelsOutOurHolding() {
  Date tradeDate = new Date();

  send(aTradeEvent().ofType(BUY).onDate(tradeDate).forStock("A").withQuantity(10));
  send(aTradeEvent().ofType(SELL).onDate(tradeDate).forStock("A").withQuantity(10));

  assertThat(holdingOfStock("A", tradeDate), equalTo(0));
}
```

The transmission and processing of a trade message happens concurrently with the test, so the server might not have received or processed the messages yet when the test makes its assertion. The value of the stock holding that the assertion checks will depend on timings: how long the messages take to reach the server, how long the server takes to update its database, and how long the test takes to run. The test might fire the assertion after both messages have been processed (passing correctly), after one message (failing incorrectly), or before either message (passing, but testing nothing at all).

As you can see from this small example, with an asynchronous test we have to be careful about its coordination with the system it's testing. Otherwise, it can become unreliable, failing intermittently when the system is working or, worse, passing when the system is broken.

Current testing frameworks provide little support for dealing with asynchrony. They mostly assume that the tests run in a single thread of control, leaving the programmer to build the scaffolding needed to test concurrent behavior. In this chapter we describe some practices for writing reliable, responsive tests for asynchronous code.

Sampling or Listening

The fundamental difficulty with testing asynchronous code is that a test triggers activity that runs concurrently with the test and therefore cannot immediately check the outcome of the activity. The test will not block until the activity has finished. If the activity fails, it will not throw an exception back into the test, so the test cannot recognize if the activity is still running or has failed. The test therefore has to wait for the activity to complete successfully and fail if this doesn't happen within a given timeout period.

 Wait for Success

An asynchronous test must wait for success and use timeouts to detect failure.

This implies that every tested activity must have an *observable* effect: a test must affect the system so that its observable state becomes different. This sounds obvious but it drives how we think about writing asynchronous tests. If an activity has no observable effect, there is nothing the test can wait for, and therefore no way for the test to synchronize with the system it is testing.

There are two ways a test can observe the system: by *sampling* its observable state or by *listening for events* that it sends out. Of these, sampling is often the only option because many systems don't send any monitoring events. It's quite common for a test to include both techniques to interact with different "ends" of its system. For example, the Auction Sniper end-to-end tests sample the user interface for display changes, through the WindowLicker framework, but listen for chat events in the fake auction server.

Beware of Flickering Tests

A test can fail intermittently if its timeout is too close to the time the tested behavior normally takes to run, or if it doesn't synchronize correctly with the system. On a small system, an occasional flickering test might not cause problems—the test will most likely pass during the next build—but it's risky. As the test suite grows, it becomes increasingly difficult to get a test run in which none of the flickering tests fail.

Flickering tests can mask real defects. If the system itself occasionally fails, the tests that accurately detect those failures will seem to be flickering. If the suite contains unreliable tests, intermittent failures detected by reliable tests can easily be ignored. We need to make sure we understand what the real problem is before we ignore flickering tests.

Allowing flickering tests is bad for the team. It breaks the culture of quality where things should "just work," and even a few flickering tests can make a team stop paying attention to broken builds. It also breaks the habit of feedback. We should be paying attention to *why* the tests are flickering and whether that means we should improve the design of both the tests and code. Of course, there might be times when we have to compromise and decide to live with a flickering test for the moment, but this should be done reluctantly and include a plan for when it will be fixed.

As we saw in the last chapter, synchronizing by simply making each test wait for a fixed time is not practical. The test suite for a system of any size will take too long to run. We know we'll have to wait for failing tests to time out, but succeeding tests should be able to finish as soon as there's a response from the code.

 Succeed Fast

Make asynchronous tests detect success as quickly as possible so that they provide rapid feedback.

Of the two observation strategies we outlined in the previous section, listening for events is the quickest. The test thread can block, waiting for an event from the system. It will wake up and check the result as soon as it receives an event.

The alternative—sampling—means repeatedly polling the target system for a state change, with a short delay between polls. The frequency of this polling has to be tuned to the system under test, to balance the need for a fast response against the load it imposes on the target system. In the worst case, fast polling might slow the system enough to make the tests unreliable.

Put the Timeout Values in One Place

Both observation strategies use a timeout to detect that the system has failed. Again, there's a balance to be struck between a timeout that's too short, which will make the tests unreliable, and one that's too long, which will make failing tests too slow. This balance can be different in different environments, and will change as the system grows over time.

When the timeout duration is defined in one place, it's easy to find and change. The team can adjust its value to find the right balance between speed and reliability as the system develops.

Two Implementations

Scattering ad hoc sleeps and timeouts throughout the tests makes them difficult to understand, because it leaves too much implementation detail in the tests themselves. Synchronization and assertion is just the sort of behavior that's suitable for factoring out into subordinate objects because it usually turns into a bad case of duplication if we don't. It's also just the sort of tricky code that we want to get right once and not have to change again.

In this section, we'll show an example implementation of each observation strategy.

Capturing Notifications

An event-based assertion waits for an event by blocking on a monitor until it gets notified or times out. When the monitor is notified, the test thread wakes up and continues if it finds that the expected event has arrived, or blocks again. If the test times out, then it raises a failure.

NotificationTrace is an example of how to record and test notifications sent by the system. The setup of the test will arrange for the tested code to call append() when the event happens, for example by plugging in an event listener that will call the method when triggered. In the body of the test, the test thread calls containsNotification() to wait for the expected notification or fail if it times out. For example:

```
trace.containsNotification(startsWith("WANTED"));
```

will wait for a notification string that starts with WANTED.

Within NotificationTrace, incoming notifications are stored in a list trace, which is protected by a lock traceLock. The class is generic, so we don't specify the type of these notifications, except to say that the matchers we pass into containsNotification() must be compatible with that type. The implementation uses Timeout and NotificationStream classes that we'll describe later.

```java
public class NotificationTrace<T> {
  private final Object traceLock = new Object();
  private final List<T> trace = new ArrayList<T>(); ❶
  private long timeoutMs;
  // constructors and accessors to configure the timeout [...]

  public void append(T message) { ❷
    synchronized (traceLock) {
      trace.add(message);
      traceLock.notifyAll();
    }
  }

  public void containsNotification(Matcher<? super T> criteria) ❸
    throws InterruptedException
  {
    Timeout timeout = new Timeout(timeoutMs);

    synchronized (traceLock) {
      NotificationStream<T> stream = new NotificationStream<T>(trace, criteria);

      while (! stream.hasMatched()) {
        if (timeout.hasTimedOut()) {
          throw new AssertionError(failureDescriptionFrom(criteria));
        }
        timeout.waitOn(traceLock);
      }
    }
  }

  private String failureDescriptionFrom(Matcher<? super T> matcher) {  [...]
    // Construct a description of why there was no match,
    // including the matcher and all the received messages.
}
```

❶ We store notifications in a list so that they're available to us for other queries and so that we can include them in a description if the test fails (we don't show how the description is constructed).

❷ The append() method, called from a worker thread, appends a new notification to the trace, and then tells any threads waiting on traceLock to wake up because there's been a change. This is called by the test infrastructure when triggered by an event in the system.

❸ The containsNotification() method, called from the test thread, searches through all the notifications it has received so far. If it finds a notification that matches the given criteria, it returns. Otherwise, it waits until more notifications arrive and checks again. If it times out while waiting, then it fails the test.

The nested NotificationStream class searches the unexamined elements in its list for one that matches the given criteria. It allows the list to grow between calls to hasMatched() and picks up after the last element it looked at.

```
private static class NotificationStream<N> {
  private final List<N> notifications;
  private final Matcher<? super N> criteria;
  private int next = 0;

  public NotificationStream(List<N> notifications, Matcher<? super N> criteria) {
    this.notifications = notifications;
    this.criteria = criteria;
  }

  public boolean hasMatched() {
    while (next < notifications.size()) {
      if (criteria.matches(notifications.get(next)))
        return true;
      next++;
    }
    return false;
  }
}
```

NotificationTrace is one example of a simple coordination class between test and worker threads. It uses a simple approach, although it does avoid a possible race condition where a background thread delivers a notification before the test thread has started waiting. Another implementation, for example, might have containsNotification() only search messages received after the previous call. What is appropriate depends on the context of the test.

Polling for Changes

A sample-based assertion repeatedly samples some visible effect of the system through a "probe," waiting for the probe to detect that the system has entered an expected state. There are two aspects to the process of sampling: *polling* the system and failure reporting, and *probing* the system for a given state. Separating the two helps us think clearly about the behavior, and different tests can reuse the polling with different probes.

Poller is an example of how to poll a system. It repeatedly calls its probe, with a short delay between samples, until the system is ready or the poller times out. The poller drives a probe that actually checks the target system, which we've abstracted behind a Probe interface.

```
public interface Probe {
  boolean isSatisfied();
  void sample();
  void describeFailureTo(Description d);
}
```

The probe's sample() method takes a snapshot of the system state that the test is interested in. The isSatisfied() method returns true if that state meets the test's acceptance criteria. To simplify the poller logic, we allow isSatisfied() to be called before sample().

```
public class Poller {
  private long timeoutMillis;
  private long pollDelayMillis;
  // constructors and accessors to configure the timeout [...]

  public void check(Probe probe) throws InterruptedException {
    Timeout timeout = new Timeout(timeoutMillis);

    while (! probe.isSatisfied()) {
      if (timeout.hasTimedOut()) {
        throw new AssertionError(describeFailureOf(probe));
      }
      Thread.sleep(pollDelayMillis);

      probe.sample();
    }
  }
  private String describeFailureOf(Probe probe) { [...]
}
```

This simple implementation delegates synchronization with the system to the probe. A more sophisticated version might implement synchronization in the poller, so it could be shared between probes. The similarity to `NotificationTrace` is obvious, and we could have pulled out a common abstract structure, but we wanted to keep the designs clear for now.

To poll, for example, for the length of a file, we would write this line in a test:

```
assertEventually(fileLength("data.txt", is(greaterThan(2000))));
```

This wraps up the construction of our sampling code in a more expressive assertion. The helper methods to implement this are:

```
public static void assertEventually(Probe probe) throws InterruptedException {
  new Poller(1000L, 100L).check(probe);
}

public static Probe fileLength(String path, final Matcher<Integer> matcher) {
  final File file = new File(path);
  return new Probe() {
    private long lastFileLength = NOT_SET;

    public void sample() { lastFileLength = file.length(); }
    public boolean isSatisfied() {
      return lastFileLength != NOT_SET && matcher.matches(lastFileLength);
    }
    public void describeFailureTo(Description d) {
      d.appendText("length was ").appendValue(lastFileLength);
    }
  };
}
```

Separating the act of sampling from checking whether the sample is satisfactory makes the structure of the probe clearer. We can hold on to the sample result to report the unsatisfactory result we found if there's a failure.

Timing Out

Finally we show the Timeout class that the two example assertion classes use. It packages up time checking and synchronization:

```java
public class Timeout {
 private final long endTime;

  public Timeout(long duration) {
    this.endTime = System.currentTimeMillis() + duration;
  }

  public boolean hasTimedOut() { return timeRemaining() <= 0; }

  public void waitOn(Object lock) throws InterruptedException {
    long waitTime = timeRemaining();
    if (waitTime > 0) lock.wait(waitTime);
  }

  private long timeRemaining() { return endTime - System.currentTimeMillis(); }
}
```

Retrofitting a Probe

We can now rewrite the test from the introduction. Instead of making an assertion about the *current* holding of a stock, the test must wait for the holding of the stock to reach the expected level within an acceptable time limit.

```java
@Test public void buyAndSellOfSameStockOnSameDayCancelsOutOurHolding() {
  Date tradeDate = new Date();

  send(aTradeEvent().ofType(BUY).onDate(tradeDate).forStock("A").withQuantity(10));
  send(aTradeEvent().ofType(SELL).onDate(tradeDate).forStock("A").withQuantity(10));

  assertEventually(holdingOfStock("A", tradeDate, equalTo(0)));
}
```

Previously, the holdingOfStock() method returned a value to be compared. Now it returns a Probe that samples the system's holding and returns if it meets the acceptance criteria defined by a Hamcrest matcher—in this case equalTo(0).

Runaway Tests

Unfortunately, the new version of the test is still unreliable, even though we're now sampling for a result. The assertion is waiting for the holding to become zero, which is what we started out with, so it's possible for the test to pass before the system has even begun processing. This test can run ahead of the system without actually testing anything.

The worst aspect of runaway tests is that they give false positive results, so broken code looks like it's working. We don't often review tests that pass, so it's easy to miss this kind of failure until something breaks down the line. Even more tricky, the code might have worked when we first wrote it, as the tests happened to synchronize correctly during development, but now it's broken and we can't tell.

Beware of Tests That Return the System to the Same State

Be careful when an asynchronous test asserts that the system returns to a previous state. Unless it also asserts that the system enters an intermediate state before asserting the initial state, the test will run ahead of the system.

To stop the test running ahead of the system, we must add assertions that wait for the system to enter an intermediate state. Here, for example, we make sure that the first trade event has been processed before asserting the effect of the second event:

```
@Test public void buyAndSellOfSameStockOnSameDayCancelsOutOurHolding() {
  Date tradeDate = new Date();

  send(aTradeEvent().ofType(BUY).onDate(tradeDate).forStock("A").withQuantity(10));
  assertEventually(holdingOfStock("A", tradeDate, equalTo(10)));

  send(aTradeEvent().ofType(SELL).onDate(tradeDate).forStock("A").withQuantity(10));
  assertEventually(holdingOfStock("A", tradeDate, equalTo(0)));
}
```

Similarly, in Chapter 14, we check all the displayed states in the acceptance tests for the Auction Sniper user interface:

```
auction.reportPrice(1098, 97, ApplicationRunner.SNIPER_XMPP_ID);
application.hasShownSniperIsWinning();
auction.announceClosed();
application.hasShownSniperHasWon();
```

We want to make sure that the sniper has responded to each message before continuing on to the next one.

Lost Updates

A significant difference between tests that sample and those that listen for events is that polling can miss state changes that are later overwritten, Figure 27.1.

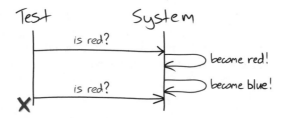

Figure 27.1 *A test that polls can miss changes in the system under test*

If the test can record notifications from the system, it can look through its records to find significant notifications.

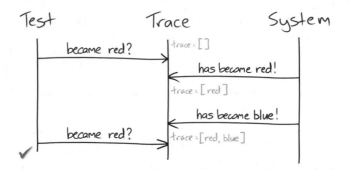

Figure 27.2 *A test that records notifications will not lose updates*

To be reliable, a sampling test must make sure that its system is *stable* before triggering any further interactions. Sampling tests need to be structured as a series of phases, as shown in Figure 27.3. In each phase, the test sends a stimulus to prompt a change in the observable state of the system, and then waits until that change becomes visible or times out.

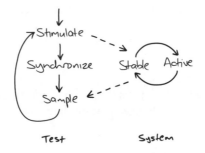

Figure 27.3 *Phases of a sampling test*

This shows the limits of how precise we can be with a sampling test. All the test can do between "stimulate" and "sample" is wait. We can write more reliable tests by not confusing the different steps in the loop and only triggering further changes once we've detected that the system is stable by observing a change in its sampled state.

Testing That an Action Has No Effect

Asynchronous tests look for *changes* in a system, so to test that something has *not* changed takes a little ingenuity. Synchronous tests don't have this problem because they completely control the execution of the tested code. After invoking the target object, synchronous tests can query its state or check that it hasn't made any unexpected calls to its neighbors.

If an asynchronous test waits for something not to happen, it cannot even be sure that the system has started before it checks the result. For example, if we want to show that trades in another region are not counted in the stock holding, then this test:

```
@Test public void doesNotShowTradesInOtherRegions() {
  send(aTradeEvent().ofType(BUY).forStock("A").withQuantity(10)
                    .inTradingRegion(OTHER_REGION));
  assertEventually(holdingOfStock("A", tradeDate, equalTo(0)));
}
```

cannot tell whether the system has correctly ignored the trade or just not received it yet. The most obvious workaround is for the test to wait for a fixed period of time and then check that the unwanted event did not occur. Unfortunately, this makes the test run slowly even when successful, and so breaks our rule of "succeed fast."

Instead, the test should trigger a behavior that *is* detectable and use that to detect that the system has stabilized. The skill here is in picking a behavior that will not interfere with the test's assertions and that will complete after the tested behavior. For example, we could add another trade event to the regions example. This shows that the out-of-region event is excluded because its quantity is not included in the total holding.

```
@Test public void doesNotShowTradesInOtherRegions() {
  send(aTradeEvent().ofType(BUY).forStock("A").withQuantity(10)
                    .inTradingRegion(OTHER_REGION));
  send(aTradeEvent().ofType(BUY).forStock("A").withQuantity(66)
                    .inTradingRegion(SAME_REGION));
  assertEventually(holdingOfStock("A", tradeDate, equalTo(66)));
}
```

Of course, this test assumes that trade events are processed in sequence, not in parallel, so that the second event cannot overtake the first and give a false positive. That's why such tests are not completely "black box" but have to make assumptions about the structure of the system. This might make these tests brittle—they would misreport if the system changes the assumptions they've been built on. One response is to add a test to confirm those expectations—in this case, perhaps a stress test to confirm event processing order and alert the team if circumstances change. That said, there should already be other tests that confirm those assumptions, so it may be enough just to associate these tests, for example by grouping them in the same test package.

Distinguish Synchronizations and Assertions

We have one mechanism for synchronizing a test with its system and for making assertions about that system—wait for an observable condition and time out if it doesn't happen. The only difference between the two activities is our interpretation of what they mean. As always, we want to make our intentions explicit, but it's especially important here because there's a risk that someone may look at the test later and remove what looks like a duplicate assertion, accidentally introducing a race condition.

We often adopt a naming scheme to distinguish between synchronizations and assertions. For example, we might have waitUntil() and assertEventually() methods to express the purpose of different checks that share an underlying implementation.

Alternatively, we might reserve the term "assert" for synchronous tests and use a different naming conventions in asynchronous tests, as we did in the Auction Sniper example.

Externalize Event Sources

Some systems trigger their own events internally. The most common example is using a timer to schedule activities. This might include repeated actions that run frequently, such as bundling up emails for forwarding, or follow-up actions that run days or even weeks in the future, such as confirming a delivery date.

Hidden timers are very difficult to work with because they make it hard to tell when the system is in a stable state for a test to make its assertions. Waiting for a repeated action to run is too slow to "succeed fast," to say nothing of an action scheduled a month from now. We also don't want tests to break unpredictably because of interference from a scheduled activity that's just kicked in. Trying to test a system by coinciding timers is just too brittle.

The only solution is to make the system deterministic by decoupling it from its own scheduling. We can pull event generation out into a shared service that is driven externally. For example, in one project we implemented the system's scheduler as a web service. System components scheduled activities by making HTTP requests to the scheduler, which triggered activities by making HTTP "postbacks." In another project, the scheduler published notifications onto a message bus topic that the components listened to.

With this separation in place, tests can step the system through its behavior by posing as the scheduler and generating events deterministically. Now we can run system tests quickly and reliably. This is a nice example of a testing requirement leading to a better design. We've been forced to abstract out scheduling, which means we won't have multiple implementations hidden in the system. Usually, introducing such an event infrastructure turns out to be useful for monitoring and administration.

There's a trade-off too, of course. Our tests are no longer exercising the entire system. We've prioritized test speed and reliability over fidelity. We compensate by keeping the scheduler's API as simple as possible and testing it rigorously (another advantage). We would probably also write a few slow tests, running in a separate build, that exercise the whole system together including the real scheduler.

Afterword

A Brief History of Mock Objects

Tim Mackinnon

Introduction

The ideas and concepts behind mock objects didn't materialise in a single day. There's a long history of experimentation, discussion, and collaboration between many different developers who have taken the seed of an idea and grown it into something more profound. The final result—the topic of this book—should help you with your software development; but the background story of "The Making of Mock Objects" is also interesting—and a testament to the dedication of the people involved. I hope revisiting this history will inspire you too to challenge your thoughts on what is possible and to experiment with new practices.

Origins

The story began on a roundabout[1] near Archway station in London in late 1999. That evening, several members of a London-based software architecture group[2] met to discuss topical issues in software. The discussion turned to experiences with Agile Software Development and I mentioned the impact that writing tests seemed to be having on our code. This was before the first Extreme Programming book had been published, and teams like ours were still exploring how to do test-driven development—including what constituted a good test. In particular, I had noticed a tendency to add "getter" methods to our objects to facilitate testing. This felt wrong, since it could be seen as violating object-oriented principles, so I was interested in the thoughts of the other members. The conversation was quite lively—mainly centering on the tension between pragmatism in testing and pure object-oriented design. We also had a recent example of a colleague,

---

1. "Roundabout" is the UK term for a traffic circle.
2. On this occasion, they were Tim Mackinnon, Peter Marks, Ivan Moore, and John Nolan.

Oli Bye, stubbing out the Java Servlet API for testing a web application without a server.

I particularly remember from that evening a crude diagram of an onion[3] and its metaphor of the many layers of software, along with the mantra "No Getters! Period!" The discussion revolved around how to safely peel back and test layers of that onion without impacting its design. The solution was to focus on the composition of software components (the group had discussed Brad Cox's ideas on software components many times before). It was an interesting collision of opinions, and the emphasis on composition—now referred to as *dependency injection*—gave us a technique for eliminating the getters we were "pragmatically" adding to objects so we could write tests for them.

The following day, our small team at Connextra[4] started putting the idea into practice. We removed the getters from sections of our code and used a compositional strategy by adding constructors that took the objects we wanted to test via getters as parameters. At first this felt cumbersome, and our two recent graduate recruits were not convinced. I, however, had a Smalltalk background, so to me the idea of composition and delegation felt right. Enforcing a "no getters" rule seemed like a way to achieve a more object-oriented feeling in the Java language we were using.

We stuck to it for several days and started to see some patterns emerging. More of our conversations were about expecting things to happen between our objects, and we frequently had variables with names like `expectedURL` and `expectedServiceName` in our injected objects. On the other hand, when our tests failed we were tired of stepping through in a debugger to see what went wrong. We started adding variables with names like `actualURL` and `actualServiceName` to allow the injected test objects to throw exceptions with helpful messages. Printing the expected and actual values side-by-side showed us immediately what the problem was.

Over the course of several weeks we refactored these ideas into a group of classes: `ExpectationValue` for single values, `ExpectationList` for multiple values in a particular order, and `ExpectationSet` for unique values in any order. Later, Tung Mac also added `ExpectationCounter` for situations where we didn't want to specify explicit values but just count the number of calls. It started to feel as if something interesting was happening, but it seemed so obvious to me that there wasn't really much to describe. One afternoon, Peter Marks decided that we should come up with name for what we were doing—so we could at least package the code—and, after a few suggestions, proposed "mock." We could use it both as a noun and a verb, and it refactored nicely into our code, so we adopted it.

---

3. Initially drawn by John Nolan.
4. The team consisted of Tim Mackinnon, Tung Mac, and Matthew Cooke, with direction from Peter Marks and John Nolan. Connextra is now part of Bet Genius.

Spreading the Word

Around this time, we[5] also started the London Extreme Tuesday Club (XTC) to share experiences of Extreme Programming with other teams. During one meeting, I described our refactoring experiments and explained that I felt that it helped our junior developers write better object-oriented code. I finished the story by saying, "But this is such an obvious technique that I'm sure most people do it eventually anyway." Steve pointed out that the most obvious things aren't always so obvious and are usually difficult to describe. He thought this could make a great paper if we could sort the wood from the trees, so we decided to collaborate with another XTC member (Philip Craig) and write something for the XP2000 conference. If nothing else, we wanted to go to Sardinia.

We began to pick apart the ideas and give them a consistent set of names, studying real code examples to understand the essence of the technique. We backported new concepts we discovered to the original Connextra codebase to validate their effectiveness. This was an exciting time and I recall that it took many late nights to refine our ideas—although we were still struggling to come up with an accurate "elevator pitch" for mock objects. We knew what it felt like when using them to drive great code, but describing this experience to other developers who weren't part of the XTC was still challenging.

The XP2000 paper [Mackinnon00] and the initial mock objects library had a mixed reception—for some it was revolutionary, for others it was unnecessary overhead. In retrospect, the fact that Java didn't have good reflection when we started meant that many of the steps were manual, or augmented with code generation tools.[6] This turned people off—they couldn't separate the idea from the implementation.

Another Generation

The story continues when Nat Pryce took the ideas and implemented them in Ruby. He exploited Ruby's reflection to write expectations directly into the test as blocks. Influenced by his PhD work on protocols between components, his library changed the emphasis from asserting parameter values to asserting messages sent between objects. Nat then ported his implementation to Java, using the new Proxy type in Java 1.3 and defining expectations with "constraint" objects. When Nat showed us this work, it immediately clicked. He donated his library to the mock objects project and visited the Connextra offices where we worked together to add features that the Connextra developers needed.

---

5. With Tim Mackinnon, Oli Bye, Paul Simmons, and Steve Freeman. Oli coined the name XTC.
6. This later changed as Java 1.1 was released, which improved reflection, and as others who had read our paper wrote more tools, such as Tammo Freese's Easymock.

With Nat in the office where mock objects were being used constantly, we were driven to use his improvements to provide more descriptive failure messages. We had seen our developers getting bogged down when the reason for a test failure was not obvious enough (later, we observed that this was often a hint that an object had too many responsibilities). Now, constraints allowed us to write tests that were more expressive and provided better failure diagnostics, as the constraint objects could explain what went wrong.[7] For example, a failure on a `stringBegins` constraint could produce a message like:

```
Expected a string parameter beginning with "http"
  but was called with a value of "ftp.domain.com"
```

We released the new improved version of Nat's library under the name Dynamock.

As we improved the library, more programmers started using it, which introduced new requirements. We started adding more and more options to the API until, eventually, it became too complicated to maintain—especially as we had to support multiple versions of Java. Meanwhile, Steve tired of the the duplication in the syntax required to set up expectations, so he introduced a version of a Smalltalk cascade—multiple calls to the same object.

Then Steve noticed that in a statically typed language like Java, a cascade could return a chain of interfaces to control when methods are made available to the caller—in effect, we could use types to encode a workflow. Steve also wanted to improve the programming experience by guiding the new generation of IDEs to prompt with the "right" completion options. Over the course of a year, Steve and Nat, with much input from the rest of us, pushed the idea hard to produce jMock, an expressive API over our original Dynamock framework. This was also ported to C# as NMock. At some point in this process, they realized that they were actually writing a language *in* Java which could be used to write expectations; they wrote this up later in an OOPLSA paper [Freeman06].

Consolidation

Through our experience in Connextra and other companies, and through giving many presentations, we improved our understanding and communication of the ideas of mock objects. Steve (inspired by some of the early lean software material) coined the term "needs-driven development," and Joe Walnes, another colleague, drew a nice visualisation of islands of objects communicating with each other. Joe also had the insight of using mock objects to drive the design of interfaces between objects. At the time, we were struggling to promote the idea of using mock objects as a design tool; many people (including some authors) saw it only as a technique for speeding up unit tests. Joe cut through all the conceptual barriers with his simple heuristic of "Only mock types you own."

---

7. Later, Steve talked Charlie Poole into including constraints in NUnit. It took some extra years to have matchers (the latest version of constraints) adopted by JUnit.

We took all these ideas and wrote a second conference paper, "Mock Roles not Objects" [Freeman04]. Our initial description had focused too much on implementation, whereas the critical idea was that the technique emphasizes the roles that objects play for each other. When developers are using mock objects well, I observe them drawing diagrams of what they want to test, or using CRC cards to roleplay relationships—these then translate nicely into mock objects and tests that drive the required code.

Since then, Nat and Steve have reworked jMock to produce jMock2, and Joe has extracted constraints into the Hamcrest library (now adopted by JUnit). There's also now a wide selection of mock object libraries, in many different languages.

The results have been worth the effort. I think we can finally say that there is now a well-documented and polished technique that helps you write better software. From those humble "no getters" beginnings, this book summarizes years of experience from all of us who have collaborated, and adds Steve and Nat's language expertise and careful attention to detail to produce something that is greater than the sum of its parts.

Appendix A

jMock2 Cheat Sheet

Introduction

We use *jMock2* as our mock object framework throughout this book. This chapter summarizes its features and shows some examples of how to use them. We're using JUnit 4.6 (we assume you're familiar with it); jMock also supports JUnit3. Full documentation is available at www.jmock.org.

We'll show the structure of a jMock unit test and describe what its features do. Here's a whole example:

```
import org.jmock.Expectations;
import org.jmock.Mockery;
import org.jmock.integration.junit4.JMock;
import org.jmock.integration.junit4.JUnit4Mockery;

@RunWith(JMock.class)
public class TurtleDriverTest {
  private final Mockery context = new JUnit4Mockery();
  private final Turtle turtle = context.mock(Turtle.class);

  @Test public void
  goesAMinimumDistance() {
    final Turtle turtle2 = context.mock(Turtle.class, "turtle2");
    final TurtleDriver driver = new TurtleDriver(turtle1, turtle2); // set up

    context.checking(new Expectations() {{ // expectations
      ignoring (turtle2);
      allowing (turtle).flashLEDs();

      oneOf (turtle).turn(45);
      oneOf (turtle).forward(with(greaterThan(20)));
      atLeast(1).of (turtle).stop();
    }});

    driver.goNext(45); // call the code
    assertTrue("driver has moved", driver.hasMoved()); // further assertions
  }
}
```

335

Test Fixture Class

First, we set up the test fixture class by creating its `Mockery`.

```
import org.jmock.Expectations;
import org.jmock.Mockery;
import org.jmock.integration.junit4.JMock;
import org.jmock.integration.junit4.JUnit4Mockery;

@RunWith(JMock.class)
public class TurtleDriverTest {
  private final Mockery context = new JUnit4Mockery();
  [...]
}
```

For the object under test, a `Mockery` represents its *context*—the neighboring objects it will communicate with. The test will tell the mockery to create mock objects, to set expectations on the mock objects, and to check at the end of the test that those expectations have been met. By convention, the mockery is stored in an instance variable named `context`.

A test written with JUnit4 does not need to extend a specific base class but must specify that it uses jMock with the `@RunWith(JMock.class)` attribute.[1] This tells the JUnit runner to find a `Mockery` field in the test class and to assert (at the right time in the test lifecycle) that its expectations have been met. This requires that there should be exactly one mockery field in the test class. The class `JUnit4Mockery` will report expectation failures as JUnit4 test failures.

Creating Mock Objects

This test uses two mock turtles, which we ask the mockery to create. The first is a field in the test class:

```
private final Turtle turtle = context.mock(Turtle.class);
```

The second is local to the test, so it's held in a variable:

```
final Turtle turtle2 = context.mock(Turtle.class, "turtle2");
```

The variable has to be final so that the anonymous expectations block has access to it—we'll return to this soon. This second mock turtle has a specified name, `turtle2`. Any mock can be given a name which will be used in the report if the test fails; the default name is the type of the object. If there's more than one mock object of the same type, jMock enforces that only one uses the default name; the others must be given names when declared. This is so that failure reports can make clear which mock instance is which when describing the state of the test.

---

1. At the time of writing, JUnit was introducing the concept of `Rule`. We expect to extend the jMock API to adopt this technique.

Tests with Expectations

A test sets up its expectations in one or more *expectation blocks*, for example:

```
context.checking(new Expectations() {{
  oneOf (turtle).turn(45);
}});
```

An expectation block can contain any number of expectations. A test can contain multiple expectation blocks; expectations in later blocks are appended to those in earlier blocks. Expectation blocks can be interleaved with calls to the code under test.

What's with the Double Braces?

The most disconcerting syntax element in jMock is its use of double braces in an expectations block. It's a hack, but with a purpose. If we reformat an expectations block, we get this:

```
context.checking(new Expectations() {
  {
    oneOf (turtle).turn(45);
  }
});
```

We're passing to the `checking()` method an anonymous subclass of `Expectations` (first set of braces). Within that subclass, we have an instance initialization block (second set of braces) that Java will call after the constructor. Within the initialization block, we can reference the enclosing `Expectations` object, so `oneOf()` is actually an instance method—as are all of the expectation structure clauses we describe in the next section.

The purpose of this baroque structure is to provide a scope for building up expectations. All the code in the expectation block is defined within an anonymous instance of `Expectations`, which collects the expectation components that the code generates. The scoping to an instance allows us to make this collection implicit, which requires less code. It also improves our experience in the IDE, since code completion will be more focused, as in Figure A.1.

Referring back to the discussion in "Building Up to Higher-Level Programming" (page 65), `Expectations` is an example of the Builder pattern.

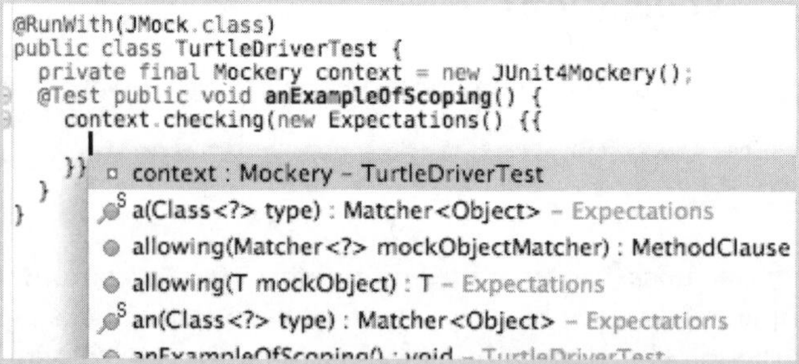

```
@RunWith(JMock.class)
public class TurtleDriverTest {
  private final Mockery context = new JUnit4Mockery();
  @Test public void anExampleOfScoping() {
    context.checking(new Expectations() {{

    }}  ▫ context : Mockery – TurtleDriverTest
  }     ⊚ˢ a(Class<?> type) : Matcher<Object> – Expectations
}       ⊚ allowing(Matcher<?> mockObjectMatcher) : MethodClause
        ⊚ allowing(T mockObject) : T – Expectations
        ⊚ˢ an(Class<?> type) : Matcher<Object> – Expectations
        ⊚ anExampleOfScoping() : void – TurtleDriverTest
```

Figure A.1 *Narrowed scope gives better code completion*

Expectations

Expectations have the following structure:

```
invocation-count(mock-object).method(argument-constraints);
  inSequence(sequence-name);
  when(state-machine.is(state-name));
  will(action);
  then(state-machine.is(new-state-name));
```

The `invocation-count` and `mock-object` are required, all the other clauses are optional. You can give an expectation any number of `inSequence`, `when`, `will`, and `then` clauses. Here are some common examples:

```
oneOf (turtle).turn(45); // The turtle must be told exactly once to turn 45 degrees.
atLeast(1).of (turtle).stop(); // The turtle must be told at least once to stop.
allowing (turtle).flashLEDs(); // The turtle may be told any number of times,
                              // including none, to flash its LEDs.
allowing (turtle).queryPen(); will(returnValue(PEN_DOWN));
                              // The turtle may be asked about its pen any
                              // number of times and will always return PEN_DOWN.
ignoring (turtle2); // turtle2 may be told to do anything. This test ignores it.
```

Invocation Count

The *invocation count* is required to describe how often we expect a call to be made during the run of the test. It starts the definition of an expectation.

exactly(n).of

The invocation is expected exactly n times.

oneOf

The invocation is expected exactly once. This is a convenience shorthand for `exactly(1).of`

`atLeast(n).of`

> The invocation is expected at least n times.

`atMost(n).of`

> The invocation is expected at most n times.

`between(min, max).of`

> The invocation is expected at least `min` times and at most `max` times.

`allowing`
`ignoring`

> The invocation is allowed any number of times including none. These clauses are equivalent to `atLeast(0).of`, but we use them to highlight that the expectation is a *stub*—that it's there to get the test through to the interesting part of the behavior.

`never`

> The invocation is not expected. This is the default behavior if no expectation has been set. We use this clause to emphasize to the reader of a test that an invocation should not be called.

`allowing`, `ignoring`, and `never` can also be applied to an object as a whole. For example, `ignoring(turtle2)` says to allow all calls to `turtle2`. Similarly, `never(turtle2)` says to fail if any calls are made to `turtle2` (which is the same as not specifying any expectations on the object). If we add method expectations, we can be more precise, for example:

```
allowing(turtle2).log(with(anything()));
never(turtle2).stop();
```

will allow log messages to be sent to the turtle, but fail if it's told to stop. In practice, while allowing precise invocations is common, blocking individual methods is rarely useful.

Methods

Expected methods are specified by calling the method on the mock object within an expectation block. This defines the name of the method and what argument values are acceptable. Values passed to the method in an expectation will be compared for equality:

```
oneOf (turtle).turn(45); // matches turn() called with 45
oneOf (calculator).add(2, 2); // matches add() called with 2 and 2
```

Invocation matching can be made more flexible by using *matchers* as arguments wrapped in `with()` clauses:

```
oneOf(calculator).add(with(lessThan(15)), with(any(int.class)));
// matches add() called with a number less than 15 and any other number
```

Either all the arguments must be matchers or all must be values:

```
oneOf(calculator).add(with(lessThan(15)), 22); // this doesn't work!
```

Argument Matchers

The most commonly used matchers are defined in the Expectations class:

equal(o)
> The argument is equal to o, as defined by calling o.equals() with the actual value received during the test. This also recursively compares the contents of arrays.

same(o)
> The argument is the same object as o.

any(Class<T> type)
> The argument is any value, including null. The type argument is required to force Java to type-check the argument at compile time.

a(Class<T> type)
an(Class<T> type)
> The argument is an instance of type or of one of its subtypes.

aNull(Class<T> type)
> The argument is null. The type argument is to force Java to type-check the argument at compile time.

aNonNull(Class<T> type)
> The argument is not null. The type argument is to force Java to type-check the argument at compile time.

not(m)
> The argument does not match the matcher m.

anyOf(m1, m2, m3, [...])
> The argument matches at least one of the matchers m1, m2, m3, [...].

allOf(m1, m2, m3, [...])
> The argument matches all of the matchers m1, m2, m3, [...].

More matchers are available from static factory methods of the Hamcrest Matchers class, which can be statically imported into the test class. For more precision, custom matchers can be written using the Hamcrest library.

Actions

An expectation can also specify an action to perform when it is matched, by adding a will() clause after the invocation. For example, this expectation will return PEN_DOWN when queryPen() is called:

```
allowing (turtle).queryPen(); will(returnValue(PEN_DOWN));
```

jMock provides several standard actions, and programmers can provide custom actions by implementing the Action interface. The standard actions are:

will(returnValue(v))
> Return v to the caller.

will(returnIterator(c))
> Return an iterator for collection c to the caller.

will(returnIterator(v1, v2, […], vn))
> Return a new iterator over elements v1 to v2 on each invocation.

will(throwException(e))
> Throw exception e when called.

will(doAll(a1, a2, […], an))
> Perform all the actions a1 to an on every invocation.

Sequences

The order in which expectations are specified does not have to match the order in which their invocations are called. If invocation order is significant, it can be enforced in a test by adding a Sequence. A test can create more than one sequence and an expectation can be part of more than once sequence at a time. The syntax for creating a Sequence is:

```
Sequence sequence-variable = context.sequence("sequence-name");
```

To expect a sequence of invocations, create a Sequence object, write the expectations in the expected order, and add an inSequence() clause to each relevant expectation. Expectations in a sequence can have any invocation count. For example:

```
context.checking(new Expectations() {{
    final Sequence drawing = context.sequence("drawing");
    allowing (turtle).queryColor(); will(returnValue(BLACK));

    atLeast(1).of (turtle).forward(10); inSequence(drawing);
    oneOf (turtle).turn(45);     inSequence(drawing);
    oneOf (turtle).forward(10); inSequence(drawing);
}});
```

Here, the queryColor() call is not in the sequence and can take place at any time.

States

Invocations can be constrained to occur only when a condition is true, where a condition is defined as a state machine that is in a given state. State machines can switch between states specified by state names. A test can create multiple state machines, and an invocation can be constrained to one or more conditions. The syntax for creating a state machine is:

```
States state-machine-name =
       context.states("state-machine-name").startsAs("initial-state");
```

The initial state is optional; if not specified, the state machine starts in an unnamed initial state.

Add these clauses to expectations to constrain them to match invocations in a given state, or to switch the state of a state machine after an invocation:

when(stateMachine.is("state-name"));

> Constrains the last expectation to occur only when stateMachine is in the state "state-name".

when(stateMachine.isNot("state-name"));

> Constrains the last expectation to occur only when stateMachine is not in the state "state-name".

then(stateMachine.is("state-name"));

> Changes stateMachine to be in the state "state-name" when the invocation occurs.

This example allows turtle to move only when the pen is down:

```
context.checking(new Expectations() {{
  final States pen = context.states("pen").startsAs("up");
  allowing (turtle).queryColor(); will(returnValue(BLACK));

  allowing (turtle).penDown();       then(pen.is("down"));
  allowing (turtle).penUp();         then(pen.is("up"));

  atLeast(1).of (turtle).forward(15); when(pen.is("down"));
  one (turtle).turn(90);             when(pen.is("down"));
  one (turtle).forward(10);          when(pen.is("down"));
}}
```

Notice that expectations with states do not define a sequence; they can be combined with Sequence constraints if order is significant. As before, the queryColor() call is not included in the states, and so can be called at any time.

Appendix B

Writing a Hamcrest Matcher

Introduction

Although Hamcrest 1.2 comes with a large library of matchers, sometimes these do not let you specify an assertion or expectation accurately enough to convey what you mean or to keep your tests flexible. In such cases, you can easily define a new matcher that seamlessly extends the JUnit and jMock APIs.

A matcher is an object that implements the `org.hamcrest.Matcher` interface:

```
public interface SelfDescribing {
  void describeTo(Description description);
}

public interface Matcher<T> extends SelfDescribing {
  boolean matches(Object item);
  void describeMismatch(Object item, Description mismatchDescription);
}
```

A matcher does two things:

- Reports whether a parameter value meets the constraint (the `matches()` method);

- Generates a readable description to be included in test failure messages (the `describeTo()` method inherited from the `SelfDescribing` interface and the `describeMismatch()` method).

A New Matcher Type

As an example, we will write a new matcher that tests whether a string starts with a given prefix. It can be used in tests as shown below. Note that the matcher seamlessly extends the assertion: there is no visible difference between built-in and third-party matchers at the point of use.

```
@Test public void exampleTest() {
  [...]
  assertThat(someString, startsWith("Cheese"));
}
```

343

To write a new matcher, we must implement two things: a new class that implements the Matcher interface and the startsWith() factory function for our assertions to read well when we use the new matcher in our tests.

To write a matcher type, we extend one of Hamcrest's abstract base classes, rather than implementing the Matcher interface directly.[1] For our needs, we can extend TypeSafeMatcher<String>, which checks for nulls and type safety, casts the matched Object to a String, and calls the *template methods* [Gamma94] in our subclass.

```java
public class StringStartsWithMatcher extends TypeSafeMatcher<String> {
  private final String expectedPrefix;

  public StringStartsWithMatcher(String expectedPrefix) {
    this.expectedPrefix = expectedPrefix;
  }
  @Override
  protected boolean matchesSafely(String actual) {
    return actual.startsWith(expectedPrefix);
  }
  @Override
  public void describeTo(Description matchDescription) {
    matchDescription.appendText("a string starting with ")
                    .appendValue(expectedPrefix);
  }
  @Override protected void
  describeMismatchSafely(String actual, Description mismatchDescription) {
    String actualPrefix =
            actual.substring(0, Math.min(actual.length(), expectedPrefix.length()));

    mismatchDescription.appendText("started with ")
                       .appendValue(actualPrefix);
  }
}
```

Matcher Objects Must Be Stateless

When dispatching each invocation, jMock uses the matchers to find an expectation that matches the invocation's arguments. This means that it will call the matchers many times during the test, maybe even after the expectation has already been matched and invoked. In fact, jMock gives no guarantees of when and how many times it will call the matchers. This has no effect on stateless matchers, but the behavior of stateful matchers is unpredictable.

If you want to maintain state in response to invocations, write a custom jMock Action, not a Matcher.

---

1. This lets the Hamcrest team add methods to the Matcher interface without breaking all the code that implements that interface, because they can also add a default implementation to the base class.

The text generated by the describeTo() and describeMismatch() must follow certain grammatical conventions to fit into the error messages generated by JUnit and jMock. Although JUnit and jMock generate different messages, matcher descriptions that complete the sentence "expected *description* but it *mismatch-description*" will work with both libraries. That sentence completed with the StringStartsWithMatcher's descriptions would be something like:

```
expected a string starting with "Cheese" but it started with "Bananas"
```

To make the new matcher fit seamlessly into JUnit and jMock, we also write a factory method that creates an instance of the StringStartsWithMatcher.

```
public static Matcher<String> aStringStartingWith(String prefix ) {
    return new StringStartsWithMatcher(prefix);
}
```

The point of the factory method is to make the test code read clearly, so consider how it will look when used in an assertion or expectation.

And that's all there is to writing a matcher.

Bibliography

[Abelson96] Abelson, Harold and Gerald Sussman. *Structure and Interpretation of Computer Programs*. MIT Press, 1996, ISBN 978-0262011532.

[Beck99] Beck, Kent. *Extreme Programming Explained: Embrace Change*. Addison-Wesley, 1999, ISBN 978-0321278654.

[Beck02] Beck, Kent. *Test Driven Development: By Example*. Addison-Wesley, 2002, ISBN 978-0321146530.

[Begel08] Begel, Andrew and Beth Simon. "Struggles of New College Graduates in Their First Software Development Job." In: *SIGCSE Bulletin*, 40, no. 1 (March 2008): 226–230, ACM, ISSN 0097-8418.

[Cockburn04] Cockburn, Alistair. *Crystal Clear: A Human-Powered Methodology for Small Teams*. Addison-Wesley Professional, October 29, 2004, ISBN 0201699478.

[Cockburn08] Cockburn, Alistair. *Hexagonal Architecture: Ports and Adapters ("Object Structural")*. June 19, 2008, http://alistair.cockburn.us/ Hexagonal+architecture.

[Cohn05] Cohn, Mike. *Agile Estimating and Planning*. Prentice Hall, 2005, ISBN 978-0131479418.

[Demeyer03] Demeyer, Serge, Stéphane Ducasse, and Oscar Nierstrasz. *Object-Oriented Reengineering Patterns*. http://scg.unibe.ch/download/oorp/.

[Evans03] Evans, Eric. *Domain-Driven Design: Tackling Complexity in the Heart of Software*. Addison-Wesley, 2003, ISBN 978-0321125217.

[Feathers04] Feathers, Michael. *Working Effectively with Legacy Code*. Prentice Hall, 2004, ISBN 978-0131177055.

[Fowler99] Fowler, Martin. *Refactoring: Improving the Design of Existing Code*. Addison-Wesley, 1999, ISBN 978-0201485677.

[Freeman04] Freeman, Steve, Tim Mackinnon, Nat Pryce, and Joe Walnes. "Mock Roles, Not Objects." In: *Companion to the 19th ACM SIGPLAN Conference on Object-Oriented Programming Systems, Languages, and Applications, OOPLSA, Vancouver, BC, October 2004*, New York: ACM, ISBN 1581138334, http://portal.acm.org/citation.cfm?doid=1028664.1028765 .

[Freeman06] Freeman, Steve and Nat Pryce. "Evolving an Embedded Domain-Specific Language in Java." In: *Companion to the 21st ACM SIGPLAN Conference on Object-Oriented Programming Systems, Languages, and Applications, OOPLSA, Portland, Oregon, October 2006*, New York: ACM, http://www.jmock.org/oopsla06.pdf.

[Gall03] Gall, John. *The Systems Bible: The Beginner's Guide to Systems Large and Small*. General Systemantics Pr/Liberty, 2003, ISBN 978-0961825171.

[Gamma94] Gamma, Erich, Richard Helm, Ralph Johnson, and John Vlissides. *Design Patterns: Elements of Reusable Object-Oriented Software*. Addison-Wesley, 1994.

[Graham93] Graham, Paul. *On Lisp*. Prentice Hall, 1993, ISBN 0130305529, http://www.paulgraham.com/onlisp.html.

[Hunt99] Hunt, Andrew and David Thomas. *The Pragmatic Programmer: From Journeyman to Master*. Addison-Wesley Professional, October 30, 1999, ISBN 020161622X.

[Kay98] Kay, Alan. *Email Message Sent to the Squeak Mailing List*. October 10, 1998, http://lists.squeakfoundation.org/pipermail/squeak-dev/1998-October/017019.html.

[Kerievsky04] Kerievsky, Joshua. *Refactoring to Patterns*. Addison-Wesley, 2004, ISBN 978-0321213358.

[Kernighan76] Kernighan, Brian and P. J. Plauger. *Software Tools*. Addison-Wesley, 1976, ISBN 978-0201036695.

[Lieberherr88] Lieberherr, Karl, Ian Holland, and Arthur Riel. "Object-Oriented Programming: An Objective Sense of Style." In: *OOPSLA*, 23, no. 11 (1988): 323–334.

[LIFT] *Framework for Literate Functional Testing*. https://lift.dev.java.net/.

[Mackinnon00] Mackinnon, Tim, Steve Freeman, and Philip Craig. "Endo-Testing: Unit Testing with Mock Objects." In: Giancarlo Succi and Michele Marchesi, *Extreme Programming Examined*, Addison-Wesley, 2001, pp. 287–301, ISBN 978-0201710403.

[Magee06] Magee, Jeff and Jeff Kramer. *Concurrency: State Models & Java Programs*. Wiley, 2006, ISBN 978-0470093559.

[Martin02] Martin, Robert C. *Agile Software Development, Principles, Patterns, and Practices*. Prentice Hall, 2002, ISBN 978-0135974445.

[Meszaros07] Meszaros, Gerard. *xUnit Test Patterns: Refactoring Test Code*. Addison-Wesley, 2007, ISBN 978-0131495050.

[Meyer91] Meyer, Betrand. *Eiffel: The Language*. Prentice Hall, 1991, ISBN 978-0132479257.

[Mugridge05] Mugridge, Rick and Ward Cunningham. *Fit for Developing Software: Framework for Integrated Tests*. Prentice Hall, 2005, ISBN 978-0321269348.

[Schuh01] Schuh, Peter and Stephanie Punke. *ObjectMother: Easing Test Object Creation In XP*. XP Universe, 2001.

[Schwaber01] Schwaber, Ken and Mike Beedle. *Agile Software Development with Scrum*. Prentice Hall, 2001, ISBN 978-0130676344.

[Shore07] Shore, James and Shane Warden. *The Art of Agile Development*. O'Reilly Media, 2007, ISBN 978-0596527679.

[Wirfs-Brock03] Wirfs-Brock, Rebecca and Alan McKean. *Object Design: Roles, Responsibilities, and Collaborations*. Addison-Wesley, 2003, ISBN 0201379430.

[Woolf98] Woolf, Bobby. "Null Object." In: *Pattern Languages of Program Design 3*. Edited by Robert Martin, Dirk Riehle, and Frank Buschmann. Addison-Wesley, 1998, http://www.cse.wustl.edu/~schmidt/PLoP-96/woolf1.ps.gz.

[Yourdon79] Yourdon, Edward and Larry Constantine. *Structured Design: Fundamentals of a Discipline of Computer Program and Systems Design*. Prentice Hall, 1979, ISBN 978-0138544713.

Index

informIT.com

LearnIT at InformIT

Looking for a book, eBook, or training video on a new technology? Seeking timely and relevant information and tutorials? Looking for expert opinions, advice, and tips? **InformIT has the solution.**

- Learn about new releases and special promotions by subscribing to a wide variety of newsletters.
  Visit **informit.com/newsletters**.

- Access FREE podcasts from experts at **informit.com/podcasts**.

- Read the latest author articles and sample chapters at **informit.com/articles**.

- Access thousands of books and videos in the Safari Books Online digital library at **safari.informit.com**.

- Get tips from expert blogs at **informit.com/blogs**.

Visit **informit.com/learn** to discover all the ways you can access the hottest technology content.

Are You Part of the IT Crowd?

Connect with Pearson authors and editors via RSS feeds, Facebook, Twitter, YouTube, and more! Visit **informit.com/socialconnect**.